# Asians Wear Clothes on the Internet

# Asians Wear Clothes on the Internet

Race, Gender, and the Work of Personal Style Blogging

**Minh-Ha T. Pham**

Duke University Press   Durham and London   2015

© 2015 Duke University Press
All rights reserved
Printed in the United States of America on acid-free paper ∞
Designed by Natalie F. Smith
Typeset in Quadraat Pro by Westchester Publishing Services

Library of Congress Cataloging-in-Publication Data
Pham, Minh-Ha T., [date] author.
Asians wear clothes on the internet : race, gender,
and the work of personal style blogging / Minh-Ha T. Pham.
pages cm
Includes bibliographical references and index.
ISBN 978-0-8223-6015-5 (hardcover : alk. paper)
ISBN 978-0-8223-6030-8 (pbk. : alk. paper)
ISBN 978-0-8223-7488-6 (e-book)
1. Fashion—Social aspects—Asia—Blogs. 2. Asians—
Clothing—Blogs. 3. Fashion writing—Asia—Blogs. I. Title.
GT525.P44 2015
391.0095—dc23   2015020933

Cover art: Photograph © Camera Press Ltd. / Alamy.

# Contents

# Acknowledgments

Writing this book involved a steep and sometimes painful learning curve that was, by turns, maddening; inspiring; lonely; and crowded with love, support, and care. My graduate school cohort of friends and allies in the Ethnic Studies Department at the University of California at Berkeley were some of the first to stand with me as I began this process. Marlon Bailey, Rebecca Hurdis, Dulcinea Lara, Rani Neutill, Victor Rios, and Gustavo Guerra Vasquez pushed and inspired me—and continue to do so—to hold my scholarly and political commitments together in service of one another. Patrick Anderson, Vernadette Gonzalez, Marie Lo, Thy Phu, Oliver Wang, and Kathy Yep showed me through their examples that intellectual rigor and intellectual generosity are not only not mutually exclusive but are in fact co-constituting.

The subject of this book is far from anything I wrote as a graduate student (including my dissertation), but I hope that Elaine Kim, Josh Kun, José Saldívar, Trinh T. Minh-ha, and Sau-ling Wong will see throughout its pages the enormous impact of their rich scholarship and meaningful mentorship.

Over these past few years, the care and attention that Lisa Nakamura, Alondra Nelson, and Thuy Linh Tu have given to reading and commenting on my research have been invaluable. They have helped me sharpen not only my own understanding of this work but also what feminist scholarship is, in practice. With their commitment to sharing their wisdom, never pulling a critical punch, and always looking and being fabulous, they are exemplary feminist scholars. I am so grateful to have them on Team Minh-Ha.

Ken Wissoker, Elizabeth Ault, and Cathy Hannabach deserve special mention, too. Whatever strengths this book may have are due in no small part to their smart feedback and unwavering support of this project through its many iterations (and, for Ken, across a number of years, lunches, and shopping trips).

Also deserving of a personal shout-out are those who have ridden with and for Threadbared as well as *Of Another Fashion* for so many years. When I began Threadbared with Mimi Thi Nguyen in 2007, I didn't expect or imagine that our online notes and brief commentary about social power through fashion would find an audience of any size. I am very thankful for Threadbared's smart, engaged, and active readers. Some of our readers have also become friends and co-conspirators in the critical race and gender blogosphere, the field of critical fashion studies, and IRL. Lisa Wong Macabasco, erin Khue Ninh, Latoya Peterson, Jorge Rivas, Jenna Sauers, Sarah Scaturro, and Jenny Zhang of (or formerly of) *Hyphen*, *Racialicious*, *Colorlines*, *Jezebel*, *Rookie*, and the Costume Institute graciously offered their personal and professional help in expanding the reach and sometimes the scope of my research and writing at crucial times.

Of course, the first reader of any of my Threadbared posts (after me) is my co-blogger and friend Mimi Thi Nguyen. It is no overstatement to say that without her amazing gifts for cultural and social analyses, her experience with HTML coding, and her willingness to share all of them, Threadbared— including the research and writing I did in and through Threadbared that would later become this book—simply would not have been.

For their thoughtful suggestions and criticism of the work at various stages of its evolution, I want to thank the faculty, students, and members of the many institutions that have invited me to present my research. Also, I am grateful for the Society for the Humanities Research Grant at Cornell University and the Mellon Foundation Research Grant at Pratt Institute which helped to defray the costs associated with the research and writing of this book.

I am lucky to have found a small but super smart, fun, and crazy stylish group of friends, allies, and colleagues in and across a range of critical race, gender, fashion, and media studies. The conversations, good cheer, and support of Aimee Bahng, Denise Cruz, Tanisha Ford, Sharon Heijin Lee, Alice Marwick, Ashley Mears, Christina Moon, Mimi Thi Nguyen, Thy Phu, Priti Ramamurthy, Thuy Linh Tu, and Grace Wang are some of the topmost scholarly and nonscholarly reasons I love being an academic.

Super colleagues in the Social and Cultural Analysis Department at New York University, especially Crystal Parikh and Lok Siu, offered me—as a very green junior scholar—kind remarks and patient advice on embryonic drafts of my academic work and a supportive place to share it.

At Cornell University, I could not have asked for a group of better colleagues than Derek Chang, Viranjini Munasinghe, and Shelley Wong. Their generous yet exacting comments on various drafts of many of this book's chapters—and especially their warmth, humor, and encouragement throughout the three years I was fortunate enough to have been part of the Asian American Studies Program (deftly and gracefully managed by Vlad Micic)—enriched my work and life in immeasurable ways. I am so grateful to have been part of this small but mighty crew. In the History of Art and Visual Studies Department, the feminist scholars Cheryl Finley, Maria Fernandez, and Jolene Rickard, who do the important work of race-ing art history day in and day out provided much-appreciated guidance, support, and warmth. Annetta Alexandridis, Judy Bernstock, Keeley Boerman, Saida Hodžić, Kaja McGowan, Lorenzo Perillo, Verity Platt, Noliwe Rooks, and Nandi Cohen Suarez shared their time, laughter, food, and fashion insights in ways that warmed even the coldest Ithaca months. Shirley Samuels is a standout colleague at Cornell in general, and especially for me. Her energy and efforts in helping me navigate the labyrinth of downtown Ithaca apartments, my first tenure-track job, and the work-life (and Ithaca-Brooklyn) balance were tireless and seemingly limitless.

While my time at the Pratt Institute has been short so far, there has been no shortage of good food, good conversations, and strong and super fun collegiality among my new colleagues in the Graduate Program in Media Studies, specifically Jon Beller, Stephanie Boluk, Ira Livingston, Mendi Obadike, Ethan Spigland, and Christopher Vitale.

During the writing of this book, some of the best times for me have been when I stopped working on it or thinking about it. Cara Faris, Melissa Fondakowski, Mike Garcia, Spencer and Katya Lum, Liz Madans, Thuy Linh Tu, and Gustavo Guerra Vasquez are always reenergizing forces and bringers of real talk and real Mexican food. Thank you, thank you.

Finally, this book and my world would be unthinkable without my family. My parents, Nguyễn Thị Thọ-Da and Phạm Minh Tân, provided strength, patience, and distraction for a writing process they did not always understand but always supported. My brother Son and sister-in-law Jina (who has never felt like an in-law); my sister Hai (who has always been more than a sister) and brother-in-law Robin; and Brian, most of all, have lived with and through the many twists and turns of the job market and writing process. Their laughter, constancy, and willingness to listen while I moan about it all are the reasons I finished writing this book. Also their promises of good Vietnamese food, sushi, and cake—those helped, too.

This book is dedicated to Anam, who entered this world breathless and has been giving me breath ever since.

# Introduction.
## Asian Personal Style Superbloggers and the Material Conditions and Contexts of Asian Fashion Work

On October 24, 2010, Susanna Lau—a London-born Hong Konger who is better known online by her childhood nickname, Susie Bubble (because she was always in her own little world)—posted a series of photographs of herself wearing lilac-and-pink-striped, 1930s-era cocktail pajamas (see figures I.1 and I.2). Shortly after the post went up, the owner of the small vintage clothing store in London where she purchased the pajamas was inundated with inquiries about the outfit. The owner recalls: "My phone was ringing off the hook. People called me from all over the country and beyond asking me for those pyjamas!"[1] As well as benefiting retailers, Lau's taste for out-of-the-box styles of dress (such as vintage pajamas as daywear) has also launched the careers of little-known independent designers. The *New York Times* reported, "Her finds have snared the attention of chains like Topshop; last year the company snapped up Angie Johnson, the [Canadian] designer of I Heart Norwegian Wood, one of Ms. Lau's discoveries, to create a line for its stores."[2] Rumi Neely, a mixed-race Japanese American, wields the same kind of sales-boosting power. Sales surge any time fashion companies like Forever 21 and Myer (an Australian department store) feature her in their advertising campaigns. Chris Wirasinha, cofounder of pop culture web channel pedestrian.tv, rightly observes, "If Rumi likes your brand, it's probably worth more than a *Harper's Bazaar* or a *Vogue* mention."[3]

1.1 and 1.2 Susanna Lau in vintage cocktail pajamas, Style Bubble, October 24, 2010.

Other bloggers like the Korean American Aimee Song and the Taiwanese American Tina Craig (who coauthors the blog Bag Snob with fellow Taiwanese American Kelly Cook) have an impact on sales simply by wearing their favorite clothes. Song has boasted that clothes she photographs herself wearing and posts to the photo-sharing site Instagram, where she has more than a million followers, usually sell out that day.[4] Although Craig's blog focuses on handbags, a Twitter photograph of her wearing DL1961 premium denim jeans not only caused a spike in sales for the company, it also launched a capsule collection called DL1961xBagsnob (in which a pair of jeans retails for $168–$225).[5] The Vietnamese American blogger Wendy Nguyen's "Promise" bracelet, designed in collaboration with Tacori (for whom she is also the brand ambassador) has become a top-selling item for the American jewelry company. The bracelet with its intertwined silver and yellow gold has also found a receptive audience among A-list celebrities like Jay Z, who purchased it as a Valentine's Day gift for his superstar wife, Beyoncé.[6]

Lau, Neely, Song, Craig, and Nguyen are part of an elite class of personal style bloggers whose tastes—represented primarily by the fashion garments and accessories they buy, wear, style, describe, admire, and broadcast on their personal blogs—carry an inordinate amount of cultural and economic influence. Like all personal style bloggers, they post photos of themselves wearing clothes, often accompanied by text describing the occasion for wearing the outfit, styling tips, or product reviews. They also share details of their personal lives that help contextualize their unique fashion perspectives. Lau has hinted on her blog that her signature eccentric style of combining "clashing" prints, colors, and categories of clothing (for example, sportswear and formal wear, or sleepwear and sportswear) "was initially an act of rebellion against my parents and the 'popular' people at school."[7] (Throughout her blog, Lau openly, if offhandedly, attributes her feelings of childhood alienation to her racial difference.) Nguyen's adolescence—spent first in poverty as a Vietnamese immigrant, whose parents worked in the garment industry[8] and later in the California foster care system—provides the tacit or overt backstory for all of her blog posts. Her personal history reframes how we understand her penchant for floaty, diaphanous dresses and other similarly feminine items. Her romantic and generally conservative style has a cheerful, even indomitably optimistic, spirit when viewed in light of her tumultuous past. In one post she acknowledges that her personal style blog helps her to "heal from some of the emotional scars" of her past.[9]

Broadly speaking, personal style blogs represent an individual's taste. Unlike the clothing featured in fashion museums or in retail spaces that is displayed on mannequins or on hangers, the clothes in style blogs are personal. They are worn on a real person's body, and they reflect a practice and convey an idea of self-composure. Clothes on personal style blogs communicate a personal style of dress as well as a style of identity and of life. They constitute what Joanne Entwistle terms "situated bodily practices."[10] Which garments bloggers wear and how they style them articulate a unique relation between the body and the individual's experience of everyday life. This approach to the media representation of clothing distinguishes personal style blogs from other popular genres of fashion blogs.

The street style blog (for example, The Sartorialist, Street Peeper, and Jak & Jil) presents a more panoramic view of fashion. It is concerned with representing the material, cultural, and aesthetic landscape of a city from a fashion perspective. It is not unusual, then, for most of the people featured in street style blogs to be unnamed and not described with any personalizing details. The primary function of street style blog images is to represent a fashion city, not a fashionable individual. The personal style blog is also distinct from the fashion news aggregate blog (such as The Cut and Business of Fashion), which focuses more on collecting and sharing links about fashion than on creating new content. These are filter blogs that presurf and presort the Internet for interesting, relevant, and recent news items. The personal style blog, street style blog, and fashion news aggregate blog are the three most common types of fashion blogs, but there are a number of derivative and minor genres including microblogs hosted on Tumblr, Instagram, and Twitter that are image-heavy and, more often than not, image-only presentations of personal style; blogs focused on fashion criticism like my own coauthored Threadbared; and blogs that combine elements of various genres of fashion, food, cooking, and lifestyle blogs. All fashion blog genres contain blogs that are independently owned, corporate owned, or some combination of the two.

The personal style blogs I'm concerned with in this book have a distinct set of common features. First, they are all privately owned and operated (though as they have become more successful, many have acquired noncontrolling corporate support). Second, they are run by Asian bloggers based mostly in the United States, although some of them are in the English-speaking Asian diaspora in England and the Philippines. And third, they constitute a highly select group of superblogs. By this, I mean that they are among the most elite blogs according to a variety of metrics, including online traffic; number of reader comments; number of subscribers or followers; the quantity and quality of fashion industry invitations, collaborations, and media attention that they attract; and their high name recognition. The blogs that are the focus of this book make up a very small and incredibly select group of personal style blogs that have the lion's share of influence and attention with respect to both the online public and the fashion industry.[11] How did this group of Asian superblogs rise to such prominence in the early twenty-first century? How did the fashion tastes of more or less ordinary Asian consumers come to have such significance in the new economies of mainstream Western fashion media and consumer markets? And how do Asian superbloggers' digital practices work to rearticulate race and gender as aesthetic strategies of value rather than locations of social difference? In other words, how are their personal style blogging practices (such as self-fashioning, posing, and writing) modes of taste work that turn their styles of gendered racial embodiment into cultural, social, and economic capital? These questions frame my investigation of Asian superblogs.

To begin, it is necessary to clarify what I mean by taste. I draw on Pierre Bourdieu's famous statement that "the idea of personal taste is an illusion."[12] What he meant is that our personal tastes are shaped by and reflect our social position and social context. Bourdieu argues that the expression of taste, materialized through our manners, comportment, speech, styles of dress, and other consumer choices, is a practice of self-classification: "Taste classifies, and it classifies the classifier."[13] Our tastes locate us in a particular social context that is itself structured by a system of sensibilities, dispositions, and values (what Bourdieu terms "habitus"). Thus, an analysis of the tastes of Asian superbloggers is an analysis of the social reality that creates the conditions for their taste as well as the cultural economic context that gives value to it. It asks both what is Asian taste in the context of early twenty-first-century fashion, and why do fashion consumers and the fashion industry have such a taste for it?

Above I described personal style blogs as representations of individual taste. But with respect to superblogs, the blogger's personal style and taste are not simply represented. As I have already indicated, elite Asian bloggers' tastes do a great deal of work. Their taste practices are value-producing activities that generate a significant though highly uneven amount of cultural, social, and sometimes financial capital for the blogger and for various entities in the fashion industry. As the fashion blog phenomenon has spread to the mainstream, fashion companies have become increasingly savvy about monetizing superbloggers' free taste labors (which involve creating media publicity, building consumers' interest and trust, and fashion modeling). Sometimes their savviness verges on the ethically dubious, as was the case when the luxury handbag company Fendi borrowed the "BryanBoy pose" (the signature pose of Filipino queer superblogger Bryan Grey Yambao) in its international ad campaign without crediting or compensating him. (I discuss this event in greater detail in chapter 4.)

In addition to producing economic value, Asian superbloggers' tastes produce economic relations between bloggers and readers and between bloggers and industry insiders. Although bloggers blog for free and readers read blogs for free, and although bloggers and readers have more or less equal social standing as ordinary fashion consumers, a superblogger is able to economicize readers' activities by turning their consumption of the blog and their admiration and emulation of the superblogger's taste into cultural, social, and financial capital—for example, when readers click on affiliate links embedded in a blog post.[14]

To examine Asian superbloggers' online taste activities as value-producing work is to place them in the longer historical context of Asian fashion work. In doing so, I want to extend the notion and history of Asian fashion work into the digital realm. This will serve to draw out the evolving roles that race, gender, and class play in structuring work opportunities and constraints for Asian fashion workers at a time when nonmaterial commodities (such as blogs and taste) have become so central to the fashion industry's accumulation of capital.

## One of These Is Much Like the Other

The Asian fashion worker—the designation likely brings to mind images of sewing machine operators; of an exploited and informal female workforce; and of a largely contingent Asian diasporic labor market concentrated in Southeast Asia, South Asia, and the United States that has been the global backbone of fashion manufacturing for the past sixty years. The work practices and conditions of this Asian fashion worker—the garment worker—are characterized by the brutal physicality of long hours, hot and poorly ventilated buildings, bent backs, tired bodies, and nimble fingers.

Since the late 2000s, the Asian fashion superblogger has emerged as a new kind of Asian fashion worker. The bloggers' online activities generate indirect and direct value for themselves and various entities connected to the fashion industry. In contrast to the earlier proletariat notion of the Asian fashion worker, the superblogger is considered to be part of a new Asian creative class. Instead of being seen as unskilled and oppressed, superbloggers are described in terms that emphasize their imagination, ingenuity, and vision. For example, when The Business of Fashion, a highly respected fashion news aggregate blog, kicked off its popular column "The Business of Blogging," the first three profile stories featured Asian superbloggers: first, Susanna Lau; second, Tommy Ton, a Vietnamese Canadian street style blogger and photographer; and finally, the Taiwanese American handbag bloggers Tina Craig and Kelly Cook. The stories focused on the bloggers' artistic vision as the driving force of their productions. In Ton's profile, the writer admired the blogger's "well-trained fashion eye" and his aesthetic sense for capturing "the little details" in his "landscape-style images," "a towering Louboutin stiletto here, a pop of colour there."[15] In Lau's profile, the writer quotes Lau as saying that her product is "my eye, my point of view, a certain taste, a certain way of documenting and presenting fashion."[16] Ton's taste for the little aesthetic details and Lau's taste for "documenting and presenting fashion" are understood in these media profiles to be work practices, highly skilled ones that are neither widely possessed nor easily learned. The high level of Ton's and Lau's taste work is what separates the wheat from the chaff, the everyday hobbyist blogger from the superblogger.

Implicit in these descriptions is a conceptual framework that separates head labors from hand labors, creative work from physical work. Accounts of Asian superbloggers' taste work as creative work, as intellectually and artistically innovative practices, are partial and misleading. They elide the ways in which taste work is physical, instrumental, and socially and culturally conditioned. Yet as narrow and inadequate as these interpretations of Asian superbloggers' taste work are, in some ways they are also refreshing and even possibly oppositional takes on Asian labor.

The Asian creative worker is a relatively new mainstream idea. Long-held Western stereotypes of Asian workers perceived them as unimaginative; docile; and predisposed to perform rote and repetitive, if demanding, work. In recent years, a spate of media and scholarly attention has focused on the Asian creative class, particularly fashion bloggers, YouTube video makers, maverick chefs, fashion designers, and software start-up founders. The literature on the Asian creative class coalesces around several themes: the mobility of second- and third-generation Asians away from traditional Asian occupations and definitions of success; a celebration of Asians' newfound individualism and freedom from—and, in many cases, rebellions against—so-called Eastern models of collectivist subjectivity; and the end of racial stereotypes as we know them (for example, new images of cool Asians are thought to supplant stereotypes of Asians as nerds). The underlying message in all these discussions is that for these Asians, race no longer poses social, economic, cultural, or personal obstacles. In effect, creativity and entrepreneurialism are perceived as social ladders that lead younger Asians out of blue- and pink-collar labor sectors. These sectors—which cross transnational boundaries and include domestic services, apparel manufacturing, and electronics assembly—have often been the only labor markets available to rural, immigrant, poor, and undocumented Asians.

Represented as personalities, productive Asian hipsters from the YouTube beauty guru Michelle Phan to the pot-smoking, accidental multimillionaire graffiti artist David Choe are imagined to embody a different relation to capitalism: one based not on gendered racial stereotypes but on individual talent. Asian creatives supposedly signal an entirely new vector of Asian labor history that is rooted in free expression rather than exploitation. Countless mainstream media articles and blog posts assert that the rising prominence of Asian creatives represents a definitive shift away from previous racial labor identities and markets. One such article written by Richard Florida, best known for his assertion that creativity is the new engine of capitalist production and urban renewal, begins this way: "Many in the West think of the Asian Pacific as the world's factory."[17] The rest of the article is dedicated to smashing that perception. For Florida, the Asian factory worker is an embodiment of an earlier formation of Asian labor that has now been superseded. Florida and other writers and scholars contrast the earlier Asian factory worker with the creative entrepreneur. Whereas Asian factory labor is closely monitored and controlled, Asian creative labor is free and self-managed. Whereas Asian factory labor is exploitative and alienating, Asian creative labor is expressive and personal.

The category of the creative class embodies an implicit ideological assumption about the democratic and even liberatory properties of creative work. Framed by ideas of individualism, agency, meritocracy, postracism, and liberal multiculturalism, creative work and success in the so-called new economy is understood as fueled by individual drive and intellectual capacity rather than capital, credentials, and other institutionally conferred privileges. Following this logic, a person's race, ethnicity, gender, and class do not hinder access to success in creative economies. They may even be assets. Re-presented through taste work practices (self-fashioning, sartorial styling, posing, and so on) race, ethnicity, and gender can be rearticulated as aesthetic positions or fashion statements that add to and enhance the value of one's identity as a personal style blogger in the new digital fashion media economy.[18]

Asian web stars stand out as success stories in the digital realms of creative economies. In mainstream media outlets like the *New York Times* and the Huffington Post as well as popular arts and culture blogs like Hyperallergic, much has been written about Asian creatives' talent, charisma, capacity to build social networks, and unique but universally appealing personal brand.[19] The common implication is that the new economy of informational or networked capitalism is far more egalitarian than the old economy of industrial capitalism that still persists in more formalized labor sectors like the manufacturing and film and television industries. Under informational capitalism, the increase and diffusion of productive forces, particularly as a result of new user-driven media technologies and knowledges, have purportedly democratized economic processes. Old barriers to success like race, ethnicity, class, gender, and lack of capital can be overcome with a certain measure of stick-to-itiveness and social media savvy. A Huffington Post story points out that "discrimination, stereotypes and exclusion are the norm for Asians, both on television and the silver screen" but "social media . . . amplifies otherwise unheard-from populations and creates an equal playing field for ethnic minorities. In this realm . . . Asian Americans (and cats) dominate."[20] Asian web stars—personal style superbloggers being some of the most highly visible among them—seem to be evidence of the new and more equitable race and labor relations under informational capitalism.

My book pushes against the assumptions of upward postracial mobility that structure popular understandings of the new Asian digital creative class. Rather than seeing personal style blogging as an altogether new and postracial job category, I situate it within the longer historical trajectory of gendered racial fashion work. Focusing on Asian personal style bloggers' practices and conditions of taste work, I highlight the historical continuities and discontinuities in the social and economic processes shaping new modes of Asian fashion labor. My aim is to demonstrate that the roles race, gender, and class play in structuring work opportunities and constraints under informational capitalism are evolving, not diminishing.

Throughout this book, I examine Asian personal style superbloggers as workers rather than digital artisans, high-tech bohemians, or even immaterial laborers. These latter categories of labor—occupations involved in Florida's lauded gentrification processes—do not adequately capture the structural similarities that both cut across and link the class relations between new and earlier forms of fashion work that I am concerned with in this book.

Personal style bloggers as a group trouble distinctions between immaterial and physical labor, and between innovative and instrumental labor. Whereas digital artisans and high-tech bohemians are explicitly marked as middle-class categories, personal style bloggers are not so easily characterized. Some come from middle-class backgrounds, but others do not (as is reflected in the style-on-a-budget blogs that feature clothes purchased from fast fashion and big-box retailers). For most bloggers, blogging constitutes a second-shift job, with all the gendered implications that term entails. All bloggers blog for free, and the most successful of them blog for more than eight or ten hours each day (again, this is often in addition to the hours they work at their "day job").

Furthermore, though they are digital or immaterial laborers, they are also embodied ones. They generate visual, textual, and aesthetic information that is located and stored in disembodied and distributed networks of algorithmic functions, personal computers, and data centers. Yet these digital, immaterial, or cognitive laborers are not laborers without bodies. Personal style bloggers' work practices involve the physical labors of posing; self-adornment; and shuttling between their homes, photo sites, and retail sites.

 Asian personal style bloggers are especially difficult to categorize in terms of conventional labor classifications. Asian superbloggers are immaterial or informational laborers, yet their gendered racial bodies are of particular importance to their work in this historical period of global fashion capitalism. Their participation in the blogosphere as well as their incorporation into the dominant Western fashion industry are conditioned to a great extent by the cultural economic value of their Asian bodies in this moment that many regard as the Asian decade, which began around 2008. (Diane von Furstenberg and others, including the *Financial Times*, are convinced that the Asian decade is really the start of the Asian century.[21]) As I will explain below, the rise of Asian fashion superbloggers has occurred at a time when the fashion industry and its various taste makers have a taste for Asian tastes.

This book is inarguably indebted to the many insights that digital and immaterial labor studies provide into the new organizations and meanings of work in informational economies. However, too many critical conceptualizations of immaterial labor are limited because they ignore race as a variable in the quality and conditions of informational or knowledge work. Terms like *electronic sweatshops* and *digital plantations* are frequently used to describe the exploitative conditions of immaterial or informational labor. But sweatshops and plantations do not simply name difficult workplaces. They designate a racially gendered system of labor organization in which owners, managers, and manufacturers dehumanize specific groups of people to extract surplus value. Race and gender shape work opportunities and constraints in physical as well as digital arenas, and scholars who ignore this risk treating Others' experiences as no more than colorful metaphors. Indeed, the historical specificity of these terms is emptied out when the sweated labor in question is that of, say, English-language Wikipedia editors (who are overwhelmingly white and male[22]) or when *netslaves* refers to the volunteer AOL community leaders and chat hosts who in 1999 sued the Internet giant for back wages.

The insights that scholars like Lisa Nakamura, Minoo Moallem, Nishant Shah, and Kalindi Vora have provided into the uneven flows and inequitable distributions of technical capital (whether skills, resources, wages, knowledge, or time) represent some of the most interesting and important work on race, gender, digital labor, and economies today.[23] Collectively, their research draws critical attention to the historical links connecting material bodies and relations with digital technologies, practices, and economies. But their discussions of Chinese gold farmers in World of Warcraft, iPhone girls, electronic assembly plant workers, call center operators, carpet weavers, and puppeteers focus on proletarianized—or at least nonelite—classes of workers. The structural marginalization these workers experience in digital economies is reflective of and compounded by the racialized and gendered materiality of their bodies.

The Asian superbloggers I focus on here are a racially gendered labor force with an inordinate amount of status, influence, and cultural power. This class of style bloggers represents not simply the 1 percent but something closer to the 0.01 percent of bloggers who have more than the lion's share of online traffic, readers, informal and formal support from fashion industry insiders, corporate sponsorships, and personal resources. Their high visibility in an economy in which attention is currency is what has made them ready examples of the postracism of the digital era.

However, I insist in this book that Asian personal style blogger is not a postracial or postpolitical labor identity but instead a historically situated, racially gendered and class-based formation. As with Asian labor in garment manufacturing industries, the labor of Asian personal style superbloggers is shaped by larger geopolitical, economic, technological, and cultural structures. Asian superbloggers' work is nonmaterial, but it is not removed from the material reality and constraints of fashion economies, social relations, and work opportunities that include the inequalities of race, class, size, and gender presentation that have always structured fashion work. The blogosphere is just as racially stratified as earlier fashion labor markets, though it exhibits a somewhat different pattern and logic of stratification.

 The difference has to do with the emergence of key luxury fashion markets in Asia, the new meanings and significance of Asianness in the Asian decade, the relative privilege of Asian fashion blog workers in relation to garment workers, and the aesthetic and personal nature of bloggers' taste work compared to the impersonal work of apparel manufacturing. What's more, elite bloggers have technological, cultural, and economic resources that industrial fashion workers simply do not. Indeed, the very work and success of Asian superbloggers rests on the promoting and buying of commodities that Asian garment workers (and electronics assembly workers) produce under highly exploitative conditions. Asian superbloggers, garment workers, and electronics assembly workers are linked together in a strange circuit of production in which one group's free, highly visible, and rewarding labor (because it offers outlets for self-expression, creativity, and social connection, as well as the possibility of lucrative side work) depends on another group's free or severely underpaid, invisible, and largely alienating labor. Put differently, the emergence of this new form of Asian fashion labor (personal style superblogging) is constitutive of and constituted by the continuation of an older form of Asian fashion labor (garment work). Yet both are positioned—hierarchically—in fashion's productive system as a racially gendered supply of unwaged or underwaged labor.

While I focus on the ways in which the structural position of these two groups of Asian fashion workers overlap, I do not want to lose sight of a fundamental reality: there are vast differences between industrial and immaterial fashion work and the conditions that shape each worker group's experiences and activities. In some ways, their differences are so great that a comparison might seem implausible. Substandard work conditions, declining wages in leading apparel-exporting countries, and the physical degradation of workers' bodies (including verbal, physical, and sexual abuse by factory managers) are structural realities for apparel manufacturing workers. Bloggers do not experience these, even in the worst circumstances.

Despite these important differences, *Asians Wear Clothes on the Internet* argues that Asian personal style superbloggers are connected to Asian garment workers—though not in the same way that other Asian fashion workers are. In *The Beautiful Generation*, Thuy Linh Tu observes that Asian American designers acknowledge and create relationships to garment workers that, for some, are based on familial histories intimately connecting the designers to the garment or apparel manufacturing industry. Whether familial or chosen, Tu explains, the kinship relations between Asian American designers and Asian suppliers and sewers who become so-called aunties and uncles challenge the fashion industry's "logic of distance" (in Tu's formulation). These relationships, for her, "acknowledge proximity, contact, and affiliation between domains imagined as distinct."[24] Asian superbloggers do not identify with or demonstrate any apparent sympathy for the hundreds of thousands of Asian industrial fashion workers around the globe who produce the material and technological products on which blog labor relies. Not only do superbloggers not acknowledge cultural, familial, or other intimate connections with the people who make the clothes featured on their blogs, but—as I discuss in chapter 5—they sometimes use the digital resources and digital work practices available to them to maintain a divide between head and hand, or innovative and instrumental, labors. Yet a structural examination of Asian fashion work and the productive systems and modes of fashion capital accumulation it sustains and that sustain it reveals that these two groups of Asian fashion workers have similar material and social positions in fashion's productive economy.

This book traces how the work practices and working conditions of Asian superbloggers and Asian garment workers—specifically with respect to their gendered and racialized implications—link them in spite of their differences. Thinking about these two groups together reveals fascinating insights into the fashion industry's changing and enduring divisions of labor, opportunity, recognition, and rewards as it is shifting from a manufacturing-based economy to one based on information or communication. Inarguably, the material conditions and social relations of power that defined fashion labor under late twentieth-century capitalism are different from those defining fashion labor under early twenty-first-century informational capitalism (more on this below). This book shows, however, that there are historical continuities in the racial and gendered dimensions of patterns of employment opportunity, wage gaps, and labor systems, suggesting that conditions of fashion production in the digital age have much in common with those in earlier stages of global industrialization.

## Economies of Asian Industrial and Informational Fashion Work

*Asians Wear Clothes on the Internet* demonstrates the complementarity of fashion's informational and industrial labor systems without conflating the two. To begin with, both systems have low start-up costs, require little to no prior training or experience, pay workers less than a living wage for physically taxing full-time jobs, prevent unionization through decentralization, discourage workers' collective identification through individualizing tasks and reward systems, and in general exploit workers. Additionally, Asian women and girls have played a significant role in both the early twenty-first-century and late twentieth-century fashion industries—suggesting a shared racial and gendered organization of fashion labor across two very different modes of work.

The entry and participation of Asian garment workers and superbloggers in both fashion production systems are results of broader shifts in global capitalism. In the 1970s, the fashion industry was transformed by the same neoliberal ideologies and policies that had begun to transform various U.S. economic and cultural sectors. Neoliberalism's inexorable march through the 1970s and 1980s cast unions as bureaucratic impediments to workplace efficiency and promoted unobstructed corporate expansion as an intrinsic right under free market capitalism. Neoliberal policies spurred the rapid growth of transnational corporations and increased global production of export goods by some of the poorest countries and people in the world. It was in this late twentieth-century period that Asians, mostly Southeast and South Asian women and girls and immigrant Asians in the United States, first entered the fashion labor force in large numbers.

The second phase of fashion's economic restructuring—which I argue is not entirely divorced from the first phase—began in the early 2000s. This twenty-first-century phase is marked by a confluence of several technological, social, and economic changes: the mass distribution of personal digital technologies, the rise in the use of social media, and the 2008 financial crash and recession in Europe and the United States that caused the fashion industry to turn its attention to Asian consumers as a new luxury market. English-speaking Asian fashion bloggers rose to prominence in the midst of this recession, enabled by these new technological, political, and economic transformations.

In 2008, at the dawn of the Asian decade, Asian personal style bloggers embodied fashion's new ideal consumer, and they unwittingly became informational intermediaries. Their blogs provide consumers, retailers, and designers with an easily accessible storehouse of up-to-the-minute information about style trends and consumer values. A few words and photographs posted to high-ranking Asian personal style blogs like Lau's Style Bubble or Neely's Fashion Toast have enhanced the cool cred of established brands while training a high-powered social media spotlight on emerging designers and little-known fashion retailers. As representative consumers of a newly significant luxury market, these bloggers' observations are of particular interest to fashion companies that are working hard to capture Asian consumers' attention and disposable income. The growing numbers of Asian models on fashion runways and in magazines—a related phenomenon in the Asian decade—can also be attributed to the new significance of Asian markets to the Western fashion industry. As Ivan Bart, the senior vice president and managing director of IMG Models Worldwide, explains, "it comes down to getting consumers to come to your brand. You have to have faces that reflect the consumer."[25] Asian superbloggers have faces that reflect the new ideal fashion consumer and do the work of promoting brands for a great deal less money than commercial fashion models or, more often than not, for free.

Asian feminized labor has been integral to the fashion industry's global expansion and development throughout the late twentieth and early twenty-first centuries. What is popularly described as an historical novelty—the Asian moment (beginning in the mid-2000s)—has a precedent in the early years of neoliberal globalization in the 1970s and 1980s. In both cases, the production of fashion commodities, one material (clothing) and the other nonmaterial (information, taste, and blogs), relies on racially gendered Asian bodies seen as particularly suited for fashion labor and the specific needs of global Western fashion capitalism. The industrial manufacture of mass-produced and mass-distributed clothing requires cheap, docile, and plentiful labor that Asian and immigrant Asian women and girls are imagined to embody and to be naturally suited to provide.

Today, English-speaking Asian superbloggers are also well positioned to provide important contributions to Western fashion's expansion into and capture of emerging and dynamic Asian markets. As I suggested above, the bloggers are racially matched with the Asian consumers whom Western fashion companies have set their sights on. At the same time, because the bloggers are English speakers, they are familiarly and knowably Western. They are just racially exotic enough to have a wide market appeal—to Asian as well as to non-Asian English-speaking consumers and retailers—yet not so foreign that their racial difference disrupts the postracial fantasy of late capitalism. Asian superbloggers' language privilege lends economic value to their racially marked bodies. Their English fluency maintains their highly marketable balance between exotic and familiar.

Finally and just as importantly, Asian superbloggers possess a sizable personal market share of the so-called attention economy as well as the capacity to accumulate more currency because they have a strong online presence, a highly engaged and loyal audience base, and a proven and significant record for promoting Western fashion brands (again, often for free). With the institutionalization of social commerce in which social media technologies and practices play key roles in shaping consumer behaviors and decisions, the Western fashion industry is increasingly (probably more than it would care to admit) relying on the unwaged labor of bloggers for its continuation and development.

It is important to underscore that personal style blog labor is always free labor—voluntarily given and unpaid. More than an economic issue, this is an issue of identity. Superbloggers' construction of their labor subjectivities as artists rests on the idea that they blog for passion, not for money. In a *New York Times* article about her, Lau describes her blogging in terms of an obsession that has "no financial motivation."[26] Similarly, while blogging provides Song opportunities for additional capital streams, she frequently points out that her main source of income is her interior design job. This job serves as Song's proof that her blog is a "genuine expression of her style."[27]

Superbloggers—an infinitesimally tiny fraction of all bloggers—have managed to create a livelihood from side jobs such as brand collaborations, affiliate links, direct ad sales, and freelancing that can be quite lucrative. Top-tier bloggers make as much as $250,000 annually (possibly more, depending on the number and types of design collaborations, paid appearances, and advertising partnerships they amass). But these are indirect earning methods that are separate from, though related to, the actual production of blogs. The actual blogging labor of superbloggers—like all bloggers—is unwaged work. In this way, superbloggers are no different from other Internet users who provide the free labor that keeps the Internet running. Now an $8 trillion[28] enterprise,[29] the Internet is built and sustained by a massive network of horizontal yet hierarchical users (as Tiziana Terranova points out) who voluntarily provide labor in the form of content creation, information sharing, communicating, buying, selling, and so on.[30]

In this era of social commerce, the various and, again, voluntary online activities of fashion media and market consumers now provide much of the advertising and promotion that fashion retailers and designers depend on to sell their clothes. According to a 2013 report by the Internet search engine company Technorati, bloggers are particularly influential. Thirty-one percent of fashion consumers say blogs influence their purchases.[31] A four-year survey conducted by the media company BlogHer (which focuses on women bloggers and blog readers, a significant number of whom participate in the fashion blogosphere) found that for the majority of female readers (53 percent), recommendations from bloggers have more weight than celebrity endorsements.[32] What this influence translates to in numbers is staggering. A top-tier blog like Craig and Cook's BagSnob can drive as much as $175 million in annual sales to retailers.[33] While retailers profit enormously, even the highest paid bloggers earn negligible fees. As with garment workers, Asian superbloggers' relationship to the broader fashion industry is characterized by sharply asymmetrical distributions of labor and earnings.

Perhaps the strongest link between Asian personal style superbloggers and Asian garment workers is the historically fraught position they share as the embodied evidence of and alibi for the racially gendered processes of transnational fashion capitalism. The two groups of Asian workers entered Western fashion's production systems in related but distinct historical moments when economic articulations of Asians represented them as Western capitalist success stories (as model minority labor) and, paradoxically, as economic competitors threatening the dominant racial order of Western capitalism (as cheap Asian labor).

Understood within a taste model of race relations, the contradictory status of Asian workers and of meanings of Asian labor in these two different fashion production systems is not surprising. Taste is flexible and fleeting—none more so than fashion taste. One person's taste is likely to be another person's distaste, but one's taste can also become one's distaste as a result of changing personal and popular tastes. One particular form of distaste is the aftertaste. These are tastes that might at first be pleasing but, after lingering too long in the mouth, throat, or public sphere (for example, through media overexposure) become unpalatable.

Historically, we have seen the increased visibility of racial Others in positions of political power, economic employment, or academic arenas turn racial admiration into racial resentment. The popular reception of model minorities provides a useful example of the slide from racial taste to racial aftertaste. In the 1960s, the U.S. paper of record, the *New York Times*, praised "Japanese American style" work ethic and academic achievements.[34] In 2007, an article published in the same newspaper expressed concerns that the overrepresentation of Asians at top-ranked universities like the University of California at Berkeley were turning these American institutions into "Little Asias."[35] More than four decades after embracing the Asian model minority and with the seeming rise in the number of model minorities at American institutions, the "Little Asias" article reflects the limits of racial tolerance when racial taste becomes racial aftertaste. The 2007 *Times* article described Asians as "the demographic of the moment," suggesting that Asians had overstayed their moment and left racial traces that were apparently neither assimilable nor repressible, and certainly not fully controllable. One such racial trace mentioned in the article is Mandarin, a language described as now "part of the soundtrack at this iconic university," heard "all the time, in plazas, cafeterias, classrooms, study halls, dorms and fast-food outlets."[36]

Racial aftertastes describe aversions to racial alterities, the features, aspects, and bodies of racial otherness that are not easily consumable either because their racial flavor is perceived as too strong or because their racial traces linger so long that they exceed the terms and limits of racial palatability. Aftertastes mark the limits of racial tolerance; they are not manifestations of blatant racial hatred. Aftertastes are taste judgments derived from perceptions that racial boundaries of social and economic power and privilege are being threatened by a figure or feature of racial alterity seen not just as out of place, but as not keeping its place because it is encroaching on places where it does not belong (like iconic American universities or job markets that belong to so-called real Americans). Racial aftertastes are the bringing to the surface of racial anxieties and apprehensions that exceed the limits of racial tolerance. Taste and aftertaste, like racial tolerance and intolerance, are contradictory yet complementary. Part of the same structure of racial power and domination, they are systemically co-operating and co-constituted.

Economic articulations of Asian fashion workers as both solutions for and problems of the Western fashion industry's productive needs are also contradictory and complementary. And if, as Bourdieu argues, taste is reflective not so much of personal preference but of "the logic of the space of [taste] production,"[37] then an examination of the taste for Asian fashion workers and its aftertaste has important implications for our understanding of the contradictory yet complementary racial logics of transnational capitalism in the late twentieth century and informational capitalism in the early twenty-first century.

While Asian personal style superbloggers are generally associated with the new Asian creative class—a labor category that supposedly distinguishes them from previous racialized categories of Asian model minority labor like the efficient and passive garment worker or electronics assembly worker—the superbloggers can be understood as a model minority labor force for the digital era. The model minority thesis emerged in the 1960s as a racial discourse that constructs an image of Asians in the United States and elsewhere as hardworking, self-driven, and self-sufficient people who maximize available opportunities for social and economic advancement (at school or in the workplace), all without fuss or friction. In the civil rights era, it functioned as a liberal alibi that countered the growing criticisms of structural racial inequalities raised most forcefully and publicly by African Americans and Latinos. Images of the Asian model minority in television news, entertainment media, and popular newspapers and magazines like the *New York Times*[38] and *U.S. News and World Report*[39] repeatedly deployed the Asian model minority stereotype as a way to obscure the racialized realities of systemically uneven distributions of political, economic, and social power, opportunities, and resources.

In the 1980s, advocates of neoliberal policies and discourses framed the transnationalization of production that shifted Western manufacturing work offshore and underground as the triumph of free-market democracy. The largely Asian and Latina workforce in the United States and abroad that fill the jobs created by the global expansion of Western apparel manufacturing constitute a model minority labor force. The workers are perceived as ideally suited to fulfill the demands of Western fashion capital for dramatically reduced labor costs, quick turnaround of a high volume of garments, and maximized profits. Richard Pierce is the former owner of a garment factory in Saipan, a U.S. territory in the South Pacific that in the 1980s and 1990s produced clothes for U.S. brands like Gap, Nordstrom, Liz Claiborne, JC Penney, Abercrombie and Fitch, Polo, Gymboree, and Sears, to name a few. Pierce boasts of the predominantly Chinese and Filipina labor force his factory had: "I remember one of the biggest manufacturers here when he visited our company. . . . He came into the factory and the first thing he did was, he kind of just listened and you can tell by the hum of the machinery there whether it's a productive place. He just got this smile on his face because our workers were actually, I think, better than his. It's a busy place."[40]

While Asian and Latina garment workers have been vocal about the brutal working conditions and criminal labor practices necessary to sustain the high level of productivity that labor contractors, designers, retailers, and consumers have come to expect, they are regularly held up as living proof that the promise of free-market democracy (in which a free, competitive market will positively influence individual and national economic and social development) has been realized. Pierce maintains that the apparel manufacturing industry's system of contract, contingent, and outsourced labor is "to the benefit of here [Saipan's economy] and particularly, I think more than anything, to the benefit of the ladies that are here in our business that come from other places."[41] Pierce's perspective is a common neoliberal stance that fails to acknowledge the ways neoliberal economic policies are directly responsible for widening the gap between the rich and the poor in the United States[42] as well as deepening the international division of labor between the Global North and the Global South (and all of that division's racialized and gendered relations of production).[43] A 1999 lawsuit filed by more than 30,000 garment workers in Saipan (the majority of whom were from China and the Philippines) clearly contradicts Pierce's claim. The lawsuit cited labor and human rights violations—including emotional abuse, dangerous working conditions, nonpayment, and debt peonage—that essentially held workers hostage in garment factories, keeping them from their children and other family members.

Uncritical celebrations about the benefits of neoliberal restructuring for (Asian) workers in other countries occurred at the same time that (white) workers in the United States in the 1980s were experiencing severe economic decline as a consequence of "the combined effects of deindustrialization, economic restructuring, and the oppressive materialism of a market society where things have more value than people."[44] The model minority worker discourse added more fuel to the flames of anti-Asian sentiment, which has a long history in the United States. In the 1980s and 1990s, a pervasive belief that Asians represented a foreign economic enemy to white American workers led to heightened anti-Asian violence, including the murder of Vincent Chin in Detroit, Michigan. (One of his attackers was heard saying, "It's because of you little motherfuckers that we're out of work!"[45]) Asian garment workers in the 1980s and 1990s were put in the contradictory position of embodying both a gendered model minority labor force and a racialized and foreign economic enemy.

The fraught position of Asian garment workers—as the racially gendered embodiment of the problem of and the solution for transnational fashion capitalism, as the alibi confirming and the evidence undermining the promise of free-market democracy, and as the model minority labor force and foreign economic competition—mirrors that of the new Asian fashion worker. Asian superbloggers such as Yambao, Lau, Song, and Neely are regularly held up as proof that the digital democratization of fashion production systems is real. The indirect earnings of Yambao, Song, and Lau are routinely the focus of news stories about fashion's digital democratization. To be sure, they provide compelling evidence for claims that social media are lowering participation barriers and allowing more people to enter the previously insular fashion industry. The fact that ordinary Asian Internet users have become superbloggers (earning six figures annually) in a historically white cultural economic field—seemingly through their own hard work and determination—is the kind of rags-to-riches trajectory that is essential to the model minority discourse. Asian superbloggers are not simply among the top earning personal style bloggers; in 2013, Yambao and Song were the two highest grossing superbloggers in the world.[46] Yambao made headlines when he admitted in the early days of personal style blogging that "he makes more than $100,000 per year,"[47] mostly from advertising and guest appearances.[48] Aimee Song, the highest-paid blogger in the world, commanded fees as high as $50,000 for a single brand collaboration a couple of years ago.[49] While there are no published data, her current fees are likely higher now since her popularity has increased in recent years.

But as with the earlier formation of the model minority fashion worker, the Asian superblogger is largely a discursive construction that conceals deep-seated asymmetries of race, color, class, and body size in the blogosphere and in the global fashion industry more broadly. Asian superbloggers are a highly visible and high-achieving group, but they are also only a tiny minority of superbloggers—which is why the same few Asian superbloggers are named over and over in the fashion media. The personal style superblogosphere, as a whole, is overwhelmingly white. At the same time, Asian superbloggers' body sizes and skin tones complement rather than challenge dominant standards of beauty. In fact, personal style blogs and other related social media platforms and practices have not so much democratized the fashion industry as they have enabled limited forms of diversification that do not upset the racialized hierarchies of fashion bodies, tastes, and economies that have historically structured the Western fashion industry.

Discursive constructions of Asian superbloggers as the embodied evidence of digital democratization also ignore the uneven social relations built into the commercial Internet, where a handful of corporations control the technical means of communication, creative expression, and sociability that millions use but will never own. While new user-driven technologies of communication and information have certainly lowered participation barriers in fashion's productive and consumer economies, they have not eliminated disparities in the quality of participation in and through the blogosphere. Henry Jenkins, Craig Watkins, and others have argued that the corporatization and mass distribution of cheaper Internet technologies and telecommunications infrastructure have narrowed the digital divide between the technological haves and have-nots.[50] These authors caution, however, that there is a growing participation gap in which certain online users and activities that serve and sustain corporate interests are privileged over others. The participation gap is unmistakable in the personal style blogosphere.

Creating a fashion blog is free and relatively easy, thanks to new on-line publishing services. Yet the corporate-run search engines' operating logic means that only the most popular sites are likely to show up in web searches. The advent of expensive search engine optimization services means that the top search result positions are for sale to sites with large bankrolls. The same websites and blogs routinely appear in the top three to five results of web searches; all other sites, as Jodi Dean puts it, are "drowned in the massive flow [of commercialized data]."[51] When I ran a search using the term *fashion blog*, the first page of Google results included only corporate and monetized blogs maintained by *Elle* magazine, *New York* magazine, the Sartorialist, and Fashion Toast (Neely's blog, which is now hosted, but not owned, by the media giant Fairchild Fashion Media). I received nearly identical results using the Bing and Yahoo search engines. Blogs owned and run by individual personal style bloggers were nowhere near the top of the search rankings. This confirms Dean's observations that digital democracy is little more than a "neoliberal fantasy": "Rather than a rhizomatic structure where any one point is as likely to be reached as any other, what we have on the web are situations of massive inequality, massive differentials of scales where some nodes get tons of hits and the vast majority get almost none."[52]

In the personal style blogosphere, fashion's traditional social hierarchies are not leveling out, nor are they becoming more democratic. Instead, these hierarchies have evolved in ways that allow them to expand into this popular digital arena. Far from being a postracial meritocracy, the personal style blogosphere is organized by highly uneven distributions of power and privilege that are not determined by blog quality. The on-line traffic of some African American fashion blogs (both personal style blogs and street style blogs) outrank or are comparable to white and Asian English-language U.S. fashion blogs, yet many of the African American blogs with the most traffic, like The Fashion Bomb, do not show up in top search results and do not receive nearly the same levels of national and global attention as do white and English-language Asian superblogs. With the notable exceptions of Street Etiquette, a style blog coproduced by Joshua Kissi and Travis Gumbs; Tamu McPherson's street style blog All the Pretty Birds;[53] and Kathryn Finney's cheap chic blog, The Budget Fashionista, African American–run blogs occupy the same marginal status in the blogosphere as African American fashion models (and Black fashion models more broadly) do on the runway.[54]

Bloggers that are not located in global media empires also have an extremely difficult time gaining the attention of the hegemonic Western fashion industry. Han Huohuo, for example, is a blogging sensation in China. His account on the strictly policed Chinese microblogging platform Weibo draws more than a million followers, yet he hardly registers in the mainstream consciousness of the Western fashion public. Because he lives in China and is subject to its state-run and heavily censored media system, Han lacks access to popular blog host sites like Blogger and Word-Press; blog-measuring sites like Technorati; and social media platforms like YouTube, Vimeo, and Twitter. Further, Weibo is not readily accessible to audiences outside of mainland China, although modified versions of it exist in Taiwan and Hong Kong.

Han and other Chinese bloggers are further disadvantaged by China's relatively low ranking on the Global Creativity Index that measures national levels of financial investment and research, among other technological infrastructural commitments. In 2011, China ranked thirty-seventh, about on a par with Latvia and Bulgaria.[55] In effect, these technological conditions structure the flows of information and communication that shape bloggers' work experiences, opportunities, and earning potential (in terms of social, cultural, informational, and financial capital). As a result, the social divisions of labor and the social stratifications that exist outside of the Internet are embedded in and supported by the operating logic of search engines and the development logic of telecommunications networks and services.

Even superbloggers who have the advantages of public, industry, and technological attention (such as a top rank in search engine results) participate in the blogosphere under highly asymmetrical and exploitative conditions. Superbloggers who generate hundreds of thousands of clicks on and in their blogs and microblogs (Twitter, Instagram, and so on) may or may not monetize their popularity, but they do create an extraordinary amount of capital for social media sites that these companies depend on for revenue. Popular platforms draw interest and funding from venture capital firms as well as major advertisers—both of which are willing to pay top-ranked Internet companies a lot of money for access to their users' information and attention. The importance of Asian superbloggers to Google has not escaped the company's notice. When the Web behemoth wanted to understand how new media are consumed and used, it turned to a small handful of experts, among them Lau, Yambao, Ton, and Ethan Nguyen.[56]

For every superblogger who can command public and corporate attention, there are thousands more (across all racial groups) who will never find a general audience, much less a livelihood. Asian superbloggers have won the "glittering prizes" in what Andrew Ross calls the "jackpot economy," but as with all jackpots, there are many more players than there are winners.[57] As I demonstrate throughout this book, the glittering prizes of substantial online traffic, corporate collaborations, sponsorships, affiliations, and paid freelance writing and speaking opportunities can distract us from noticing that the game is rigged against bloggers, even those who have achieved considerable success. The dominant fashion industry rigs the game in a way that recalls Marx's notion of worker alienation: as Mark Andrejevic puts it, workers' labors are turned back on them.[58] Ironically, the more successful bloggers are, the better positioned they are for increased self- and corporate exploitation.

Asian superbloggers have acquired a substantial number of privileges within the fashion industry. Yet these privileges come at a cost. The corporate Internet, as Andrejevic has argued, is structured to accelerate and channel users' behaviors for commercial profit. Online publishing services encourage bloggers to make their sites visible to search engines; use tags and categories (a classification system that groups similar blog posts together and makes them searchable); post often; respond to readers' comments; link to other blogs; and even pay for web traffic using services like StumbleUpon, which forwards web content to users. These activities can help increase and sustain high levels of blog traffic—a key goal for superbloggers—but they also demand more and more free labor from the bloggers in the form of more blog posts as well as more Tweets, Instagram photographs, and other social media content. These diverse but converging social media platforms provide additional channels for online traffic to the blog and different possibilities for brand collaborations. In February 2014, for example, Song—whose Instagram account attracts more than four million weekly hits and has more than a million followers—took over the Instagram account for the online fashion retailer Revolve Clothing. These are temporary guest worker arrangements that are in addition to the personal style blogging that bloggers do for their own social media channels.

Rather than hiring a full-time, permanent employee (who earns a regular salary and benefits), retailers, brands, and designers turn to high-profile superbloggers as short-term contract workers to fill a variety of jobs including social media managers, models, and spokespeople. Asian super-bloggers, as I suggested above, have a structural advantage in fashion's casual labor markets. Not only does their strong online presence provide the all-important personal customer touch points that familiarize consumers with fashion brands, but their racially marked bodies also link them to the kinds of consumers that brands are particularly targeting. In other words, their racial advantage makes them more vulnerable to the exploitative features of casual labor.

In the section that follows, I briefly revisit the history of Asian garment workers. While *Asians Wear Clothes on the Internet* focuses on the contemporary forms and practices of Asian fashion work seen in personal style blogging, the history of an earlier mode of Asian fashion work is crucial. Presenting this history even briefly provides an important contextual backdrop for examining the historical continuities, global forces, and racially gendered frameworks that structure the taste work of Asian superbloggers today.

To be sure, Asian garment workers' fashion tastes play no role in their production of fashion products. Asian garment workers' bodies—the sites at which taste is perceived, performed, and socially constructed—are fragmented and ultimately alienated from the productive processes of apparel manufacturing. Apparel manufacturing industries exert enormous amounts of control over and abuse of garment workers' bodies (even their bodily functions are controlled by routine denials of bathroom breaks). The near total devaluation of their bodies reduces hundreds of thousands of Asian women and child workers to little more than their labor power. Yet the history of Asian fashion work in apparel manufacturing sectors is worth reviewing in an investigation of Asian personal style superblogging for what it can reveal about changing and enduring racialized hierarchies that structure the political economic and social terrain on which even some of the most elite levels of Asian fashion work take place.

## A Critical Review of Asian Fashion Labor

Since the 1970s, Asian women and girls have made major contributions to the global expansion and development of the U.S. fashion industry—now a dominant cultural, economic, and aesthetic power in global fashion. The Asian and Asian American history of the U.S. garment industry is a long and complex story that has been the subject of numerous academic and popular texts. The Asian fashion worker and the garment industry are critical topics in and across development studies; globalization studies; urban studies; feminist labor studies; immigration studies; sociological, political economic, and cultural studies of fashion; and comparative ethnic studies. The Asian garment worker holds a central position in the critical imaginary of Asian American studies and disciplines that intersect and overlap with the field. When *Amerasia* conducted an inventory of Asian American and Asian diaspora studies publications, the journal's editors found that research "related to the labor issues [surrounding] contemporary garment workers [got] the most attention."[59] The Asian garment worker also appears in Asian American studies scholarship that is not specifically about labor and economy. For example, literary, media, and cultural studies texts like Darrell Hamamoto's *Monitored Peril: Asian Americans and the Politics of TV Representation* and Laura Hyun Yi Kang's *Compositional Subjects: Enfiguring Asian/American Women* invoke the Asian garment worker as a figure representing global capitalism's transformations. Throughout Asian American and Asian diaspora studies, the Asian garment worker embodies globalization's cultural, social, and economic effects.

Western academic literature, films, news reports, and documentaries about garment workers in general regularly focus on the Asian female fashion worker. In a scholarly essay on digital labor's political significance, David Hesmondhalgh pits the feminized Asian factory worker against (positive) free digital creative labor: "Are we really meant to see people who sit at their computers modifying code or typing out responses to TV shows as 'exploited' in the same way as those who endure appalling conditions and pay in Indonesian sweatshops?"[60] The gendered racialization of garment workers in these sites accurately reflects contemporary workforce demographics in which Asian women are now a majority (though they have not always been). Such gendered racialization is also present in assumptions about Asian women's natural facility for gendered manual labor—for example, stereotypes about their nimble fingers. In reducing Asian women to their racial and gendered bodies, the fashion industry has made them both vital and vulnerable to fashion's material conditions and productive economy.

Despite their now ubiquitous presence, Asians have not always participated in the U.S. garment industry. From 1870 to 1965, Asian workers made up a very small minority of the multiracial and multiethnic apparel manufacturing workforce. Beginning in 1882, Asian exclusion laws—which included special bars against Asian women and Asian workers—kept Asians from establishing a foothold in this growing industry. Before the 1965 Immigration and Nationality Act reversed these anti-Asian immigration policies, the U.S. garment industry was powered first by Italian and Eastern European Jewish immigrant labor and, following World War I, by African American and Puerto Rican labor.[61]

During World War II, Italian and Jewish workers and members of other white ethnic groups left the industry for better-paying jobs related to the war effort, and African Americans who had left the South as part of the Second Great Migration and Puerto Ricans who were emigrating in increasingly large numbers to New York City filled most of the garment industry jobs.[62] Though African American and Puerto Rican workers formed the majority of the workforce, they rarely occupied management positions, which members of white ethnic groups held until the 1970s. And though the fashion industry turned to Southeast Asia for cheap labor as early as the 1950s (when postwar prosperity increased the demand for clothing and other personal goods), it was not until the late 1960s and early 1970s that Asian women became a visible presence in the garment industry.

In the mid-1960s, several key events facilitated Asian women's entry into the garment industry: the passage of the 1964 Civil Rights Act, affirmative action policies, and the 1965 Immigration and Nationality Act. Encouraged by recent civil rights victories, African Americans left the garment industry for better employment opportunities, creating a labor shortage that Asians soon alleviated. Chinese, Korean, and Southeast Asian immigrants who were just arriving in the United States after the passage of the Immigration and Nationality Act took jobs in the garment industry, primarily in Los Angeles and New York City. According to a 1969 Columbia University survey, 23 percent of New York's Chinatown residents were working in the apparel industry at that time.[63] Chinese factory owners in New

York's Lower East Side and Chinatown tended to hire Chinese American workers. Korean factory owners who opened shops in midtown Manhattan hired mostly Mexican and Ecuadoran workers.[64] The ethnic hiring networks and work environments of Chinese-owned garment factories provided Chinese workers with some flexibility in their work time. Margaret M. Chin notes that Chinese factory owners offered courtesies to members of their ethnic group, such as permitting workers to run errands in the middle of the workday or bring their children to work on school holidays. Chinese workers, however, complained that Chinese factory owners often took advantage of them. They worked more hours at piecework rates, earning less money than Latino workers at Korean garment factories who received hourly salaries.

Trade and capital liberalization throughout the 1980s and 1990s shrunk an already faltering U.S. garment industry. When the North American Free Trade Agreement (NAFTA) took effect in 1994, its impact on the weak U.S. garment industry was almost immediate. In the first year after the U.S. Congress ratified NAFTA (alongside the Canadian Parliament and the Mexican Senate), Los Angeles lost tens of thousands of jobs, while wages plummeted in the jobs that remained.[65] The 1995 creation of the World Trade Organization, which was designed to expand labor and consumer markets, was another blow to the U.S. garment industry. Between 1997 and 2007, the New York City garment industry lost 650,000 apparel jobs[66]—and it had already lost an average of 2.8 percent of its jobs every year between 1970 and 1987.[67] Most of these jobs moved to Southeast Asia, South Asia, Mexico, or Central America, where fashion companies found the lower wage, work, and environmental standards easier on their bottom lines. In the 1990s and early 2000s, workers in Asia and Latin America were paid an average of about $7,200 per year.[68] In 2005, when the Multi-Fibre Arrangement that had been governing world trade in textiles and garments since 1974 ended, U.S. imports from China of cotton trousers increased by 1,500 percent and imports of cotton shirts increased by 1,350 percent.[69] As Asia became a world supplier of apparel (with the United States its biggest consumer), the United States lost more textile jobs as well as jobs in ancillary services such as cutting, laundering, and finishing operations.[70]

The apparel manufacturing jobs that remained in the United States after trade liberalization relied, by and large, on the sweated labor of women of color and nonwhite immigrants. A 1998 U.S. Department of Labor study of seventy Southern California garment factories found that 61 percent violated provisions of the Fair Labor Standards Act: owners violated the minimum wage law; failed to pay overtime; did not pay some workers for work; and denied workers standard benefits like sick pay, health insurance, disability protection, and worker grievance systems. Social Security and vacation pay were nonexistent in these factories. Based on this report, Edna Bonacich and Richard Appelbaum estimate that the Los Angeles garment industry was accruing about $72.6 million in unpaid wages per year.[71] In addition to wage violations, the investigators found that hazardous work conditions were prevalent in most of the factories: blocked and locked exits, nonfunctioning doors and windows, dangerous electrical wiring, and uncapped gas lines. They also found malfunctioning toilets, some of them in the same room where workers worked, ate, and slept.

Bonacich and Appelbaum estimate that the actual percentage of garment factories operating under sweatshop conditions was likely much greater than 61 percent. For example, the Department of Labor survey did not include unregistered and underground firms that accounted for 25–33 percent of the Los Angeles garment industry.[72] Also uncounted were the makeshift garment factory outposts hidden in the homes of workers. While industrial home work was outlawed in the 1940s because officials found it too hard to monitor wage and work violations (especially involving child labor), home work not only persists today, it is a standard practice in the garment industry.

Ironically, personal style blogging has revived home fashion work not only as an acceptable but also as a lauded mode of fashion labor. The story of Yambao's beginning his blog in 2004 from his parents' home in Manila (at the age of seventeen or twenty-four[73]) has become more than a personal blog origin story. Frequently invoked in the "how to make it as a fashion blogger" media stories that have become their own genre, the image and idea of this Asian superblogger working from home (voluntarily) underscore Yambao's initiative and passion and the extraordinariness of his rise to superblogger status, as well as functioning as a racially loaded moral tale about the value and practice of the Third World Asian work ethic. As a popular racial mythology, Yambao's story plays an important role in the construction of Asian superbloggers as the new model minority of the digital economy.

The myth of the Asian work ethic (to which Yambao contributes to some extent in the construction of his identity as a fame-taxed fashion celebrity) places extra burdens on superbloggers whose high level of productivity, in turn, creates greater demands for more and faster production. This is something that both Yambao and Lau have directly addressed on their blogs. In one blog post, Yambao admits that he "sometimes feel[s] like packing up and calling it a day because of the horrible, unreasonable demands by [blog] audiences."[74] In another entry, he posts screenshots of his various e-mail and Facebook in-boxes, some showing more than 600 new messages.[75] By his own account, the "horrible, unreasonable demands" of his readers include: "Why are you so slow updating? How dare you not update in days? Why have you changed the way you blog? Why haven't you replied to my emails? Why don't you want to follow me on twitter? Why aren't you replying to my tweets? Why won't you accept my facebook request? Why is your content so different now than what it was three years ago? Why do you have ads? Why do you have lots of ads? Why can't you post more pictures? Why can't you post better pictures?"[76]

Yambao's description of the ever increasing and seemingly relentless expectation for productivity reminds me of the experiences of garment workers interviewed in Tia Lessin's documentary *Behind the Labels*: "Today he [the factory manager] would say that the quota was sixty pieces. Tomorrow he would increase the quota to sixty-five pieces. You reach sixty-five and the next day, he would say seventy. . . . They always yelled at us: 'Why can't you reach 2,000?' The supervisor punched our table and shout[ed] at us . . . 'You work so slow!' His insults were more than you can bear."[77] Meeting their quotas, the women explain, often require working inhumane hours: "We worked forty hours straight. Two days without eating, sleeping, without changing anything, without toothbrushing. But most of the time, I work like twenty hours, twenty-two hours, twenty-six hours." Long work hours exacerbated the likelihood of accidents such as workplace fires and industrial needles puncturing fingers. Most days, first aid supplies and medicine were padlocked in a cabinet. Locks were removed and air conditioners turned on only in preparation for scheduled investigations by employees of the Occupational Safety and Health Administration.

Asian fashion workers in the information economy do not have to contend with domineering bosses and a hostile work environment. For superbloggers, the pressure for productivity is both internalized as well as distributed across blog readers. Yet in the examples above we see that Asian superbloggers who do different kinds of fashion work under different operating conditions share with garment workers racialized demands for productivity.

To clarify, I am not arguing that the expectation for constant and high productivity is unique to Asian superbloggers or garment workers. As Jonathan Crary argues, this expectation is a condition of our times, made more widespread by the advent and use of digital communications and the idea that "productive operations . . . do not stop" in our 24/7 world.[78] Crary means both technological and human productivity. What I am pointing to in the shared experiences of these two distinct groups of Asian fashion workers is that the racialization of their labor power—the idea that Asian fashion workers have a predisposition to hard work and high levels of work demand—is both a source of advantage and of mistreatment in their respective fashion labor markets. They occupy a common fraught position as a model minority labor supply believed to be oriented to hard work, yet racial assumptions about their natural facility for hard and difficult work put them in a position where they must bear the burden of demands (often discourteously made) for unreasonable amounts of work.

Racial and gendered stereotypes about Asian model minority workers have structurally advantaged them in hiring decisions while historically disadvantaging African Americans, Puerto Ricans, and (to a lesser extent) Dominicans seeking jobs in the garment industry, who suffer from corresponding stereotypes about laziness and a quickness to complain. Typically, Asian garment workers are darker skinned due to their working-class, rural background, and/or Indigenous ancestry, and they have little education. Stereotypes about this socially disenfranchised group of workers' racially gendered docility and willingness to accept substandard work conditions have resulted in a new international division of labor in which the largest portion of the world's apparel manufacturing is done in Asia. Currently, the four largest exporters of clothing to the United States—which provide a whopping 97.7 percent of the clothing Americans purchase[79]—are all countries in Asia: China, Viet Nam, Indonesia, and Bangladesh (in that order).[80]

The advantage that Asians have in the garment industry is a cruel irony in light of the oppressive work conditions and workplace arrangements that they endure on a daily basis. In 1995, seventy Thai immigrants were held in a Southern California apartment complex in El Monte that served as a covert garment factory. They were forced to work seventeen-hour days for $1.60 per hour (the 1995 California minimum wage was $4.25 per hour). The Thai-Chinese owners of the makeshift factory also charged workers a hundred dollars per month for food and housed sixteen workers in one room. By one account, the apartment complex was "ringed with razor wire and fences with spiked bars turned inward as if to prevent escape. The building's windows had been covered with cardboard, and the interior had been converted into a fiberboard-and-plywood rabbit warren of crowded living areas and sewing work spaces."[81] While the owners promised workers they would be freed after paying off their transportation debts, Bonacich and Appelbaum point out that their rock-bottom wages and the vastly inflated costs of food and other supplies "virtually assured that they would never get out of debt peonage."[82] Garments manufactured in the El Monte factory were sold at Nordstrom, Sears, Target, and Mervyn's. They also bore the coveted "Made in the USA" label, which was meant to assure consumers that garments were manufactured in compliance with strict employment, wage, and environmental standards.

What the El Monte factory and other sweatshop factories continue to do illegally in the United States, trade liberalization policies allow U.S. companies to accomplish legally overseas. The garment factories in Saipan are a representative example. In the 1990s, Saipan's $1 billion per year garment industry was the island's economic backbone. Most garment workers were women from China and the Philippines. They paid as much as $3,600 in recruitment fees (borrowed from friends and family) to travel to Saipan. Their base salary at that time was $6,350 per year. After paying for room and board (approximately $2,400 per year) and paying off their recruitment fee debts, workers might earn a net salary of $350 in their first year.[83]

Saipan garment workers believed that U.S. employment and wage laws protected them, since Saipan is a U.S. territory and they were making clothes for U.S. companies such as Gap, J. Crew, and Walmart. When workers arrived, however, they discovered that U.S. territories were exempt from U.S. immigration laws, import duties, and federal minimum wage laws. In fact, Congress passed the minimum wage exemption in the early days of 1970s neoliberalism to attract businesses to Saipan and similar locales.

Saipan is an exemplary sign of neoliberalism in Aihwa Ong's sense of the term. Ong understands *neoliberalism* as a global system of exception in which political and economic liminality is a standard feature of life.[84] Saipan's guest worker economic structure and legislative shell game produce a neoliberal exception by deterritorializing labor and thereby stripping migrant workers of rights they might have under U.S. law or the laws of their origin countries. In so doing, the Saipan garment industry and the U.S. fashion industry operate within a context of exception with respect to wage and employment laws. This state of exception allowed them to disregard U.S. manufacturing standards while still assuring consumers that their clothes were "made in the USA."

In fact, the "Made in the USA" label has long been a cover for severe corporate abuses. Throughout the 1990s, Saipan garment workers' essentially free and round-the-clock labor enabled the all-American fashion company J. Crew to expand into international markets and the Gap Corporation to become the second-largest-selling apparel brand in the world.[85] While these brands bear the "Made in the USA" label because they were made in a U.S. territory, the label conceals workplace abuses and hazardous workplace environments that are the reality of Asian garment workers' lives. In Lessin's film, a Filipina woman describes her first impressions of a Saipan factory and living barracks: "As we were driving towards the barracks, I was really surprised. I'm asking, 'Is this United States territory?' It's like a rural area in the Philippines. . . . The barracks is [sic] squalid, unsanitary, rat-infested and cockroach-infested. We have ten bunk beds, so twenty people stayed in that place." Another woman notes the unsafe noise levels that workers were subjected to in their rooms: "Next door to my barracks is a sewing workshop. It sounds like a machine gun firing away. Next to my bed is a window with an exhaust fan that sounds like an airplane. I couldn't sleep well for three months. . . . It's not a place suitable for living."[86]

The "Made in the USA" label functions as the kind of spectacle that George Lipsitz identifies as a key feature in "the new patriotism" of the 1980s and 1990s in the United States. He points out that the "nationalistic rhetoric and patriotic display" is odd in an "era of economic and political internationalization."[87] Yet the new patriotism emerged when it did because it served to provide a feeling and discourse that deflected "attention and anger away from capital" and the racial and gendered configurations and consequences of massive unemployment, wage stagnation, and homelessness that so many Americans experienced at this time, as a result of deindustrialization and deregulation policies. "Made in the USA" labels obscure the economic realities wrought by neoliberal policies and the racially gendered labor that constitutes the production of fashion commodities bearing the labels. The very policies that move garment work offshore to exceptional sites like Saipan, where Asian female workers are specifically recruited through contractors who promise attractive salaries and work environments, are also the policies that make it possible to devalue this labor force and make it invisible.

Globalization has been disastrous for garment workers in the Global South as well as in the Global North. By all accounts, the number of sweatshops in the United States has increased in the years since the birth of NAFTA and the World Trade Organization. In garment industries abroad, there has been a steady decline in wages, while corporate greed climbs unchecked. A 2013 study prepared by the Worker Rights Consortium found that "garment workers still typically earn only a fraction of what constitutes a living wage—just as they did more than 10 years ago."[88] Living wages are salaries that afford workers minimum necessities such as adequate nutrition and decent housing. Most garment workers earn about one-third of a living wage. In places like Bangladesh and Cambodia, where wages are lowest, workers make only about one-sixth of a living wage. In nine of the fifteen countries that the 2013 study investigated, real wages had decreased: Bangladesh, Cambodia, the Dominican Republic, El Salvador, Guatemala, Honduras, Mexico, the Philippines, and Thailand. In the countries where wages increased—China, Haiti, India, Indonesia, Peru, and Viet Nam—the gains were less than 2 percent when adjusted for inflation. As a consequence, the report concludes, "while wage gains for workers in Indonesia, Vietnam, and Haiti were more substantial [than those in other countries], it would take more than 40 years for the prevailing wage rate to equal a living wage even if their recent rates of real wage growth were sustained."[89] Together, trade liberalization and the interlocking hierarchies of race, color, gender, and class have shaped both the work opportunities and work constraints that characterize Asian fashion work in the apparel manufacturing industry.

Today, it is not trade and labor liberalization but a confluence of several shifts in popular and consumer culture that is shaping the work opportunities and constraints of Asian personal style superbloggers. As I discuss in chapter 1, the global spread of Asian cute culture, the emergence of new fashion markets in Asia as a result of the rapid rise of some

Asian economies, and social media–connected consumers' growing influence on fashion companies' behaviors and strategies have culturally and economically restructured the Western fashion industry around the tastes and Internet activities of Asian fashion consumers. The Asian superbloggers who are the focus of this book are structurally advantaged with respect to the broader context in which the business and culture of fashion now operates. They are prime beneficiaries of these shifts and the changing dynamics of race, gender, and labor that are the shifts' effects.

The influence of basically ordinary Asian consumers on fashion advertising, retail, and consumer behavior is both historically unprecedented and historically conditioned. These consumers are the flavor of the Asian decade or Asian century, depending on one's view of global economic forces. Yet their heightened visibility and success have also left a racial aftertaste for fashion industry insiders and media pundits who have tacitly and overtly suggested that they are racial threats to fashion journalism and the standards of taste, decorum, and work ethic that the industry purports to uphold. The fraught positions that Asian superbloggers occupy as beneficiaries of racialized preference and targets of racial discrimination, as a racialized labor force in a postracial digital media economy and as signs of the progressive democratizing development of fashion media and markets, as well as symptoms of their decline (for example, lowered barriers to participation mean lowered standards of knowledge and practice), are the focus of chapter 1. First, I argue that their fraught positions signal a continuation of the historically contradictory relation of Asian fashion workers to the fashion industry. Second, I argue that Asian superbloggers' fraught positions illustrate the contradictory reality of liberal multicultural and postracial celebrations of diversity and difference (such as the digital democratization of fashion). The paradox that underlies these fraught positions as the subject of popular tastes for racial difference and  the object of racial aftertaste demonstrates the implicit conditionality and limits of celebrations of multiculturalism, diversity, and racial tolerance.

After chapter 1 historicizes these blogs and shows their context of global Asian labor and the changing social dynamics of global consumer capitalism, chapters 2 through 5 unpack different elements of the personal style blog and Asian superbloggers' negotiations of race, class, gender, and sexuality. Asian superbloggers are not passive bystanders of the structural forces that condition their participation in contemporary fashion media.

Their blogs are tools for shaping, negotiating, and managing stereotypes of Asian cheapness in the linked terms of taste, work ethic, and morals. How specific blogging practices work to produce and perform Asian superbloggers' taste and their fashionable embodiment as a distinct but not radically different racialized tastemaker is the subject of chapters 2 through 5.

Each of these chapters documents, reveals, and carefully analyzes major features of the personal style blog and the specific taste work practices associated with them: the style story, the outfit photo, the blogger pose, and the outfit post, respectively. These are not frivolous formalities of the style blog but rather a complex set of aesthetic, representational, and commercial strategies that reveal the particular ways in which the work of Asian superbloggers is raced, gendered, and class-based as well as how the style blog genre, more generally, is at once a cultural form and a commercial product. My critical attention to Asian superbloggers' taste work is intended to uncover the shifting and enduring relations of race, gender, class, and labor in one of the most popular spheres of the Internet.

Chapter 2 begins the discussion of Asian superbloggers' taste work. I analyze bloggers' style stories—the text that accompanies their outfit photographs—as a complex mode of taste work that involves textual, computational, and identity work in the form of code switching. Drawing on Roland Barthes's theory of "written fashion"[90] and Bourdieu's formulation of fashion language as a site where the struggle for fashion meanings takes place, I argue that Asian superbloggers' style stories are the means by which they articulate themselves as racialized fashionable bodies, as embodiments of legitimate difference.

The code switching in Asian superbloggers' style stories is not necessarily about shifting between languages; instead, the shift is in how the bloggers express their Asianness, from a racial difference to a style of racial embodiment. In close analyses of Song's and Yambao's style stories, I argue that the stories function to aestheticize Asianness by recasting racial difference as a style of Asianness that is distinct in terms of taste and, tacitly, class. The bloggers' style stories indicate an important shift in the signification of race in the personal style blogosphere, from the physical and social body to the practices of aesthetic sartorial choice.

Style stories suggest that Asian superbloggers wear their race on their sleeves, but as with all things in fashion, how race is worn matters. Chapter 3 focuses on the class-based dimensions of superbloggers' taste work practices. Analyzing the aesthetic forms and technocultural structures of outfit photos—the essential feature of personal style blogs—I consider what these photos might tell us about how racialized eliteness is constructed in the personal style blogosphere and what kinds of Asianness are valued when they are attached to eliteness.

Stylistically and formally, all outfit photos look pretty much the same. Some of their most characteristic aesthetic and formal conventions have been credited to Asian superbloggers and reproduced ad infinitum throughout the blogosphere. Yet hierarchies in the personal style blogosphere—between hobbyist bloggers and superbloggers, for example—suggest that outfit photos are almost the same but not quite. Analyzing the formal features of outfit photos produced by the memetic repetition of photographic practices like Lau's mirror shot technique, I argue that there is a difference in the repetition of camera angles and distances. This difference is understated because it is located not on the surface of outfit photos' formal qualities but in the distinction of informational mobilities—of the frequency and extent of the photos' circulation. Outfit photos demonstrate that Asian eliteness in the blogosphere balances distinction with relatability; it is the embodiment of a difference that looks familiar. As with their style stories, Asian superbloggers' outfit photos and other taste work practices are ways to construct the bloggers' legitimate difference as racialized taste makers and style leaders.

Chapter 4 focuses on fashion blogger poses, particularly the brand-name poses Lau and Yambao invented—the Susie Bubble pose and the BryanBoy pose. The significant amount of cultural, social, and financial capital these bloggers have accrued through the poses and their memetic repetition suggest that the poses function as job performances that have the power to heighten bloggers' status and role in the blogosphere. I argue that fashion blogger poses in general reflect the changing values and gendered attitudes related to knowledge, expertise, and authority in informational capitalism. However, the brand-name poses bear the marks of the ongoing racial disparities in the blogosphere, even for elite bloggers. As I explain, they were created in response to and are performances of racial ambivalence. As job performances, then, they represent the added racial and gender dimensions of impression management against stereotypes that workers belonging to minority groups are often pressed to perform in traditional workplaces.

Chapter 5 returns to an early and central premise of this book: that while there are structural similarities that link new and earlier forms of fashion work, Asian superbloggers do not necessarily acknowledge these links. In fact, bloggers actively maintain the divide between digital and physical labors. An investigation of the technological and aesthetic conventions of the primary mode of personal style blogging called outfit posting demonstrates that bloggers use the digital technologies and practices available to them to render invisible the spaces and times they move through in doing the work of blogging and self-fashioning (for example, driving to retail sites and trying on clothes). Outfit posts represent personal style blogging as an effortless activity. Their spatial and temporal conventions suggest that bloggers come by their stylishness easily and effortlessly, confirming the idea of the personal style blogosphere as a site of real and natural style.

The construction of blogging as effortless has two contradictory implications that I examine in chapter 5. It has the positive effect of disassociating the concept of Asian fashion work from sweated labor, but it also has the negative effect of deskilling personal style blogging in ways that have historically defined and justified the devaluation of women's work. This produces a doubly negative effect for Asian superbloggers. First, it deskills the very significant knowledge and expertise they have with respect to media work, bodily work, and taste work. And second, the racial hierarchies that have historically organized women's work (often performed not just by women but also by Asian men, for example, as laundry workers and domestic workers) especially devalues Asians in ways that raise the racialized specter of cheap Asian workers. In outfit posting, the primary mode of media production for personal style bloggers, the structural intersections of race, gender, and class that shape Asian fashion labor in manufacturing sectors are both disrupted and reinforced by Asian fashion labors in the blogosphere.

# Chapter 1.
## The Taste and Aftertaste for Asian Superbloggers

The message on the sign American designer Marc Jacobs was photographed holding read: "I love you BryanBoy! I wish you were here. (I did write it!!!)."[1] The photograph, taken by V magazine fashion photographer JD Ferguson backstage at Jacobs's fall–winter 2008–9 fashion show in New York City, is just one of hundreds of tokens of affection that fans have sent to the queer Filipino personal style blogger. Like the others, it exemplifies the public's taste not only for the blogger's fashion choices but especially for the blogger himself. What makes this fan message stand out from all the others that Bryan Grey Yambao shares on his blog is that it comes from within the Western fashion industry. The message, created backstage at one of the most important fashion events in the world by one of the most illustrious designers in the world, indicates the reach of the blogger's mass appeal into the citadel of establishment fashion. In two more incredible acts of fanboying, Jacobs created a $4,800 army green ostrich leather handbag that he named BB (in honor of the blogger) and styled the white American male model Cole Mohr to look like the spitting image of Yambao in his Marc by Marc Jacobs ads (shot by the preeminent photographer Jürgen Teller).[2] See figures 1.1 and 1.2.

The Marc Jacobs "I love you BryanBoy" photo and the media frenzy it ignited introduced the practice of personal style blogging to the mainstream

 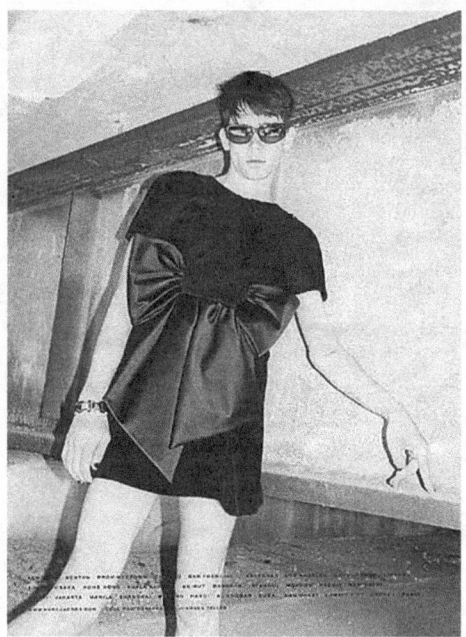

1.1 (*left*) Yambao in the Singapore edition of *Style* magazine, December 2008, 197.
1.2 (*right*) Mohr in the Marc by Marc Jacobs autumn-winter 2008 ad campaign for both men's and women's lines.

fashion public and changed Yambao from an ordinary personal style blogger to a celebrity personality. Media outlets from the mainstream (such as the *New York Times Magazine*[3]) to the alternative (*Schön!*[4]) began referring to him using the new title of superblogger.

Not until about a year later would another blogger—also Asian—garner similar levels of public and industry attention. Audiences watching the fall 2010 fashion shows live and online couldn't help see Susanna Lau (aka Susie Bubble) as a source of inspiration for some of what appeared on the most exclusive runways. The models for luxury brands like Lanvin (at Paris Fashion Week) and Erin Fetherston (at New York Fashion Week) all wore Lau's signature long straight hair with blunt-cut bangs. One blogger enthusiastically observed, "susie bubble [*sic*] you know you are doing something right when half the runway shows from the big leagues had your hair, I think unconsciously or consciously you got them!"[5]

Not long after the fashion shows ended, ads appeared on the Internet seeming to confirm that Lau's style had become the taste of the Western fashion industry. In one such ad for California-based indie online retailer Moxsie, the featured model bore a striking resemblance to Lau, physically and sartorially. For the fashion news aggregate blog Racked New York (owned by Vox Media), the ad was a cultural signpost. One of the blog's headlines declared, "Moxsie's Nod to Blogger Susie Bubble Is the Sign of the Times."[6] While the ad doesn't mention Lau or her blog, most took the omission as an indication of her prominence. As the blog's article explains, "So maybe the ad doesn't mention Susie's name because it doesn't have to—Moxsie expects shoppers to recognize her look on their own."

The fashion public's and industry's taste for Asian superbloggers Yambao; Lau; and the third member of the blogosphere's holy Asian trinity, the mixed-race Japanese American Rumi Neely (the first blogger to appear in a national advertising campaign of a major retailer—Forever 21—and the first to appear on a Times Square billboard) coincides with and is strengthened by broader shifts in the context in which Asians' relations to the global economy are understood. This is a time when, as Mimi Nguyen and Thuy Linh Tu write, there is a strong "popular appetite for all goods Asian in both the United States and the West more generally" and Asian Americans are "being courted by the corporate marketplace" as never before.[7] In the introduction, I discussed a particular focus of this manifestation of the cultural taste for Asian creativity in the critical and public attention to the Asian creative class. The discursive construction of this new labor class as a group that is both racialized yet seemingly unaffected by racial barriers or racial discrimination serves to legitimate claims about the postracial yet liberal multicultural structure of the so-called new economy. It also reflects the constitutive contradiction of Asian superbloggers' fraught position in contemporary Western fashion economies. The emergence of the Asian personal style superblogger indicates the Western fashion industry's continued dependence on racialized labor (Asian superbloggers are a pivotal workforce in the Asian moment of fashion) as well as the image of the new postracial fashion economy (in which anyone—even a gay Filipino kid—can reach the heights of fashion cultural and economic influence).[8] While queerness is normative in Western fashion industries, the racial and regional difference Yambao represents as a young Asian man from a Third World country was headline news.

An article from *Agence France-Presse* has the headline "Philippine Blogger Stirs a Fashion Revolution,"[9] and another from *Gawker* is suggestively titled "Marc Jacobs Wrapped around Finger of This Gay Filipino Blogger."[10]

I begin this chapter by elaborating on the context within which the cultural and economic influence of Asian superbloggers emerged. How did Asian superbloggers' styles and tastes become so significant in the early twenty-first century? What I am concerned with is what Pierre Bourdieu describes as "the logic of the space of [taste] production"[11] and the location of Asian superbloggers within these logics and spaces of production. In other words, what are the conditions that set the stage for Asian superbloggers to become the flavor of the decade (or century)? In the latter half of the chapter, I consider the logic of conditionality and tolerance implicit in the discourses of liberal multiculturalism and postracism that frame the meanings of Asian superbloggers' prominence in the historically white cultural domain of fashion media and imagery. My argument is that the backlash against Asian superbloggers can be understood as both the evidence and end of conditional tolerance. In other words, the backlash or the racial aftertaste following the multicultural taste for Asian superbloggers is a marker of the inherent limits of tolerance as an approach to diversity and difference. This chapter momentarily sets aside questions about the ways Asian superbloggers position themselves within taste production spaces. How Asian superbloggers position and negotiate their racial and labor identities through their taste work is the focus of the chapters that follow. The purpose of this chapter is to understand the context and extent of Asian superbloggers' rise to some of the most rarefied spheres of Western fashion media and markets.

Asian superbloggers' elite status cannot be understood through racial generalizations about their talent for media production and media relations, their work ethic, or their fashion sensibility. They are beneficiaries of cultural economic shifts that began in the late 1970s and that have accelerated rapidly in the early years of the twenty-first century. As I explain below, the global diffusion of Japanese cute culture, the ascendancy of Asian creative industries and luxury markets that have turned the Western fashion industry's economic focus toward Asia, and the social media–led expansion of ordinary consumers' power to drive fashion advertising and marketing have created space for some Asian bloggers to flourish. This does not discount the very significant ways Asian superbloggers have built on and expanded their roles as new tastemakers, but it provides a context for understanding the practices and significance of their taste work.

## The Globalization of Cute Culture and Cute Work

Asian and Asian-like commodities have been produced and consumed transnationally for centuries. Chinese porcelains and tea sets and innumerable chinoiserie objects have been circulating globally since the seventeenth century as symbols and practices of "patrician Orientalism."[12] In the context of Western fashion, Asia-inspired clothing styles and design motifs have been recurring themes. Some notable examples include Paul Poiret's 1911 *jupes sultan* (harem pants), Jean Paul Gaultier's 1999 kimono bikini ensembles, and Prada's 2013 coats embroidered with origami flowers.[13]

What is distinct about the contemporary global market of Asian commodities and consumers is that it is driven by the aesthetic practices and productions of Asians themselves, rather than non-Asians. The most widely recognized Asian commodities today are those of Japanese cute culture, and none is more recognizable than that cute cat with the marshmallow-y head named Hello Kitty. For Christine Yano, Hello Kitty is "the global icon of cute"[14] because it invites multiple modes of relating to it. Hello Kitty is a site of nostalgia, generational bridging (between mothers and daughters, for example), irony, sexual fetish (as an ideal feminine figure because it is "a mute presence that does not look back at you or judge"[15]), and a site for reclaiming a postfeminist "girl power" that doesn't mutually exclude "frilliness and dominance."[16] All of these consumer relations are built into and expressed through the Hello Kitty global empire of products that target multinational and multiracial markets for girls, women, men, and so-called adult girls (adult women who identify with girl culture). Among the 15,000 or so Hello Kitty products are plush toys, board and video games, furry slippers, plastic fly swatters, sanitary napkins, body fat monitors, exhaust pipes, lawnmowers, men's underwear, and a Boeing 777 jet plane operated by a Taipei-based EVA Airways crew. Product sales alone net the Sanrio Corporation $2.86 billion annually.[17]

The economic power of Asian cute culture can also be seen in Pikachu, the small, chubby, yellow bunny-like Pokémon[18] character with small, black, shoe-button eyes and rosy pink cheeks. Pikachu is the fastest-selling game in the Pokémon franchise, which holds the record for the second-most-popular game franchise (in terms of sales) in the world. Mario, another Nintendo creation, holds the number one spot.[19] In the broader popular culture beyond video games, Pikachu is also an economic powerhouse. In *Time*'s list of "The Best People of 1999" (ranked, in part, by each contender's earnings that year), the magazine listed Pikachu second, following Ricky Martin but beating J. K. Rowling and Prince William.[20]

As should be clear by now, cute culture crosses continents and oceans. Its transnational spread—what Yano describes as "pink globalization"[21]—means that it represents an Asian global market rather than a niche one. One of the largest markets for Japanese cute culture is the United States. When *Pokémon: The First Movie* opened in the United States in November 1999, observers noted that "it played on over 3,000 screens (in contrast to 2,000 in Japan) and was the week's top-ranked movie, grossing close to first week sales for *Star Wars, Episode I* (and surpassing those of *Lion King*)."[22]

The global economic impact of cute culture is only one dimension of its significance. For academic and popular observers, the global phenomenon of Japanese (as well as Korean and Taiwanese) cute culture indicates that the global hegemony of the Western ideal of masculine cool is giving way to a new and differently racialized and gendered ideal of Asian feminine cuteness. As one *Newsweek* article gushes, "Western-style cool is out. Everything Japanese is in—and oh, so 'cute!'"[23]

Scholars argue—rightly, I believe—that the phenomenon of Asian cute culture is both a reflection and an extension of the rising "soft power" of Asian markets in the global economy. Rather than the "hard power" of military or other coercive forces, cute culture represents Asia's "soft power" of economic co-optation through feminized personal and entertainment consumer goods and feminine shopping activities.[24] Consumers turn to Asian cute cultural products not because they are forced to but because these commodities fulfill consumers' personal desire for the cute, the sweet, the feminine, and the soft.[25] Cute culture's mass appeal has to do with its promotion of warmth and intimacy in an increasingly cold and technologically intensive world. In Yano's words, it "can be seen as part of a more generalized nostalgic reaction to a highly technologized, depersonalized world. Thus, 'cute'—Japanese or otherwise—can represent a turn to emotion and even sentimentality."[26] This echoes Larissa Hjorth's observation that Asian Pacific consumers' cute customization of mobile devices with *kawaii* wallpaper, toy attachments, phone covers, and so on "is about personalising impersonal technologies, and rendering 'cold' dehumanised new technologies friendly, human or 'warm.' "[27]

Studies of cute culture have not taken notice of the fashion blogosphere. This is a surprising oversight, since that blogosphere's visual, textual, sartorial, and body language is steeped in the aesthetic logic, goals, and judgments of cute. Cuteness is apparent in bloggers' linguistic and kinesthetic practices. These include the extensive use of nonstandard words (for example, "logo-a-go-go"; "bargainous printastic sweater"; and Yambao's signature sign-off, "baboosh"—an onomatopoeic word describing the sound that blowing a wet kiss makes); spelling (such as "gonna" and "kewl"); "backchannel sounds" (like "ah," "hmmm," "ugh," and "grr"); and emotional icons including emoticons, graphic symbols, and the linguistic shorthand for hugs and kisses ("xo"). The photographic poses that personal style bloggers perform are also cute. In front of the camera—one that is always either controlled or directed by the blogger—they construct a visual rhetoric of cuteness in the ways they position their heads, bodies, and faces. Their poses suggest youthfulness, modesty, informality, and guilelessness. Some of the most common blogger poses are the pigeon-toed stance; the "elsewhere gaze," which avoids eye contact with the camera lens and viewer; and the "sugar bowl," pose in which the blogger places two hands on the front of his or her hips, making the body appear smaller and thus younger.

In addition to, and perhaps more important than, the physical configurations of the body, personal style bloggers' poses can be understood within the context of cute culture because they exhibit what Gabriella Lukács identifies as a central feature of cuteness, "semantic flexibility."[28] Lukács's critical insight about the semantic flexibility of cuteness provides an important key to understanding the racial and gender dimensions of the production of cute, or cute work. Lukács's analysis focuses on the Net Idol phenomenon in Japan in the 1990s and 2000s. Net Idols are young Japanese women who produce their own websites that feature personal photos and narratives characterized by cute aesthetics and practices. "Net Idols offer diverse styles of care and cater to different types of needs" by creating online personas (sometimes even fictitious biographies) and digital images that are tailored to the expectations and requests of predominantly male audiences.[29] Lukács's informants stress that they are not sex workers, underscoring this point with examples of times they have taken individual viewers to task for requests that they felt were too sexually suggestive or provocative.

For Lukács, the essential cuteness of Net Idols' activities is not located in the visual aesthetics of their practices and productions but in the quality of their work ethic. Drawing on the more nuanced meaning of cute (kawaii) in its original Japanese context, Lukács states: "I challenge the assumption that cute connotes a particular physical appearance of behavior that can be described using a stable set of signifiers. Instead, I stress that semantic flexibility is a central feature of the notion of cute." The word kawaii is not limited to describing babies; small animals; and small, soft, fuzzy things. Quoting Koga Reiko, Lukács contends that "kawaii is a magical word because it can designate almost anything that is round, weak, bright, small, smooth, warm, or soft."[30] Thus, Lukács concludes, "cute is a signifier that accommodates."

Net Idols are engaged in productions of cuteness because they embody an accommodating and highly gendered service-oriented worker who is "approachable, gentle, soft, and even submissive."[31] What's more, Net Idols provide these services of care work for little to no money. While cyberentertainment companies have exploited opportunities to capitalize on the Net Idols phenomenon by skimming profits from Net Idols' entrepreneurial ventures (such as paid fan events, CDs, DVDs, postcards, T-shirts, and so on that are sold on their websites), sales of these items are rarely enough to provide Net Idols with a livelihood. Still, Net Idols cite intangible rewards such as self-exploration, self-realization, and fun as motivating factors for their production of cuteness. Some of the Japanese women that Lukács spoke to said that the tedium of their paid office jobs became so unbearable that they quit to pursue their Net Idols activities on a full-time basis. As Lukács puts it, "unpaid work in the digital media economy is for some Net Idols the only possibility for finding self-fulfilling work."[32]

Through her analysis of the Net Idols phenomenon, Lukács illuminates some of the ways that the gendered dynamics of cute culture are reshaping the new economy. She locates in cute culture "an emerging form of rationality (the foundational logic of neoliberal governmentality) within which individuals accept and even celebrate the end of job security as a marker of a shift from the postwar order of 'working to find pleasure' to the neoliberal imperative to 'find pleasure in work.'"[33] The Net Idols phenomenon is, in Lukács's formulation, producing and reproducing a gendered labor supply that embraces the conditions and forms of economic precarious-ness that is endemic to digital media economies.

The numerous ways in which personal style blogging overlaps with Net Idols activities is uncanny to me. Both are highly gendered forms of labor in which processes of capital accumulation converge with and rely on pro-cesses of social reproduction. The payoff for the vast majority of personal style bloggers, like Net Idols, is negligible at best. The time and energy they devote to fashioning their bodies and images, building social networks, communicating with their audiences, and being attentive to the audiences' needs generate almost entirely only immaterial rewards for workers. With the institutionalization of these activities, however, companies have found a way to squeeze out profits from what is mostly free labor. Website hosting companies, branding and marketing companies, and the various retailers that sell the cute clothes and accessories that are key components in the production of cute have capitalized on these Internet users' self-expressive practices. Strikingly, even some of the cute poses that Net Idols perform in front of their webcams are similar to bloggers' poses. While there are no hard-and-fast rules for Net Idols poses—or for blogger poses, for that matter—the performance and production of cuteness through these bodily practices suggest that cuteness is an unspoken rule in both work environments.

While I have never come across any evidence that Net Idols have directly inspired Asian superbloggers, I see the influence of cute culture in the gen-dered work rationale that Lukács so helpfully identifies. For me, though, work modes of accommodation (toward taking on multiple and varied tasks, meeting an audience's needs and expectations, and learning and improving on skills as needed) are not just gendered expectations but also particularly racialized ones. Asian women, more than other groups of women, have been racially stereotyped as more (and happily) inclined to accommodate, serve, and care for others for little other reason than that they want to.

The phenomena of Japanese Net Idols and Asian superbloggers indicate that cute culture—and the digital technologies and cultural practices now so integral to its production and circulation—has extended and strength-ened the link between Asian women and labors of accommodation. The especially high visibility of both groups of Asian cute workers suggests that this link is not coincidental but structural, resulting from systems of knowl-edge and power that racially gender Asian women as especially suited for and good at accommodation work. The global popularity of Asian cute culture has whet the Western consumer's appetite, cultivating the taste for Asian cuteness that Asian superbloggers embody to a tee. Asian superbloggers—for all their differences in ethnicities, dress styles, and shopping habits (some preferring to mix "high" and "low" fashion, others sticking to luxury brands)—are all conventionally cute. Their bodies and faces generally reflect rather than challenge Western standards of beauty (including thinness, youthfulness, and cuteness) that the fashion industry rigorously promotes. While Asian superbloggers are all attractive and incredibly successful, they are not immune from feelings of racial ambivalence. Lau's sartorial and posing style, as I have briefly mentioned above and will discuss in greater detail throughout this book, stems from her racial ambivalence about her face and especially her eyes. Yambao has expressed the desire for racially implicated plastic surgery: "I really need to get a fuckin nose job and chin implant soon."[34]

In the Asian moment of fashion, these superbloggers' Asian (but not too Asian) subjectivities have important value to Western fashion companies. This may be why they have found their most receptive audiences in the West, particularly in the United States and Canada.[35] Yambao has noted in his blog that the consumer and retail publics in the Philippines don't even know he exists.[36] This is an exaggeration, but his statement suggests the importance of Euro-American tastes for the production and circulation of Asian cute culture.

The racially gendered logic of cute work—the notion that Asians exemplify feminine qualities of service and are sweetly willing and happy to work hard for others for little or no pay—structurally advantages Asian superbloggers. Outside of cute culture's sphere of influence, the same racially gendered stereotype has benefited Asian garment workers. Though garment workers are not engaged in cute productions (of language, behavior, body, or affect), the link between Asian women and accommodation work connects garment workers to cute workers. As I discussed in the introduction, Asian garment workers are advantaged in hiring decisions because they are perceived to embody the accommodating worker in all its racially gendered dimensions. The rise of cute culture has facilitated the continuation and expansion of this racially gendered logic of labor into digital realms, to the "benefit" of Asian superbloggers. I use quotes because, as I have tried to make clear, the structurally advantageous position that Asian fashion workers occupy also puts them in the position of being more vulnerable to self- and corporate exploitation.

While there is significant overlap between the cute productions of Net Idols and the work of Asian superbloggers, there is an important difference between the gendered meanings of their unwaged yet corporatized labors. According to Lukács, Net Idols' unwaged work has gendered associations of weakness and submissiveness (qualities that Net Idols perform on their websites as part of their accommodative aesthetic and approach to their work). The unwaged work of personal style bloggers articulates a different but still gendered racial meaning—in this case, about passion, not weakness. For bloggers, even superbloggers, not earning a blogging income and not caring about this fact serves as a badge of authenticity. Bloggers stress on their blogs and in interviews that they produce their blogs not for money or fame but for the genuine love of fashion, of connecting with other fashion enthusiasts, and of creative expression. Yambao, the superblogger whose indirect earnings were the first to be made public (and sensationalized), insists in an interview that "for me money is really not the issue, it's about getting material and getting my content." He notes, too, that he'd even be willing to forgo his fees: "If it's something or somebody that I support, then of course I'm not going to charge."[37] Whether or not his statements are sincere is irrelevant. The salient issue is his expression of a cute work rationale that emphasizes a willingness to be flexible and accommodating—taking on a variety of different jobs that were once the highly specialized work domains of writers, photographers, trend forecasters, and fashion models—even if it means working for free. (Despite repeated claims about his artistic passion, Yambao and other Asian superbloggers have borne the brunt of critics' accusations about bloggers' fame mongering. As I discuss below in this chapter, the aftertaste of Asian superbloggers is also racialized.)

### Fashion's Asian Moment

In addition to cute culture, the taste for Asian superbloggers has been conditioned by the ascendancy of Asian economies and markets that has convinced many observers that the future of the global economy is in Asia. The Asian decade (or century) in the fashion context has seen the meteoric rise of Asian fashion workers across multiple creative labor sectors, including fashion designers, models, and editors. What's more, Asian consumers across countries and class groups (because not all luxury consumers have luxury-level salaries[38]) constitute a vast, geographically dispersed, and growing market that is supporting the multibillion-dollar global Western fashion industry.

Asian fashion designers are perhaps the most distinguished contributors to this Asian moment. Asian American designers in the United States—including Vera Wang, Anna Sui, and Jason Wu (the designer of Michelle Obama's first and second inaugural gowns), Phillip Lim, Alexander Wang, Peter Som, Derek Lam, and Humberto Leon and Carol Lim, are recognized and largely respected as global fashion powerhouses. Wang's presence in Europe was recently strengthened by his appointment as creative director of the Paris fashion house Balenciaga; similarly, Leon and Lim took the reins of the Paris-based luxury goods and clothing company Kenzo. Asian brands based in Asia, notably Couronne (Korea) and Woo (China), are also becoming popular in European fashion markets. Likewise, designers from China, India, Malaysia, and Singapore such as Jenny Ji, Lu Xiaoyu, Lili Lee, Stella Lam, Zheng Xiaodan, Zhang Yuhao, Masaba Gupta, Tanvi Kedia, Farah Khan, and Feng Zhu have all captured global attention in recent years. Much of the attention Chinese designers are receiving around the world is due to the support and visibility of China's first lady, Peng Liyuan. Peng regularly turns to Chinese designers rather than European or American ones when she needs an outfit for a public event. These fashion choices, like those of the U.S. first lady, Michelle Obama, are widely observed and have a considerable impact on retail sales.[39]

Asia's design boom is the result of a deliberate economic strategy put in place by state officials and international investors. As Thuy Linh Tu explains in *The Beautiful Generation*, state and business actors responded to "free market heightened anxieties" in the 1990s: "As nervous leaders began strategizing about how to contend with the open market, they repeatedly stressed the need to 'move up the value chain.'"[40] Because designing and branding are value chain pinnacles, "Asian government leaders increasingly saw access to this sector as the key to gaining long-term advantage, meaning long-term profit."[41] Rather than compete with apparel-manufacturing countries like Viet Nam and Bangladesh, where labor costs are much lower, countries like China, India, Thailand, and Sri Lanka began developing their creative sectors by opening new design schools and developing partnerships with U.S. and European design schools. Global fashion events like Design by Shanghai at London Fashion Week in 2013 are the outcomes of these efforts.

The rising prominence of Asian fashion producers globally is matched by the growing market power of Asian consumers in the global fashion economy. Since about 2008, Asian fashion consumers in key cities have moved from the periphery to the center of public fashion discourse. Today, considerations of Asian consumers shape decisions across the global fashion commodity chain. As I have written elsewhere,[42] the confluence of debt crises, record unemployment levels, and diminished consumer confidence felt in the United States, Europe, and Japan, as well as the massive economic growth in parts of Asia, has enabled cities like Beijing, Shanghai, Manila, Mumbai, and Hong Kong to emerge as new luxury markets.[43] In fact, China is on track to become the second-largest luxury market by 2017. Western designers are doing whatever they can to court these highly valuable consumers, including designing exclusive lines sold only in Asia.[44] These Asia-only collections are, in the words of the Los Angeles Times, "infus[ed] . . . with Asian sensibilities in look, feel, and size."[45] Economic growth is quite a bit slower in Southeast Asia than in East and South Asia, but Thailand is also attracting interest from fashion companies as a site for luxury stores. In 2012, the number of such stores in Thailand grew 17.6 percent, outpacing the global average of 8 percent.[46]

Western fashion companies are not just designing for and opening stores in key Asian markets. They are also launching their initial public offerings in Asia-based stock exchanges. Prada, Salvatore Ferragamo, Jimmy Choo, and Coach all pursued initial public offerings in Hong Kong. With a 2011 combined market capitalization of nearly $17 trillion, the Hong Kong Stock Exchange is Asia's second-largest stock market (just behind the Tokyo Stock Exchange) and the sixth-largest stock market in the world.[47] As the Financial Times, Forbes, and the Atlantic's Wire have all reported, fashion companies look to the Hong Kong Stock Exchange to be closer to their new consumer base.[48]

As well as seeking the home-field advantage in Asian stock markets, luxury fashion companies are attempting to court Asian consumers through advertising. Western brands are buying up ad pages in the Asian editions of U.S. and European fashion magazines like *Vogue* (*Vogue China* was launched in 2005 and *Vogue Thailand* in 2013) as well as in special Asia-themed issues like V magazine's summer 2011 issue. The Asian moment in fashion has also seen an increase in the hiring of Asian models for both print media and runway shows—though the increase is not as significant as it is generally perceived to be. Still, a small handful of Asian models like China's Du Juan, Shu Pei Qin (Maybelline's spokesmodel), and Liu Wen (Estée Lauder's first Asian face); South Korea's Hyoni Kang, So Young Kang, and Lee Hyun; Japan's Tao Okamoto; and Canada's Geoffrey Gao have risen to supermodel status in recent years.[49] As fashion news journalists and fashion modeling agents have noted, the rise of Asian models follows the rise of Asian luxury markets.[50]

The interest in having faces that reflect Asian consumers in fashion ads does not always lead to the hiring of Asian models. The highest echelons of the fashion modeling industries remain glaringly white even in fashion's Asian moment.[51] In major fashion spreads such as those in the American (September 2011) and Japanese *Vogue* (October 2011), as well as fashion films like *Paris-Shanghai: A Fantasy* (a short film accompanying the Chanel 2009 prefall runway show), white models Karlie Kloss, Crystal Renn, Freja Beha, and Baptiste Giabiconi achieve the Asian look through yellowface makeup techniques.[52] Not surprisingly, all of these fashion events were directed by white editors and designers (respectively, Tonne Goodman, Anna dello Russo, and Karl Lagerfeld).

While some attempts to attract Asian consumers have been wildly misguided, the industrywide interest in the Asian consumer fashion market has generated new opportunities for some of the most highly visible Asian consumers as brand ambassadors. Asian superbloggers like Neely, Lau, and Aimee Song have fronted national advertising campaigns for American brands like Forever 21, Gap, and Michael Kors, respectively (Neely was the first ever personal style blogger to do so). Highlighting the authenticity of products by using a real person rather than a fashion model has become a popular strategy in the age of social commerce. The influence of social commerce is the third factor and last point I will discuss that played a role in the rise of the Asian personal style superblogger.

## Personal Style Bloggers Are Real People, Too

The first known use of the term *social commerce* was in 2005, when Yahoo launched its online store.[53] But the practices of social commerce—the employment of social networking technologies and their capacities (such as online posting, linking, sharing, following, and commenting) as tools for buying and selling products online and offline—began at least a decade earlier. In 1995, Amazon.com was the first company to let customers post reviews of products on its site. With the launch of the social networking site MySpace in 2003 and the online review site Yelp in 2004, peer-to-peer product promotions became an everyday aspect of the consumer experience.

Product and service endorsements by so-called real people rather than actors, star athletes, or other celebrities are of course not new. People have long exchanged product referrals with friends, neighbors, and family members. In the earliest days of radio and television, product endorsements by the randomly chosen average man, woman, or housewife were a regular part of the mediascape, and for good reason. The use of real people in advertising is an effective marketing and branding strategy. It lends credibility to the endorsement and a sense of authenticity to the brand. It suggests that the company prioritizes the consumer's point of view.

Social media have amplified the reach and engagement of real-person advertising, also called reality advertising. Rather than wait for a reality ad to air on the radio or television, consumers with access to social media are able to seek out, create, and share product reviews to audiences that can circulate across time zones and continents. Today, reality advertising takes many forms, including blog posts, tweets, Yelp reviews, Facebook status updates, and print and television ads. More often than not, these ads are broadcast or shared across media systems. If a company is lucky, the ad will go viral, traveling a great distance from its target market to reach new consumers.

The fashion industry was slow to embrace social media. With their peer-to-peer communications and its tolerance, if not outright welcoming, of the amateur opinion, social media and commerce are structurally opposed to the fashion industry's top-down, hierarchical, and highly guarded organization of taste and value. But by 2009, social commerce had become the predominant business model for designers, retailers, and editors, who were all openly endorsing the social media values of connection, collaboration, and public engagement. When an Ann Taylor Loft customer placed a comment on the retailer's Facebook page complaining

WTF?
Why?

that its new silk cargo pants "look great, if you're 5'10" and a stick like the model," the company's manager of digital programs responded the following day by posting Facebook photographs of Loft employees (who ranged in size from 2 to 12, and in height from 5'3" to 5'10") modeling the pants. The company's responsiveness to regular customers and its use of "real women" to model the pants made headline news in a wide range of media outlets from the social media news site Mashable[54] to the business news site Forbes[55] and the Huffington Post.[56] Consumers rewarded the company's attentiveness with praise in social media (effectively, consumer-initiated viral marketing) and with increased sales. In the second quarter of 2010, following the Facebook photos, the company saw a 16 percent rise in same-store sales and a 55 percent increase in its e-commerce sales.[57]

The discourse of real women signals a shift but not a complete overhaul in the aspirational values of the fashion industry. While fashion companies and magazines still draw on aspirational fantasies, brand approachability or relatability has emerged as a key concern in the industry. There is a strong sense in fashion commercial markets of the importance of relatability in building and strengthening customer relations. Such relatability is established in various ways from the use of amateur models to the ease with which users navigate a company's website to the pleasantness and speed of a company's social media responsiveness. Brand approachability and corporate relatability have as much to do with meeting current commercial standards for customer service as with demonstrating the company's cultural relevance in the social media age. The importance of projecting an image of cultural relevance cannot be underestimated for companies competing in an industry that imagines itself as "a bellwether for modernity and a mirror of its (future) time."[58] Cultural relevance is the lifeblood of fashion companies.

Today, real women are not only a feature of fashion advertising and marketing strategies, but they have also become a main fashion event. As one journalist observed, the " 'real woman' is . . . greeted with much fanfare and acclaim and frenzied discussion."[59] But as critics have rightly argued, for all the attention that the fashion industry is devoting to real women, its discursive and embodied construction remains discouragingly narrow.[60] The real women in fashion media are generally not represented by, for example, disabled women, obese women, or women whose gender presentation is nonnormative. Nonetheless, the discourse of real women circulates widely in the fashion industry. National ad campaigns like the 2010 Jones New York "Empowering Your Confidence" campaign (which featured ordinary career women in their favorite Jones New York outfits) and fashion shows by Donna Karan, Betsey Johnson, Alberta Ferretti, Rick Owens, and many others that replace fashion models with nonmodels keep the discourse of real women alive in fashion media and consumer culture.

Personal style bloggers benefit from and contribute to the reality culture of social commerce. Indeed, personal style bloggers are a key real people constituency. Every day, they post tens of thousands of real person ads that can be shared, searched, and shopped (when they are linked to retail sites). Their blog posts demonstrate in intimate detail how products fit into and enhance the everyday lives of real people. This is what advertisers call brand storytelling, and bloggers provide these stories every day for free. In the age of social commerce, when peer-to-peer consumer communications and consumer-generated connections with brands are the driving forces of consumer behaviors, personal style blogs are an important sphere of social commercial activity. Whereas peer customer reviews and endorsements are just one of a multitude of activities that take place in other social media sites, these are the primary activities in the personal style blogosphere.

But unlike conventional reality ads or other forms of reality media—such as reality television—that are created for a general audience, personal style blogs are addressed to an imagined and bounded audience. Studies of self-presentation in social media have found that social media users do not write into a digital abyss but to an imagined or, as danah boyd describes it, "cognitively constructed" audience.[61] Alice Marwick and danah boyd explain in their study of Twitter users that "in the absence of certain knowledge about audience, participants take cues from the social media environment to imagine the community."[62] For bloggers, these cues include readers' comments, online traffic sources (the ways in which readers come to the blog, such as via Twitter, Instagram, or Facebook), keywords in searches (the search terms readers use to find the blog), and the relative popularity of blog posts or blog subjects. From this information, bloggers derive some sense of their audience and construct their presentations of self, identity, and taste with this imagined audience in mind.

Likewise, audiences take cues from personal style bloggers that help them feel like they know the blogger, discerning the blogger's favorite fashion trends, designers, pet peeves, phrases, and events in his or her personal life from blog posts, About Me webpages, comments, and external interviews. The blogger's construction of the self is a social and interactive practice that is constituted alongside audience practices of reading, responding, and—often—not responding. The idea that having nothing nice to say should deter readers from commenting on the blog is implicit in the posted warnings against trolling behavior (online harassment) that are common fixtures on many blogs. The construction of the imagined blog community relies on a mostly unspoken social contract that Internet trolls will keep themselves or be kept by others at bay.

In addition to the presence of an imagined audience in the coproduction of personal style blogs, another key difference between these blogs and reality ads is their subject matter. Blogs emphasize the person, while ads focus on the products promoted in blogs. To be more accurate, the main product in personal style blogs is the person producing the blog.  The bought products function as materials—matters of taste—that aid in the online production of the self. They are material representations of the blogger's taste that create and communicate the blogger's character, level of fashion knowledge, and identity. All the blog posts together create an image of the blogger's taste, style, and character—all the qualities that make the blogger unique, identifiable, and appealing. This is what bloggers call their personal brand. Recall that Lau identifies "my eye, my point of view, a certain taste, a certain way of documenting and presenting fashion" as her product. In her words, "that's what I'm selling."[63] Thus, the many formal and casual product endorsements that constitute blog content are not just visual texts (as ads are) but also social and cultural practices of taste work. All the activities of personal style blogging—from creating visual, textual, and design content to posing in front of a camera and responding to readers' comments—are modes of taste work. These activities generate value, though how much value and for whom, as I've already discussed, is highly variable and socially conditioned.

If personal style bloggers are a key real people constituency, then Asian superbloggers are a privileged (and minority) group among this constituency. They have "faces that reflect the [Asian] consumer" whom fashion companies are actively pursuing.[64] At the same time, their Asian faces are made less foreign by their English-language names and fluency. To put this another way, their Asian difference—which is not too different—is within the acceptable limits of racial tolerance. In the next section, I explain where and how the limits of racial tolerance are set. For now, what is important is that in this historical conjunction of the Asian moment in fashion and the age of social commerce, the exotic but not too exotic Asianness of Asian superbloggers provides just the balance between brand distinction and brand approachability that fashion companies now want to establish. What's more, the massive, transnational audiences that Asian superbloggers have built over the years make them very appealing to fashion companies that want to increase their exposure to mass markets.

The aim of this chapter so far has been to describe the wider context that conditions the cultural and commercial taste for Asian superbloggers. The particular confluence of Asian cute culture, the Asian moment in fashion, and the reality effect of social commerce on the fashion industry and media has rearticulated the economic meanings of Asianness, gendered Asian labor, and Asian fashion consumers in ways that have structurally advantaged some Asian personal style bloggers. But the new economic meanings of Asianness are nevertheless racialized. That is, the success of Asian superbloggers is not a sign that race no longer matters in fashion media economies. Just the opposite. The phenomenon of Asian superbloggers demonstrates clearly that race, particularly gendered ideas of Asianness, continues to matter a great deal in fashion economies—but in different, though historically linked, ways.

The taste for Asian superbloggers has not done away with the historical distaste for Asianness. As we know from Bourdieu and have seen in many examples of scholarly books and articles analyzing fashion, food, and visual cultures through the critical lens of ethnic studies,[65] the fields of taste production and consumption are constituted in and by racial, gender, and class relations of power in which the meanings of taste—and, connected to them, the meanings of style, fashion, and beauty—and the right to determine these meanings are struggled over. Thus, the souring taste for

Asian superbloggers (what I'm calling racial aftertaste) is part and parcel of the Asian superblogger phenomenon. "In matters of taste, more than anywhere else," Bourdieu writes, "all determination is negation . . . disgust provoked by horror or visceral intolerance ('sick-making') of the tastes of others."[66] He goes on to describe the negative reaction to the tastes of others as "aesthetic intolerance." I take Bourdieu's formulation of "aesthetic intolerance" or "the visceral intolerance . . . of the tastes of others" to include racial aftertastes, the souring of public tastes toward what was once a curious novelty and that now threatens to become a permanent feature of the new fashion and fashion media economy. Pushing at the limits of racial tolerance for otherness, racial aftertastes exemplify the aesthetic intolerance that, in Bourdieu's words, "amounts to rejecting others as unnatural."[67]

The unnaturalness of Asian superbloggers—the racial incongruity of the idea that the fashion tastes of Asians not only matter but are playing important roles in shaping the wider space of taste production and consumption—has been hinted at and stated outright throughout the Asian moment in fashion. An investigation of racial aftertastes with respect to Asian superbloggers is important for what it can tell us about the changing and enduring racialized hierarchies of fashion and digital labor markets.

### After the Taste, There Is the Aftertaste

The headline blasts in that ironically tabloid, insidery tone that has become a hallmark of mainstream feminist digital media in the post-Jezebel.com era: "We All Know Fashion Bloggers Have No Integrity, Right?"[68] Immediately below the headline is a photograph of two Asian superbloggers (Lau and Yambao), dressed in a riot of vivid colors and prints and standing backstage at a fashion show (figure 1.3). This is the sole image in a three-page web article published in the corporate-owned and -operated website, Gloss .com, in 2012. The choice of the photograph and its placement directly following the headline imply an affirmative answer to the question. The visual emphasis on the bloggers' eccentric dress (due in part to the way the photograph is harshly lit from the front) hints that they may have other outré tendencies like going where they don't belong (such as the front rows of fashion shows) and ignoring journalistic standards (for example, selling one's opinion for freebies)—the two main points the article makes.

# We All Know Fashion Bloggers Have No Integrity, Right?

2 years ago by Ashley Cardiff | 9 Comments | Share a Tip

— WEAR DOLCE & GABBANA. DRINK DIET COKE

During fashion month, when every fashion site with a photo department publishes slideshow after slideshow of "street style," in and around the tents, you pretty quickly note the recurring

1.3 Partial screenshot of the Gloss.com article of March 12, 2012.

The tone and substance of the article is like many other antiblogger missives that began springing up in the early 2010s. Unlike the more positive news stories about bloggers and the democratization of fashion culture and industries in the mid-2000s (which nonetheless treated bloggers as mostly pet curiosities), later stories are noticeably more circumspect about the blogger phenomenon. Consider the following article published on the website Fashionista.com, part of a larger network of websites run by Breaking Media Corporation. Its headline is nearly identical to the Gloss .com piece: "Can You Trust the Editorial Integrity of Personal Style Blogs? A Closer Look at How Bloggers Make Money." And like the former article, its opening shot is directed at Asian superbloggers. The article begins by saying that blogs, "once the provenance of earnest fashion fans on the fringes of the industry, . . . have evolved into legitimate media sources and, more importantly, big moneymakers. Just look at today's . . . 'hot fashion bloggers' like Bryan Boy and Susie Bubble [Yambao and Lau]," and it later notes that" as blogs make the transition from personal style diaries to profit-turning businesses, some readers have begun to feel that original and unbiased content . . . has taken a hit."[69] Who these skeptical readers are remains unclear in the article. Many of those quoted are anonymous, including a blogger who admits that blogging has become "a slightly vicious cycle of bribery." Other bloggers who are quoted and identified insist that all their endorsements are from the heart. Yambao and Lau are not quoted. Nor is Neely, though the article takes a gratuitous jab at her as well, quoting a *Women's Wear Daily*'s comment that she "has never had a job that's lasted more than a month."

Of the many antiblogger invectives that have circulated, the one that the renowned fashion journalist Suzy Menkes wrote for the *New York Times Magazine* in 2013 is perhaps the most damning. In "The Circus of Fashion," Menkes slams bloggers for bringing into being a world governed by "the survival of the gaudiest." As with so many other denunciations of bloggers, in this case the critic's finger wags in the general direction of all bloggers but points to Asian superbloggers as specific examples. For Menkes, one of the gaudiest leaders of the fashion circus is Yambao. In a broad description of bloggers that includes lines like "gagging for . . . attention"; "peacocks . . . [who] pose and preen, in their multipatterned dresses, spidery legs balanced on club-sandwich platform shoes"; and "the cattle market of showoff people," she suggests that her readers "think of the über-stylish Filipino blogger Bryanboy, whose real name is Bryan Grey Yambao." Another superblogger who Menkes mentions by name is Lau. In the same sentence in which she describes Lau as "the sharp Susie Bubble," Menkes admonishes her as a representative of all bloggers who have made "judging fashion . . . all about me: Look at me wearing the dress! Look at these shoes I have found! Look at me loving this outfit in 15 different images!"[70]

Nowhere in Menkes's description of bloggers' digital self-regarding and self-promotion is an acknowledgment that these activities are endemic to social media culture, as well as built into the architecture of social media platforms in the form of profile pictures, "about me" webpages, status update features, and so on. Menkes's concern is not about digital narcissism writ large. Her problem is that the gatekeeping mechanisms meant to separate, to use her analogy, the monochromatic "group of dedicated pros—dressed head to toe in black" from the "multipatterned" poseurs seem to be failing.[71]

Her aversion for bloggers is not restricted to their sartorial style but extends to their ostensible willingness to accept "trophy gifts and paid-for trips"—or "bribes," in Menkes's estimation: "Adhering to the time-honored journalistic rule that reporters don't take gifts (read: bribes), I am stunned at the open way bloggers announce which designer has given them what."[72] At best, this is an exaggerated statement of protest; at worst, it is an insincere one. Fashion editors and journalists have never made a secret of the fact that they receive gifts daily in the form of free samples, gratis services, and guest passes to big-ticket events. Yet Menkes blames bloggers for this practice and makes an example of Yambao: "When [Marc Jacobs] named a bag after Bryanboy in 2008, he made the blogger's name, and turned on an apparently unending shower of designer gifts, which are warmly welcomed at bryanboy.com."[73]

It's worth mentioning that Asian superbloggers were made to represent the fashion blogger phenomenon even in earlier news stories, in which they were mostly perceived as a cultural novelty rather than a nuisance. When the mainstream media first took notice of bloggers, it was the bodies and physical presence of Asian superbloggers that the media gave much of their attention to. Screenshots of some of the earliest news articles about bloggers illustrate the centrality of Asian superbloggers in media representations of fashion bloggers.

Some blog readers have defended Asian superbloggers by rejecting their critics as nothing more than wrenches in the wheels of progress. In a comment posted to Style Bubble on February 20, 2013, one of Lau's readers calls them "not-to-be-modernised PR companies" and "veteran journos . . . who can't bare [sic] the thought of modernization." In a position piece for Vogue a year later, Lau is equally dismissive, describing the criticism of bloggers as "the noise of a few grumbling industry insiders."[74] But it would be a mistake to see attacks on bloggers that target Asian superbloggers as just the arbitrary or subjective acts of a few intransigent relics. To do so would be to ignore the fact that they are part of a long history of racializing Asian labor. I argue that these attacks are not isolated ones against a new and distinct labor identity, but instead evidence of the persistence and mutability

# LIFE&STYLE

Beauty | Bridal | Design | Diet | Drive Life | Fashion | Gifts | Health | House & Home | Parenting | Peo

10:39PM  Sunday Jul 13, 2014 | 170 online now | Do you know more about a story?  ▼ | Real Estate | Cars

## Have laptop, will travel: bloggers arrive on fashion's front row

✉ 🖶 A A

Blogger Bryanboy backstage at the Camilla parade at Australian Fashion Week.
Photo: Edwina Pickles

Rachel Wells
May 4, 2008
Page 1 of 2 | Single page

1.4 Yambao backstage at Australian Fashion Week in Rachel Wells, "Have Laptop, Will Travel," the *Age*, May 4, 2008.

of racial hierarchies as a structuring force in fashion labor markets and in digital media economies more generally. Furthermore, they express for me not the failure of the liberal viewpoint but the logical conclusion of liberal approaches to tolerance, difference, and diversity. As I demonstrate below, the distaste for Asian superbloggers—what I'm calling racial aftertaste—is not a reversal of the popular opinion about and interest in Asian superbloggers but is instead structurally continuous with them. Racial aftertastes always follow from the taste for racial difference.

The popularity and success of Asian superbloggers are conditioned by broader cultural, economic, and technological factors, but they are sus-

InStyle   FASHION ▾   CELEBRITY ▾   HAI

FASHION

# Bloggers Take Over the Front Row

1.5  Lau, Neely, and Yambao in Joyann King, "Bloggers Take Over the Front Row," *InStyle*, September 10, 2009.

## Today I'm wearing...

Style blogger Susie Lau is headed for fashion's front row

Eva Wiseman
The Observer, Saturday 7 February 2009

Style blogger Susie Lau Photograph: Suki Dhanda

Every day, 10,000 people read what 25-year-old Susie Lau thinks about clothes. Every day, Susie Lau logs on to her blog, Style Bubble (stylebubble.typepad.com), photographs her outfit, raves about a new designer and inspires her international fanbase - they post their excited

1.6 Lau in Eva Wiseman, "Today I'm wearing . . . ," *Guardian*, February 7, 2009.

tained by the discourse and value of social progress. As I argued above, media stories about superbloggers often focus on Asians as evidence of the progressive development of the industry. In the words of Robin Givhan (the only fashion journalist to be awarded a Pulitzer Prize), they show that "fashion has evolved from an autocratic business dominated by omnipotent designers into a democratic one."[75] These media stories textually and visually represent Asian superbloggers' achievements and successes as technologically enabled by digital media. They frame the phenomenon of Asian superbloggers as an effect of digital democratization. The under-

Dennis Valle

**TRUCE** The bloggers Bryan Boy, third from left, and Tommy Ton, right, in Milan. More Photos >
By ERIC WILSON
Published: December 24, 2009

🐦 TWITTER

1.7 Yambao and streetstyle blogger Tommy Ton are the only bloggers shown in the photograph sitting with elite fashion editors—including Menkes; Michael Roberts (*Vanity Fair*); and Sally Singer, Anna Wintour, and Hamish Bowles (*Vogue*)—at Milan Fashion Week in Eric Wilson, "Bloggers Crash Fashion's Front Row," *New York Times*, December 24, 2009.

standing is that technologies have lowered the barriers to participation, helping make the various spheres of fashion (from fashion journalism and fashion modeling to fashion consumerism) more racially inclusive and diverse. Asian superbloggers are supposedly the embodied evidence of a more racially tolerant and more democratic industry.

Yet implicit in the celebrations of tolerance and egalitarianism are narrow and rigid standards for what differences and behaviors are deserving of tolerance and who is entitled to equality (and how much). To be

*The Taste and Aftertaste for Asian Superbloggers* 67

tolerated, Rey Chow incisively observes, "is to be granted a radical . . . kind of *recognition* . . . based on clear-cut, hierarchical boundaries."[76] What she means is that the subject granted tolerance is necessarily positioned as inferior, as someone in need of and determined to be reasonably deserving of tolerance (from a superior who is in the position to offer tolerance and acceptance). Using the example of the ethnic subject, Chow explains that the liberal framework of tolerance depends on—even as it overtly disavows—boundaries separating us and them, the cosmopolitan West (distinguished by its liberal tolerance) and the rest (all the backward places that are ethnically marked by their cultures of intolerance).

In liberal frameworks of tolerance (and all the names they go by, such as multiculturalism, postracialism, and diversity), the boundary between us and them is built into the discursive and ideological structure by its implicit assignment of who is the agent of tolerance and who is subject to tolerance. The contradiction in liberal approaches to difference is that they depend on clear and durable hierarchies of difference. Tolerance is contingent on the fulfillment of conditions of acceptablity that legitimize or normativize difference. Liberal approaches to difference and diversity are conditionally bound. What lies on the other side of the field of tolerance's conditions is intolerance. In this way, intolerance is systemically coconstituted with tolerance in liberal frameworks. Difference provides the occasion for both tolerance and intolerance.

To relate this more specifically to the taste for and aftertaste of Asian superbloggers, I turn to Bourdieu's concept of legitimate difference. In his essay, "Haute Couture and Haute Culture,"[77] he describes fashion trends as "legitimate differences" that operate through a central and contradictory logic, much like that identified by Chow as operating in relation to tolerance. Because legitimate differences are conditionally bound by determinations of what is legitimate and what is illegitimate, the threat of becoming an illegitimate difference is a constitutive feature of being a legitimate difference. That is, legitimate and illegitimate differences are two ends of the same spectrum of difference.

Bourdieu's legitimate difference exemplifies for me the fraught position Asian superbloggers occupy in the fashion industry and helps explain how the popular taste or preference for them necessarily leads to the souring of tastes for them. The Asian superbloggers I have been discussing embody a legitimate difference. They are exotic but not too exotic. They are different but legitimately and legibly so, because they are English-speakers; are cute (in appearance and work practice); and blog, live, shop, and fashion themselves in and through Western sites of culture and communication. They embody difference but one that is knowable, familiar, and  thus legitimate.

As the public and media buzz about Asian superbloggers illustrates, legitimate differences are highly lauded in the fashion industry. Indeed, they are crucial to the continuance of the industry. "The struggle for the monopoly of distinction, that is, the monopolistic power to impose the latest legitimate difference, the latest fashion," Bourdieu explains, is "the motor of the field."[78] Fashion trends challenge previous ones, but not to the detriment of the fashion system because they adhere to and remain within the parameters of legitimacy that leave the system of fashion trend cycles intact. In this way, fashion trends are distinct from fashion transgressions. Rather than a destructive force (though some may see and experience them that way), they are actually a productive force. The constant emergence of new trends and the decline of old ones are essential to the continued cultural and economic operations of the fashion industry. But its continuation depends on limited degrees of change and a narrow range of difference that disrupts without damaging. Legitimate fashion trends remain within the field of acceptability; they keep their place.

Racializing processes of differentiation are not only spatially articulated (for example, through residential segregation) but also temporally constructed. As we know from Chow and others (notably, Johannes Fabian, with his crucial theory about anthropological constructions of otherness through "the denial of coevalness"[79]), tolerable differences conform to spatial and temporal designations of acceptable behavior, social relations, and—as I discuss below—labor and consumer practices. Tolerable or legitimate differences are temporally distinct from universalized norms, which are privileged as spatially and temporally transcendent. To put this another way, the legitimacy of universal norms is not subject to conditionality and so is not in need of tolerance. Their legitimacy goes without saying.

The rise of Asian superbloggers is timely insofar as the phenomenon is temporally correlated with wider cultural, economic, and technological shifts. Understood in this way, a crude interpretation of Asian superbloggers is that they are trendy. And just as trends are fundamentally ephemeral and temporary, so too are superbloggers, who are bound to spatial and temporal conditions. Paradoxically, while trends are fleeting, the idea of fashion trends is a structural fixture of the fashion industry. In fact, the only thing constant about fashion trends is that there is always a next one, so the emergence of a fashion trend is also the beginning of its decline. We can say that a fashion trend is a legitimate difference—is institutionally recognizable—when another one takes its place, when it is shown to be a fleeting part of a succession of trends.

Like all good trends, predictions of Asian superbloggers' demise inevitably followed celebrations of their rise to prominence. Media stories about superbloggers describe them as the latest new thing while also anticipating (explicitly or implicitly) their eventual metamorphosis into the old thing. Examples include "Is Fashion Blogging Dead?," "Why The Era Of Personal Style Blogs Must Come To An End," and "The Golden Era of 'Fashion Blogging' Is Over."[80] These stories, as former *New York* writer Amy Odell makes clear, are about Asian superbloggers whether they are specifically named or not: "When the industry talks about fashion bloggers, they're referring to . . . the likes of Susie Bubble, Bryan Boy, Fashion Toast [Neely]."[81] This is quoted from an article whose headline reads, "Finding the Next Bryanboy." If trends are characterized by their inevitable succession, then this is perhaps the clearest evidence of Asian superbloggers' trendiness.

The spatial and temporal conditionality of Asian superbloggers as a legitimate difference helps explain the backlash against them. The extraordinary span of their achievements and the length of time they have spent in the fashion media spotlight (due in part to their own efforts in controlling and directing the spotlight) has exceeded, according to insiders like Menkes, the spatial and temporal bounds of acceptability. Lingering too long and too far outside the parameters of acceptable taste, they have left an aftertaste. Attacks on bloggers indicate a souring of popular feeling toward superbloggers. Implied is a determination that the time and place for the trend has passed. Asian superbloggers, while once novel and interesting, have overstayed their welcome.

The aftertaste left by Asian superbloggers' continued presence in the fashion media and public consciousness can be traced to a longer history of racial aftertastes regarding Asian labor. Attacks on bloggers like that of Menkes express disgust for bloggers' tastes for loud, attention-getting clothes ("multipatterned dresses"), for fashion as an attention-getting device rather than an art for its own sake, and for freebies and the media spotlight. In short, these attacks are taste judgments about the cheapness of bloggers' taste, style, and work practices. Menkes's characterization of bloggers as a group governed by "the survival of the gaudiest" is highly suggestive of the judgment of cheapness. In what follows, I investigate the gendered and racial dimensions of cheapness that the discourse of ethics that frames attacks on bloggers (using such terms as "integrity" and "time-honored journalistic rule") simultaneously implies and obfuscates. Tracing the gendered and racial dimensions of taste judgments that condemn bloggers and their cheapness will clarify the historical continuities of race and gender hierarchies that link nondigital and digital economic and labor markets.

## Cheap Talk about Asian Labor

Previous studies have shown that in the term Asian labor, the word Asian functions as both a racial and a class qualifier.[82] Historically, Asian labor (or Oriental labor or Asiatic labor) has been synonymous with degraded, cheap labor. This class-based racial identity has been reinforced and naturalized through economic, legal, and social exclusions that confine Asian workers to the lowest-paying and most precarious labor market sectors. In the nineteenth century, Indian workers on sugar plantations in Trinidad, Jamaica, British Guiana, and Mauritius; Chinese and South Asian coolies in the Caribbean and Louisiana; and Chinese miners in California all embodied cheap labor in the imaginaries of industrial and state employers. In the twentieth and twenty-first centuries, Filipino migrant agricultural laborers in the U.S. Pacific Northwest; Filipina domestic workers around the world; Chinese and Korean garment workers in the United States; and Chinese, Bangladeshi, Thai, Vietnamese, and Sri Lankan garment workers and electronics manufacturing workers in Asia embody cheap labor both in the global economy and the global imaginary. In 2014, Ethiopian workers at a Chinese shoe factory located outside Addis Ababa have also become the embodiment of cheap Asian labor. As Chinese factory owners are moving their operations to Ethiopia, where wages are staggeringly low (garment workers in Addis Ababa make 10 percent of what Chinese workers do), scholarly, corporate, and media representations have described them as the Chinese of Africa. A *Bloomberg* article reports "Ethiopia Becomes China's China in Global Search for Cheap Labor," a title that probably draws on a quote in the article by a professor of international development, who characterizes Ethiopia's future in the global economy in this way: "It could become the China of Africa."[83]

So-called Chinese gold farmers exemplify the digitalization of cheap Asian labor. Chinese gold farmers are online gamers who may or may not be Chinese or Asian but are, as Lisa Nakamura has explained, racialized online as Chinese.[84] They are typically from the Third World and are paid by First World gamers to do the tedious tasks necessary to build a high-level character, including playing the game when the First World gamer is sleeping. Here we see not only the transmigration of stereotypes of cheap Asian labor into digital realms but also the Asianization of cheap labor, even in cases where the laborers themselves are not Asian. The Asianization of cheap labor exemplifies Chow's concept of the "ethnicization of labor," in which dividing labor into hierarchical categories (cheap labor, low-level labor, domestic labor, and so on) has an ethnicizing effect that marks certain workers as socially inferior.[85] We see this in the digital economy with Chinese gold farmers as well as in the material economy with Ethiopian shoe factory workers. The designation of Chinese marks both groups as cheap laborers at the same time that their perceived cheapness racializes these workers, who may not actually be Asian, as Asian labor.

The variety of nationalities, ethnicities, and jobs that have been designated as cheap Asian labor indicates that it is not simply a labor identity designation but instead a product of economic racialization. The term is a racial expression of and a justification for social and economic divisions of labor. While the racial and economic articulation of cheap labor has not been exclusively applied to Asians, it has been a feature of Asian racialization for centuries. The current race to the bottom triggered by free trade and globalization has only reinforced the Asianization of cheap labor. Today, it is not just China but also Viet Nam, Indonesia, and Bangladesh (the four largest exporters of clothing in the world) that are the world's factories.

Strikingly, though, Asia is no longer identified just with cheap labor. It is becoming a crucial market for luxury goods as well. A 2013 report released by the Economist Intelligence Unit, the market analyst firm that publishes the *Economist*, predicts that Asia will account for 50–60 percent of luxury revenue worldwide within ten years.[86] The growing middle class and wealthy elite in China, Japan, India, Malaysia, Thailand, and Indonesia are expected to drive more than half of the luxury goods economy worldwide. Jon Copestake, chief retail and consumer goods analyst at the Economist Intelligence Unit, concludes that "with Europe stagnating and North America subdued, the focus is firmly on Asia's potential."[87]

Today, the racial and economic designation of Asian labor as cheap exists alongside the ascendancy of Asians into the higher rungs of fashion labor markets such as fashion design, fashion modeling, and fashion blogging. (Although designers, models, and bloggers do not necessarily earn high incomes, their status in the creative sectors is higher than that of Asian fashion laborers in manufacturing sectors.) Does the ascendancy of some Asians in the creative sectors of fashion's labor markets mean that the economic articulation of Asianness as cheap labor is shifting? Yes and no.

The discursive and visual construction of cheapness in attacks on bloggers suggests, on one hand, that cheap continues to be the economic description of Asian difference and, on the other hand, that the racialization of cheapness operates differently in creative labor segments. In one register of meaning, *cheap* indicates low value and worth. Cheap Asian labor is devalued as inferior, unskilled, and expendable labor (as in the contexts of the garment and electronics assembly industries). The designation of cheap Asian labor justifies the rock-bottom wages paid to these workers.

The devaluation of Asian labor as cheap also has specifically gendered meanings. Just as to feel cheap is to feel used and powerless, to be classified as cheap Asian labor is to be perceived as powerless, subordinate, and docile. In the stereotype of the docile Asian worker, femininity is presented as an inferior as well as an intrinsic quality of Asian workers. At the same time, as we saw in the racial hiring patterns in apparel manufacturing industries throughout the latter half of the twentieth century (discussed in the introduction), the feminization of cheap Asian labor structures Asian workers' relative valorization in relation to Black labor, even cheap Black labor, which is racialized as difficult and demanding.

The U.S. Page Act of 1875 institutionalized a moral valence of the term *cheap Asian labor* by legally categorizing Asian women as likely prostitutes. The act imposed a blanket prohibition on the immigration of all Asian women ("any subject of China, Japan, or any Oriental country"[88]) on the presumption that they were immigrating for the purposes of prostitution. The popular perception of Asian women as the embodiment of cheap labor and cheap morality has not gone away, as the countless representations and widespread circulation of Asian prostitute stereotypes attest.[89]

The moral dimensions of cheap Asian labor are also found in its third register of meaning, in which *cheap* signifies fakeness or fraudulence. A cheap win is not a real win, but one that is attained by some unprincipled or unscrupulous means. Asian labor has similarly denoted a cheapness of work ethic, of cutting corners and evading rules. Thus, the expression *cheap Asian labor* not only refers to the low wages Asian laborers historically have been paid, but it also implies that Asian laborers are immoral and deviant as well as dishonest and untrustworthy. Bret Harte's much-cited 1870 poem "Plain Language from Truthful James,"[90] about the Chinese immigrant card shark Ah Sin, reflects this perception. Harte does not specify Ah Sin's occupation, but the character stands in for Chinese laborers in California at the time. In the poem, Ah Sin's cheating is discovered, and he is brutally punished. But before his white card–playing counterparts Bill Nye and Truthful James beat him up, Nye wails, "we are ruined by Chinese cheap labor." The poem's conflation of *cheap* and *cheat* illuminates the historically negative ethical valence of *cheap Asian labor*.

As the earlier examples of antiblogger discourse demonstrate, it is the third register of meaning (with shades of the second meaning) that dominates articulations of cheap Asian labor in the Asian moment in fashion. Critics of personal style bloggers accuse them of unethical practices designed to extract free gifts and free publicity. There are vague insinuations of their whoring for attention and for fashion labels. These kinds of condemnations are meant to discredit personal style blogging, in general, as fake journalism and inauthentic expressions of taste and identity. But by focusing their fire on Asian superbloggers, critics racialize cheapness in ways that are historically specific and historically continuous.

As the Ah Sin literary example suggests, the charge that Asian superbloggers do not come by their skills, talents, and successes honestly is not unique in the history of Asian labor, particularly Asian immigrant labor. We see the same racialization of cheap Asian labor in the context of laundry, railroad, agricultural, and mining work in the United States in the nineteenth century. Chinese, Japanese, and Filipino workers who were willing to work for less pay and longer hours, and in harsh conditions, were accused by their Euro-American counterparts, politicians, and the mainstream media of taking unfair advantages in their respective labor markets. These advantages were also unfairly acquired, according to mainstream perceptions, since they were understood as the results of racial cunning and prowess.[91]

More than a century later, Asian fashion workers from superbloggers to star designers are subject to the same kinds of accusations. When the Asian American fashion designer Alexander Wang was named creative director of Balenciaga in 2012, industry pundits and lay observers suggested (and sometimes overtly stated) that his appointment had nothing to do with talent and business acumen and everything to do with his Chineseness.[92] (Wang, who was born in California, identifies himself as Taiwanese American.) Lurid speculations about Wang's exploiting and deriving benefits from Chinese connections underlie and sometimes appear explicitly in media stories about Wang's new job. One widely circulating article had this headline: "New Evidence That Alexander Wang's Chinese Connections May Have Helped Land Him Balenciaga."[93] Not surprisingly, the article presented no evidence of these supposed connections.

In the age of social commerce, when consumer activities are also value-producing activities, it is worth noting that the economic racialization of Asian labor extends to Asian consumers as well. As I have written elsewhere, Chinese fashion consumers—a catchall term for Asian fashion consumers—have been simultaneously hailed as the saviors of the global luxury economy and derided as gaudy, tacky consumers with cheap tastes.[94] Valentine Fillol-Cordier's comments in a Style Council discussion published in Bon in 2011 illustrate what has become a commonplace criticism of Asian fashion consumers. Discussing Chinese consumers, the stylist sniffs: "You can't pretend to have lots of taste if you're simply buying all that shit and spending tons of money."[95] Such judgments of Asian fashion consumers (with their "pretend" tastes) reveal social anxieties about the possible threat that Asian consumers' rising market power poses to fashion's established racial order. I suggest that attacks on bloggers that target Asian superbloggers betray the same kinds of racial anxieties about what the enduring presence and power of these new fashion leaders might mean for the historically white fashion industry and culture.

The persistent associations of cheapness with Asianness even in a context in which Asians are ascending fashion status ladders illustrates my point here that the word *cheap* is not only an economic designation but also a racially charged one. In addition, it illustrates the general point of this book, that the presence of Asian superbloggers in the top tiers of fashion's new informational economy marks the continuation—not the diminution of—racial hierarchization as a structuring force in fashion's processes of capital accumulation. Indeed, the history of fashion capitalism has always been a history of racial capitalism.

Cedric Robinson's magisterial work in *Black Marxism* demonstrates the ways in which racializing processes of differentiation have been integral, not incidental, to the historical development of capitalism. Tellingly, some of the earliest systems of what Robinson calls "racial capitalism" can be found in the histories of textile and clothing manufacture.[96] In the early sixteenth and the seventeenth centuries, Flemish cloth workers and, later, Huguenot handloom weavers in London made up the large and expendable reserve supply of immigrant labor that fueled these early industries. While there has been little research on the racialization of early modern European working classes—a critique that both Robinson[97] and Immanuel Wallerstein[98] make—there is evidence that Flemish workers were specifically targeted by these industries due to popular perceptions that they were capable as well as controllable. John Aubrey, a mid-seventeenth-century antiquary and amateur local historian in Wilts County in the southwest of England, jokingly compared Flemish cloth workers to the sheep they sheared for wool: "If our nation in times past was the most famous for the greatest quantity of wool in ye world, this county had the most sheep of any other." To maintain their economic advantage, "successive English rulers, even for centuries, did all that lay in their power to encourage Flemish and other foreign cloth workers to settle in this country."[99]

Today, the racializing processes of differentiation on which late Euro-American capitalism is based are structured, paradoxically, by the cultural logics of postracism and multiculturalism. Describing this era of "neo-liberal multicultural capitalism," Jodi Melamed explains that in current articulations of race with capitalism, "racism constantly appears as disappearing according to conventional race categories, even as it takes on new forms that can signify as nonracial or even antiracist."[100] This is borne out in the competing conceptualization of Asian superbloggers as, on the one hand, representative of a highly valued and entirely new formation of creative Asian worker and, on the other hand, a historically consistent class of cheap Asian workers.

The tendencies to valorize and devalue Asian superbloggers may be contradictory, but they have the same aim. Both sets of expressions (of the taste for and aftertaste of Asian superbloggers) preserve the myth of late capitalism that free market economies spur social and material progress while also maintaining fashion's dominant racial order. The existence of Asian superbloggers in one of the most cutthroat and racially stratified industries in the world proves that social progress is being made (that is, racism is disappearing) and that the fashion industry is the vanguard cultural, social, and economic force it imagines itself to be. Attacks on bloggers that focus on the personal ethical failings of bloggers retain the discourse of progress while reasserting fashion's dominant racial order, in which white Euro-American experts and consumers are the true arbiters of fashion and style.

The reassertion of the traditional racial hierarchy of taste and style is achieved in the closing text and image of Menkes's "Circus of Fashion." Hinting that Yambao (an exemplar of Asian superbloggers) is a cheap knockoff of real fashionistos and fashionistas, Menkes suggests that even his identity is fake, referring to "Filipino blogger Bryanboy, whose real name is Bryan Grey Yambao."[101] The fashion-centric *New York Times Magazine* has many readers who are sure to know as much or more about Yambao than Menkes, who has made her disdain for personal style bloggers well known. Given this, her comment about Yambao's name seems unnecessary, except to underscore her main point that he's a fake, a cheap Asian imitation, a knockoff of real fashion workers (like Menkes herself, presumably).[102]

The final image of Menkes's article illustrates what real fashion people look like, according to Menkes and the *New York Times Magazine* editors. The image shows three white European fashion editors: Emmanuelle Alt (*Vogue Paris*), Virginie Mouzat (French *Vanity Fair*), and Ludivine Poiblanc (*Interview*). Above the image is a caption that reads: "The opposite of look-at-me fashion: leave it to the French to master understated chic" (figure 1.8). Wholly rejecting the general understanding of personal style blogging as real style by real people, Menkes's article reasserts that real fashion is the preserve of white Western media and industry professionals (people with access to teams of stylists and hair and makeup artists). The binary oppositions the article sets up between real and fake fashionability and what is chic and what is cheap are clearly divided along gendered

*The opposite of look-at-me fashion: leave it to the French to master understated chic.*

1.8 The embodiment of normative chic, from Suzy Menkes, "The Circus of Fashion," *New York Times Magazine*, February 10, 2013.

racial lines. Fakeness and cheapness are Asianized and feminized in the figure of a queer Filipino man and pitted against straight white feminine authenticity.

The cheap, unethical blogger is a nonracial form of racialization that enables "racism to appear as constantly disappearing."[103] What disappears or is erased by attacks on bloggers are the conventional, more familiar categories of race as well as the histories of economic racialization in which the discursive construction of cheap Asian labor is rooted. But it is the disappearance of old racisms that enables new racisms to appear (under the covers of postracism, multiculturalism, and the seemingly nonracial discourse of ethics).

*Cheap*, as an economic and racial concept, links personal style bloggers to a longer history of Asian labor in fashion industries and beyond.

At the same time, the particular significations of *cheap* have shifted to accommodate neoliberal late capitalist rationalities of individualism, self-responsibility, and postracism. It is the shifting meanings of *cheap* that allow the term to endure as mechanism of economic racialization. The incorporation of Asian superbloggers into the top and highly visible tiers of fashion media serves the pluralistic and competitive imperatives of global and multicultural capitalism. They substantiate the inclusionary nature of fashion's business and culture to its global and increasingly Asian consumers and investors. The designation of cheap Asian labor (in all the registers of the term's meaning) ensures, however, that the racial structure of power and privilege is not altered. Thus, the incorporation of Asian superbloggers provides the multicultural cover for the upward distribution of resources, opportunities, rewards, and respect. Judgments about cheap Asian labor naturalize this hierarchical system. In this way, the racialization of Asians as cheap labor has not prevented them from participating in the fashion industry's manufacturing or digital media labor markets. To the contrary, racialization has been and continues to be the condition of Asians' economic participation.

# Chapter 2.
## Style Stories, Written Tastes, and the Work of Self-Composure

Roland Barthes begins his investigation in The Fashion System with the observation that fashion in its written form—what he calls "written clothing"—provides the clearest representation of its meaning in a society. Unlike "real clothing" (that is, actual garments), which is "burdened with practical considerations (protection, modesty, adornment)," written clothing's only function is signification.[1] According to Barthes, if a "magazine describes a certain article of clothing verbally, it does so solely to convey a message whose content is: Fashion."[2] He capitalizes Fashion here because he intends it to represent what he calls a "supercode"—a system of words and meanings that "take over" the garment.[3] The forcefulness implied in the term "take over" is appropriate. Barthes understands the function of written clothing—of descriptions of fashion—to impose meaning that blocks out other possible interpretations: "every written word has a function of authority insofar as it chooses—by proxy, so to speak—instead of the eye . . . words determine a single certainty."[4] He continues: "Fashion text represents as it were the authoritative voice of someone who knows all there is behind the jumbled or incomplete appearance of the visible forms."[5]

Several years after Barthes published The Fashion System, Pierre Bourdieu gave a talk in Arras, France, titled "Haute Couture and Haute Culture," in which he attributes to fashion descriptions much the same social, cultural, and ideological functions as Barthes does. Analyzing the adjectives most often associated with fashion designers and products in fashion magazines, Bourdieu argues that these adjectives refer less to the designer or product and more to the "aesthetic position" of the agent or institution doing the describing.[6] Fashion descriptions, according to Bourdieu, are the means by which "the possessors of legitimacy" reproduce and secure their legitimacy, and by which those who want to attain legitimacy ("the newcomers") make their way into the field of fashion. By gaining control of the meanings of fashion and the right to define its meanings, newcomers challenge "the possessors of legitimacy," being careful to "destroy the hierarchy but not the game itself."[7] In other words, fashion descriptions are both a site where the struggle over the meanings and limits of class, taste, beauty, and distinction take place and a site circumscribed by the delineation between legitimate difference (what is fashionably distinct) and illegitimate difference (what is distinctly not fashion).

I begin my discussion of the taste work of Asian superbloggers with Barthes's and Bourdieu's characterizations of the power and politics of fashion language because they provide a critical point of departure for evaluating what is an underexamined and sometimes totally ignored feature of personal style blogs: the personal style story, the text accompanying the photos that describe how bloggers choose a particular outfit, how they style it, and the occasion for wearing it. Recall that when the fashion journalist Suzy Menkes chides Susanna Lau (aka Susie Bubble) for contributing to the circus she believes fashion shows have turned into now that bloggers have come onto the scene, she skewers Lau with this taunt: "Look at me wearing the dress! Look at these shoes I have found! Look at me loving this outfit in 15 different images!"[8] Menkes is referring to the outfit photos that are the defining feature of personal style blogs. But even a casual reader of Style Bubble, Lau's blog, will notice that outfit photos make up a minority of the blog; in contrast, the number of words Lau produces for her style stories is legion. As I discuss below, Lau is an exceptionally prolific blogger in terms of the length of her stories, but she is in no way exceptional in the creation and use of them. Personal style stories are a primary component of personal style blogs, though they receive little public or scholarly attention.

The stereotype that personal style bloggers are vain and superficial attention seekers whose fashion sensibility, in Menkes's words, is nothing more than "look-at-me fashion" maintains the authoritative position of those in the fashion establishment and the structural organization of the establishment. By ignoring the literary work of these newcomers who are creating fashion language that contributes to the popular meanings of what is fashion and who is fashionable, Menkes and others like her suggest that their power to determine fashion meaning and knowledge is unopposed. The purpose of this chapter is to examine how Asian superbloggers' writings about their style and tastes challenge—and do not challenge—the dominant fashion system. Thus, part and parcel of my goal will be an investigation of how race, gender, class, and sexuality are constructed in and through these narratives of personal style in ways that maintain and accumulate capital for the blogger. In short, I am concerned with how different Asian superbloggers' literary modes of taste work function as expressions and embodiments of legitimate difference.

Asian superbloggers, as I discussed in the previous chapter, embody Bourdieu's notion of legitimate difference. As Asians in a white-dominated cultural and economic field who are expert English speakers and expert users of popular Western media technologies and practices (including popular fashion language), they are exotic, but not so exotic that they are foreign. It is their legitimate difference—their distinctiveness but not radical difference—that underpins their superblogger-level audiences, blog traffic, commercial partnerships, design collaborations, and mainstream media attention. Asian superbloggers' practices of taste work, I argue, function to negotiate and manage their fraught position as legitimate differences and to maintain their position as racialized others who are recognized in, if not always accepted by, the dominant fashion industry.

## The Anatomy of a Personal Style Blog

Personal style blog content consists primarily but not exclusively of what are called outfit posts. Generally, outfit posts have two major components: the personal style story and photos of the blogger's outfit of the day (or simply *outfit photos*). Typically, a single outfit post includes one story and several outfit photos. The stories explicitly or obliquely refer to outfit photos in much the same way that Barthes's "written clothing" refers to "image clothing,"[9] except that in personal style blogs the conceptual referent is not an article of clothing but a unified style of dress and embodiment. The clothes featured in personal style blogs (in all their structural forms) are significations of an individual's taste and personal style, not of fashion itself.

Style stories are a key but not necessary element of personal style blogs. Blair Eadie's well-regarded blog *Atlantic-Pacific* (so named because of her U.S. bicoastal life and style) does not include any style stories, yet it is recognizably a personal style blog because it has the essential feature of such blogs: outfit photos. Without outfit photos, the genre's key characteristic and by far most distinguishable feature, there is no personal style blog. When style stories are present, they might be as short as a single sentence or as long as two thousand words. Often, bloggers intersperse outfit photos throughout longer style stories, breaking up the text to make it easier to read online. And just as there is no standard length for a style story, there are no standard numbers of stories and story words that bloggers must produce.

To get a sense of the variability of style stories and outfit posts, consider that in the span of one year, Lau published a total of 237 blog posts, 65 of which were outfit posts (see table 2.1). The remaining 172 blog posts focused on a subject other than herself (such as a fashion collection, designer, retailer, event, or some other fashion news item). In the same year, she generated a total of 49,060 words, giving her an average of 207 words per blog post. In roughly the same year, Aimee Song published 197 blog posts, 191 of which were outfit posts. Her total word count was 23,754, making her average words per blog post 120. Similarly, Bryan Grey Yambao published 90 blog posts of which 52 were outfit posts. With a total of 7,459 words, his average words per blog post was 83. The ratios of outfit posts to not-outfit posts and words per blog post for other Asian superbloggers like Wendy Nguyen and Rumi Neely are about the same as Yambao's. These numbers clearly show that Lau is a superblogger both with respect to her status and her productivity. The productivity of other non-Asian superbloggers falls somewhere between Song's and Yambao's levels. For example, Jane Aldridge (Sea of Shoes) created 125 blog posts, 94 of them being outfit posts. She generated a total of 7,245 words or an average of 58 words per blog post. Leandra Medine (ManRepeller[10]) is the only other superblogger to come close to Lau's word count, but since Medine's blog is now produced by a team of people, this is not an apt comparison.

Table 2.1. A Year of Style Stories and Outfit Posts

|  | Style stories | Outfit posts | Total posts | Average word count per post | Total word count |
|---|---|---|---|---|---|
| Susanna Lau | 172 | 65 | 237 | 207 | 49,060 |
| Aimee Song | 6 | 191 | 197 | 120 | 23,754 |
| Bryan Grey Yambao | 38 | 52 | 90 | 83 | 7,459 |
| Jane Aldridge | 31 | 94 | 125 | 58 | 7,245 |

*Survey of Lau's posts taken from June 29, 2013–July 2, 2014; Song from July 2, 2013–June 29, 2014; Yambao from June 18, 2013–June 16, 2014; Aldridge from July 2, 2013–July 3, 2014.

Style stories involve literary modes of taste work. Bloggers write, edit, and revise texts that represent and constitute their identities as fashionable people, fashion consumers, and style authorities. Which garment details, brands, retailers, fashion events, and social relationships they emphasize and how they highlight them creates a literary representation of their taste identity. The linguistic form of written taste bears some relation to written clothing—in fact, bloggers sometimes adopt the popular vocabulary and turns of phrases of fashion magazines as a way of speaking to, by speaking like, the possessors of legitimacy. Song's outfit posts (97 percent of all her blog posts) are peppered with sartorial idioms and proverbs that convey the popular expressions and familiar sentiments of fashion magazines. Song frequently uses phrases like "pop of color" and "my go-to Fall jacket/blouse/studded boots/etc." and actively promotes the conventional wisdom of fashion magazines that clothes should flatter the body—that is, make it appear slender. Song's style stories simultaneously explain and demonstrate her knowledge of how to choose colors, prints, cuts, and lengths of garments that create the illusion of longer legs, a smaller waist, and curves on her "boyish shape."[11] Through her personal stories, she occupies both inspirational and instrumental roles: those of style muse and style guide. Readers write sometimes hundreds of comments on a single outfit post, remarking on how beautiful Song is and how much they love the way she styled her outfit. Just as often, they thank her for being "an inspiration" or, as was the case with a comment on a July 7, 2014, outfit post, for teaching them something new about wrap rompers, about a new exotic vacation spot in Morocco, and about how to wear a necklace as a ring ("I'll definitely be adding that to my jewelry box").

Arguably, print fashion magazines also serve the dual role of providing both style inspiration and guidance, but personal style bloggers carry out these functions differently. The production of style stories involves both textual and computational modes of taste work. This may be an obvious point, but it is one worth emphasizing since the tendency to compare fashion blogs and fashion magazines (like comparisons between bloggers and print journalists) elides the crucial difference between them. Unlike the fashion magazines that Barthes and Bourdieu analyze and that some bloggers like Song rhetorically emulate, personal style blogs are not a print medium. They are, in Katherine Hayles's words, "digital born"[12] texts that are not meant to be printed. There are no PDF versions of outfit posts, as online fashion magazines sometimes have, and there are no "print" buttons anywhere on the screen. Of course, it is possible to print out a blog post or a page of blog posts, but a print version of a personal style blog post would be a poor and only partial translation of the digital text. Lost in the translation from digital to print media are hyperlinks, affiliate marketing links (explained in the introduction), GIFs (graphics interchange formats, or animated and looping computer images), video and audio files, and the reader comments feature that allows multidirectional conversations to take place in real and asynchronous time. These are more than a blog's digital features—they constitute bloggers' taste work.

Bloggers' choice of which brands and garments to blog about, which to add hyperlinks and affiliate links to, and which audio and video files to upload are value-producing taste expressions. The most obvious message they convey is the blogger's sartorial and fashion preferences. Dedicated readers of some of the Asian superblogs know that Lau favors and is friendly with independent designers and that Yambao is "obsessed" (as he often puts it) with establishment houses like Balenciaga, Chanel, and Givenchy. And of course his friendship with Marc Jacobs has been well documented on his blog. Neely's style stories typically emphasize her laid-back Californian approach to style, in which she mixes luxury and mass-market labels, as well as her strong fan base in Japan, where she has been featured in numerous ad campaigns and fashion editorials—all of which are described in her style stories. Song also represents herself and her style as "California girl," which, as she has written a number of times, explains her "obsession with palm prints."[13]

Style stories also indicate the levels of influence and privilege a blogger's taste has. If, as Bourdieu has argued, there is a corresponding relation between taste and status—that group membership is indicated and enacted through taste—then the videos, affiliate links (or the lack thereof), and so on that constitute style stories demonstrate a blogger's relative position in the field of taste production. An uploaded video showing a blogger interviewing a top designer after a major fashion show confers a very different level of influence, status, and access than a video shared from YouTube. Likewise, the quality and quantity of affiliate links in a style story indicates a blogger's level of entrepreneurial savvy and industry support. All of these taste work practices generate cultural, informational, and—in the case of affiliate links—financial capital for bloggers. For example, behind-the-scenes videos at exclusive fashion shows, in designers' studios, or at the headquarters of a fashion house can draw new and repeat readers (as well as traffic) to the blog, thus increasing the blogger's reputation as well as the quality and quantity of his or her opportunities for side work. Uploading videos, creating GIFs, and embedding affiliate links are practices of taste work that require bloggers to do some basic to intermediate code and system administration work. For digital media to operate, computational work is needed. Print versions of personal style blogs suppress some of the key processes, practices, and skills of bloggers' taste work and, with them, bloggers' lines of capital accumulation.

With regard to the experience of the blog reader, a printed web page imposes the structural constraints of print-mediated communications onto a digital media form and practice. Online reading habits, as Internet studies have shown, differ from modes of reading print. Christian Vandendorpe adapts Mark Heyer's descriptions for the three distinct modes of information gathering—grazing, browsing, and hunting[14]—to explain methods of "reading on screen."[15] In the grazing mode, readers read continuously through a piece of text. This reading method has been transported from print to digital media and is less commonly practiced online than the other two reading modes. In the browsing mode, readers scan the text, pausing to read only those parts that interest them. In the hunting mode, readers actively search for specific information. They might use the Web browser's search tool or website's search box to find particular words or phrases. Online reading habits are also shaped by what Vandendorpe calls the "feedback effect" in which "a culture of questioning" encourages and enables Internet readers and writers to interrogate, critique, and challenge each other.

One of the effects of feedback on digital writing is the open-ended process of revision that continues even after a blog post has been published. Sometimes the revision process is highlighted by the blogger through the use of strikethrough lines or addendum notes that indicate changes have been made. A blog's changing content, particularly in the context of personal style blogs, is suggestive of the liveness of the blogger's style of dress and of embodiment. It conveys the blogger's style and life as genuinely lived in the moment. These qualities mark the personal style blogger and blog (the digital double of the blogger) as authentic. Print versions of outfit posts freeze the dynamic and dialogic processes of reading and writing in static form. In so doing, they structurally privilege linear and continuous forms of reading, imposing a method of reading print onto a digital form.

Style stories are a nonlinear and often nonsequential literary form. The noncontinuous succession of outfit posts, as I discuss in chapter 5, is an important structural characteristic that shapes the organizational representation of the personal style blogosphere as a creative labor sector. Outfit posts emphasize the art of self-styling by showing only the finished look. The physical work (traveling, shopping, trying on clothes, and so forth) that underpins the production of outfit posts—and that happens in between each outfit post—is removed from view, giving the impression that self-styling is an effortless activity.

To return to the point about the experience of reading style stories, because each outfit post is not necessarily connected to the one before or the one after it, the posts can be read in any order. Furthermore, the tags of keywords and terms (often brands, retailers, a style of clothing, and so on) that most personal style bloggers use to organize their blog posts give readers options for how to arrange their reading experience. Readers interested only in posts about TopShop garments or skinny jeans can click on those tags to filter out irrelevant posts. Another feature of style stories that gives readers the ability to customize their reading experience is hypertext. Clicking on an affiliate link will take readers immediately to a retail site (usually in a different window, so the blog remains open) where the specific garment can be purchased. Depending on which links readers choose to click on and in which order, each blog reading experience is unique.

Topshop Palm Jacquard A-Line Skirt (dress version here)
Dolce Vita Lace Top (similar here and here)
7 For All Mankind Denim Jacket (love this light one too!)

2.1 Screenshot from "Calamigos Ranch, Malibu," Song of Style, April 21, 2014.

Song's style stories include an additional feature that many others' stories do not. She provides hypertext links not only for the garments spotlighted on her blog but also for alternative versions of these garments. When she does include suggestions for alternatives, they usually appear in a footnotes list at the end of her style story. This list includes source and supplementary source information.

The difference between the featured garments and their alternatives might have to do with cost, brand, and/or design (for example, a dress version of a miniskirt; see figure 2.1). Saving her readers the time, energy, and potential frustration of combing through the Internet for versions of her outfit that better fit their budgets and/or style, Song surfs the Internet for them, giving her implicit imprimatur to these alternative fashion choices. With these links, she acts as style inspiration, search engine, and personal shopper, using her personal tastes as a rubric with which to sort, reduce, and organize the Internet's ocean of fashion choices for her readers, an audience of sartorially like-minded consumers.

This is a free service Song provides to her readers—and if readers' comments are any indication, it is a service that readers not only appreciate but also have come to expect. When bloggers don't note the brand or retailer carrying the garment featured, readers frequently use the comments feature of the blog to ask for this information. It is not uncommon for readers to respond to other readers' questions, sometimes providing additional information about the fit, color, or sizing of a garment. These are everyday interactions in the era of social commerce. Personal style blogs are key sites for mediating these one-to-many and many-to-many consumer communications. The interactivity of personal style blogs—communications between bloggers and readers, among bloggers and designers and retailers, between readers, and between different websites (blogs, news websites, online retailers, and so on)—characterizes for many fashion observers the democratizing effects of personal style blogs on the business and culture of fashion.

Yet the interactivity that bloggers facilitate through the work of creating, assigning, and managing hypertext links (and, in Song's blog, supplementary links to alternative garment choices) is not entirely a complimentary service. While these links are free to click on, and readers are free to click or not on any links they want, superblogs are fully and carefully monetized to convert readers' attention and activities into financial capital for the blogger, fashion and other retailers, and Internet companies. Even when a reader does not click on any links or purchase any items from affiliate retailers, just going to a personal style blog can create value for the blogger. For example, it can help to provide a search engine optimization boost (helping the site rise in the ranks of search engine results). Alternatively, bloggers who have cost per impression (as opposed to cost per click) arrangements with retailers can earn money based on the number of views an ad gets on their site (like in the case of a television commercial).

Just as important to bloggers' monetizing efforts as the hyperlinked text is the nonlinked text. When descriptions of garments or brands featured in an outfit post are not hyperlinked to a brand or retailer, this means that the blogger does not have an affiliate relationship with them. Because bloggers are not compensated for Internet activities that readers do off their site, static text is one way to make the most of blog reading activities. Hyperlinking only the text that will lead to value creation is a strategy for relegating (and regulating) blog readers' activities, directing them only to what creates value for the blogger. This demonstrates Espen Aarseth's important point that hypertext is best understood as a "fiction of interactivity."[16] The affiliate links in personal style blogs mean that readers are not free to traverse the blog however they want. Bloggers use hypermedia to attempt to control the experience of blog reading by limiting the choices people can make as readers and fashion consumers.

Personal style blog "hobbyists"—those who produce outfit posts casually and do not actively seek to attract large audiences—often are not interested in or do not know how to monetize their blogs. As I noted above, superbloggers' style stories are practices of taste work that require some level of coding and system administration skills. Even popular advertising programs like Google's AdSense (which automatically places ads based on a site's content and audience) require some code work. Once bloggers have been approved for an account (based on a wide range of criteria having to do with the site's language, content, and use and activity level), they still have to know how to install plug-in extensions or components that enhance the operations of their blogs so they can accept affiliate links and how to manually code links so that they are trackable. Some bloggers also manually code links to cloak affiliate partnerships so that they do not trigger ad blockers, spam filters, and search engine penalties.[17]

The textual and code work involved in superbloggers' style stories—as well as the computational work they perform or actively and passively agree to having others perform—are difficult to classify into traditional labor categories. They are free labor because readers do not pay for these services. However, they are paid labor inasmuch as bloggers are indirectly compensated by commercial affiliates for the work they and their readers do for free. Though bloggers are not paid to write their style stories or manage their system's online content and relationships, they stand to earn informational capital (for example, a higher search engine optimization ranking), cultural capital (such as more readers and more online traffic), and—once the style stories are posted and tracking scripts (for affiliate links, banner ads, and so on) are in place—financial capital for themselves and their commercial sponsors. Likewise, superbloggers' style stories are inarguably creative modes of labor, but they are also thoroughly instrumental modes of labor, literally designed (using computer codes) to accumulate capital.

The variety of work practices that superbloggers employ in the production of style stories highlights the porousness of traditional labor categories as well as some of the overlap between Asian fashion workers in digital media and those in apparel manufacturing sectors in terms of work arrangements. Both groups work on a temporary and contract basis, for which compensation is conditioned to a great extent on consumer demand (measured in terms of outbound clicks and/or retail sales). And just as the work of making clothes is done by wage-insecure outsourced labor, so too is the work of marketing and promoting clothes.

The more salient point for this discussion about the permeability of labor categories with respect to digital media and manufacturing fashion work is that digital media in general and digital interactivity in particular have not so much transformed the dominant fashion industry as they have been incorporated into, and put to work for, it. That is, if personal style bloggers and their readers are empowered by new media technologies to express their own fashion opinions and style stories and to communicate more directly with retailers and other consumers, this empowerment is conditioned on the willingness to work at all hours of the day for little to no money. The taste work practices that superbloggers apply to creating style stories, like generating and coding varieties of hypermedia, and the work that readers do just by going onto the site or clicking hypermedia are all potentially value-adding activities of which fashion companies are the ultimate beneficiaries.

Having discussed the literary and computer code work that bloggers do to construct style stories in ways that represent their taste, I want to turn now to a discussion of a different kind of code work that Asian superbloggers engage in. As racial minorities in a white-dominated cultural and economic field and in the upper echelon of the personal style blogosphere, Asian superbloggers' taste work involves practices of code switching not necessarily between languages but between expressions of their identity. Code switching is a common linguistic practice of identity work that minoritized people engage in online and offline to preemptively manage the negative and stereotypical perceptions others may have about them and to convey group belonging. (I discuss fashion blogger poses as nonverbal job performances of impression management in chapter 4.)

In the context of the personal style blogosphere, Asian superbloggers code-switch racial difference with sartorial distinction. Categories of race, gender, class, and sexuality are recoded and depoliticized into individual style. A blog post Lau wrote on January 31, 2011, called "Chinoiserie Query" illustrates what I mean. Discussing the reappearance of Chinoiserie on fashion runways that year, Lau acknowledges that while these collections "might not sit all that well with actual Chinese women," she was "dazzled." Still, she concedes that she would not be wearing any of these clothes since "I don't really wish to wear my ethnicity on my sleeve." For Lau, both her taste and distaste for Chinoiserie are individuating devices. Unlike "actual Chinese women," she appreciates the aesthetic value of these Western adaptations of Asian design ("so much of Louis Vuitton was decorative in all the ways that tickled my fancy").[18] But by preferring not to wear her ethnicity on her sleeve, she also sets herself apart from Chinese women who do (maybe the same or a different group of actual Chinese women). In any case, Lau constructs or recodes her Chineseness as individual and individuating taste. Lau's Chineseness, her personal style of being Chinese, distinguishes her individuality from the collectivity of "actual Chinese women."

Such practices of code switching often involve balancing on a razor's edge between legitimate and illegitimate difference. In their style stories, Asian superbloggers must strategically recast their racial difference as an element of style and social distinction—something that helps them stand out in an increasingly crowded and highly competitive marketplace where, as has been so often stated, attention is currency. At the same time, their stylization of difference helps them stand out without making them stand out too much. To draw mainstream audiences, maintain high volumes of readers and traffic, and acquire lucrative contracts with top fashion and marketing companies, Asian superbloggers' style must be distinct but not different, exotic but not too exotic. As the enduring, if hackneyed, examples of the lists of the best dressed and worst dressed make crystal clear, there are good and bad ways of sartorially standing out.

There is an irony in Lau's statement about preferring not to wear her ethnicity on her sleeve. In disassociating her racial identity from the broader category of group identification and recoding it as a feature of her personal style, she and other Asian superbloggers use practices of taste work to move the signification of race from the physical and social body to the sites of aesthetic sartorial choice. If the visible evidence of Chineseness or Asianness is found in the clothes one chooses to wear or not wear, then Lau and other Asian superbloggers are in fact wearing their now individuated ethnicities and race. How they wear and style (materially, textually, visually, and so on) their Asianness as a legitimate difference is the work that Asian superbloggers' taste practices do.

To give a sense of the wide range of creative ways that Asian superbloggers approach and perform the task of written taste work, I turn to two very different modes of textual taste work in the style stories of Song and

Yambao. A comparative discussion of their code switching also has important implications for our understanding of the ways in which social difference is generated and circulated in digital popular culture as value-adding style.

## When Peacocks Twirl and Camp

In this book, I have mentioned Suzy Menkes's anti-blogger article "The Circus of Fashion" a number of times. The article stirred up a considerable amount of controversy and debate that has continued up to the time of this writing. The blogger-editor feud began mildly enough in the mid-2000s, but by 2011 it had become an anxiety-laden preoccupation with whether bloggers (above all Asian superbloggers, with their cheap work ethic and cheap fashion sense) had the right to share space with credentialed fashion journalists. Treading on this familiar battleground, Menkes's 2013 article stirred up old grudges and unresolved feelings. Not surprisingly, it easily gained traction in the fashion and social media. Controversies about whether or not bloggers belong at major fashion events have been largely one-sided debates. Op-eds and news stories written by fashion and lifestyle journalists and published in a wide range of Western media outlets dominated the public discourse.[19] Bloggers have publicly downplayed these controversies as media inventions, but this does not mean that they have not reacted to the controversies.[20] Song's and Yambao's style stories provide some understanding of the complex ways in which Asian superbloggers have responded to and, sometimes, rearticulated perceptions of themselves and their style.

One of the more common tactics Asian superbloggers employ to express and enact their legitimate difference is to adopt the linguistic and broader ideological norms of fashion discourse (for example, Song's "pop of color"). Devon Carbado and Mitu Gulati, legal scholars who have published widely on the ways in which people of color "work their identity" to manage subtle and overt workplace discrimination, describe this tactic as a mode of "partial passing." Partial passing, unlike complete passing, does not involve fully claiming a white identity but rather "selectively 'escaping' the attributes of their Outsider identity." People might do this by distancing themselves from other members of their group or "by affirmatively identifying or associating with institutions, cultural practices, and social activities that are stereotypically perceived to be white. They might, in other words, express an affinity for 'stuff white people like.' "[21]

Song's habits of using popular fashion idioms like "pop of color"[22] and "boyfriend jeans/sweatshirt"[23]; of enumerating wardrobe "essentials"[24] and of providing tips for a seemingly endless list of "appropriate" clothes (from "business appropriate"[25] and "dinner appropriate"[26] to "fall appropriate"[27] and "appropriate for music festivals"[28])—along with her constant refrain about keeping her style "simple,"[29] "polished,"[30] and "flattering"[31]— demonstrate her knowledge of and facility with popular fashion language as well as her conformity to normative presentations of identity. In short, Song's style stories are constructed through partial passing. They suggest that her racially marked difference makes no real difference at all. She is just a California girl whose style is also just like California: easy, simple, and—as she regularly describes it—"casual chic" (as in the case of the palm prints). This is not to say that she conceals her Asianness. Although Song rarely discusses her social identity, the massive numbers of outfit photos posted to her blog (recall that a full 97 percent of her blog posts are outfit posts) and to her Instagram account (seen by 1.9 million followers) are visual affirmations of her Asianness. More to the point, they are representations of her style of Asianness.

If we understand style stories as Barthian systems of signification and meaning making, then Song's stories function as descriptions both of her personal style and of a broader idea about her style of embodiment. Taking care to be "appropriate," "polished," and "simple" while still maintaining some element of distinctiveness that is interesting but contained in ways that ensure it is inoffensive (for example, "casual chic" and "pop of color") and so harmless in Bourdieu's sense of not destroying the fashion institution writ large involves more than a style of dress. The qualities of appropriateness, inoffensiveness, and harmlessness have long characterized a gendered style of Asian embodiment. To invoke Gabriella Lukács again, we can say that Song's style is "cute." Her style stories exemplify the "semantic flexibility" and accommodative nature (toward both the fashion norms and expectations of mainstream fashion blog readers) that Lukács argues are the definitive qualities of Asian cuteness.[32] Historically, the attribution of these aesthetic qualities to Asian women (represented as small, soft, compliant, and vulnerable) has engendered a popular racial perception that they are naturally predisposed to service labor. What is distinct about Asian cuteness as an aesthetic of gendered racial service in Lukács's discussion of Net Idols (see chapter 1) and in the present discussion of Asian superbloggers is that it is attached not to working-class identities but to elite social and economic statuses. This is not a radical distinction, though. The elite status of Asian cuteness in these contexts says more about the value of service work in informational economies than about a real rise in the value of Asianness.

The fact that Asian cuteness now stretches to encompass elite as well as subordinated labors underlines the essential character of this racial semantic system. Historically, the term *Asian* has accommodated multiple and contradictory subject positions, including Asians who are honorary whites (for example, model minorities) to whites who are politically and socially Asian (such as the Asian Republican Coalition, whose members are almost exclusively affluent white men). *Asian* has also embodied a wide range of threats to the economy, to the racial and linguistic composition of universities and workplaces (for example, the "Little Asias" discussed in the introduction), to national security (such as spies), and to white Americans' public health (for example, severe acute respiratory syndrome, better known as SARS). Asian accommodation makes the racial category of Asianness particularly flexible and so uniquely suited to postracial definition and rearticulation.

*Appropriate, polished,* and *simple*—like *Asian*—are terms whose specific meanings can be interpreted in a wide range of ways. We see this in Song's style stories. Rather than using a stable set of sartorial signs, Song articulates her style as a jumble of opposing qualities: casual and chic, girly but also edgy, rock and roll grungy but also chic, monochromatic but with "a pop of color." Just as Lukács's Net Idols do, Song's style of dress and of embodiment accommodates: it offers something for everyone while offending no one. Not surprisingly, Song is seldom targeted in attacks on bloggers. Her taste for moderate styles of dress and embodiment leaves no racial aftertaste. Also not surprising is her mainstream popularity among readers and corporate entities, which seek her out, willing to pay a lot of money to have her as a brand partner. Her style of embodiment—like her vaunted style of dress—is ethnic but neutral, and according to branding and marketing standards, this is a virtue of mainstream multicultural appeal.[33]

Song's construction of her personal style and style of embodiment is consistent with the logics of racial neoliberalism theorized by Imani Perry, David Theo Goldberg, Herman Gray, and others.[34] Under racial neoliberalism, race and racialized markers of difference are tied to market logics of consumer sovereignty, personal branding, and freedom of expression through a free market of endless consumer choices. As Gray explains, "within racial neoliberalism, we celebrate identity as post-racial multicultural difference with a small 'd.'" Race is not historically or structurally distinct, but is just one of many "proliferating diversities" that are reduced to fashion and lifestyle choices.[35] Gray characterizes neoliberal projects of racial identification, recognition, and visibility as projects of self-enhancement undertaken by the "self-crafting entrepreneurial subject whose racial difference is the source of brand value celebrated and marketed as diversity."[36]

Song's written taste articulates a racial and class-based identity that is sartorially coded as normative—ever appropriate and polished. Her descriptions of "boyfriend jeans" and "flattering" clothes that show off her waist, legs, and bottom imply a heteronormative gender identity in which women have boyfriends and are attentive to the physical qualities that represent and conform to standards of ideal white femininity. Song's frequently stated preference for dresses that inspire her to twirl are another example of sartorial expressions of heteronormative middle-class feminine identity. Twirling in a full-skirted dress is girlish and suggestive but not overtly sexy, since it only plays with the possibility of exposure.[37]

Song's construction of her racial and ethnic identities as an Asian American and Korean American are depoliticized and privatized as universal forms of kinship. Through her sister, father, and grandmother (whom she writes about and, in the case of her grandmother, visits in Korea), she is Korean and Asian. But by these standards then, as Rey Chow writes, "everyone is ethnic." The liberal attitude that everyone is something, simply by dint of being born into a particular racial or ethnic group, "implies there should be no more violence and no more discrimination; there should only be humanistic tolerance."[38] Song's style of dress and embodiment express a neoliberal multicultural Asianness in which Asian identity is celebrated, incorporated, and neutralized as one possible style choice among many. Chow describes this in terms of the "protestant ethnic" self that is defined not by subjecthood but consumer objecthood.[39] Song's neoliberal multicultural Asianness is perhaps best illustrated in her numerous style stories and outfit posts dedicated to kimonos.

Song mentions a number times in her blog that the kimono is one of her favorite garments. Unlike Lau, who eschews Asian and particularly Chinese fashion design features because she worries about "looking like a waitress in a dodgy restaurant or a roleplay actor in a theme park,"[40] Song seems to have no such concern about being stereotyped. In fact, Song's kimonos are a way to manage and shape perceptions that others might have about her Asianness. The kimono, a Japanese garment, is recoded in her style stories as a fashion sign of consummate flexibility. Tellingly, none of the garments she wears in her outfit posts are actual kimonos; rather, they are kimono-style garments designed and sold by UK-based designers and fashion companies. Her kimonos are thus Japanese without being too Japanese, exotic but not too exotic. In their moderate neutrality, they express her taste for styles of dress and embodiment that are different but still within the bounds of Western fashion legitimacy.

In and through Song's style stories, kimono-style garments are described to be as perfectly suited for a yacht ride in Mexico as they are for a trip to Morocco.[41] For her visit to the Huntington Botanical Gardens in Southern California, she also wears a "kimono." As she puts it, "what better place to wear this beautiful floral print kimono to than the botanical gardens?"[42] In another outfit post, the kimono is just the right garment for "running (and driving) back and forth working on my day job" (as an interior designer), and in yet another post, it is the ideal garment for sort of helping her boyfriend build a deck in their backyard ("I tried to help him shovel but instead, I had him take a photo of me!").[43] Though all the kimono-style garments featured in these outfit posts are different pieces, they are unified by their ability to fit into and be aesthetically pleasing in a variety of contexts. In Song's stories, the kimono-style garment is the sartorial sign par excellence of racially gendered accommodation. Not only are these (somewhat) Japanese women's garments universally and equally appropriate in a wide range of contexts, but they are also presumably an appropriate fashion choice for the wide range of consumers that her mainstream audience of readers represents. In providing affiliate links and supplementary source information about the kimonos she is wearing and those she is not, Song—who is not Japanese or Japanese American but is an influential Asian American superblogger with strong public and industry support—gives her implicit approval to readers and anyone else who wants to wear kimono-style garments. As with her approach to kimonos, Song approaches her self-representation from the standpoint of neoliberal multiculturalism. Her style stories empty the material signs of Asianness (both the kimono and her body) of their social, cultural, and political specificities. Her gendered racial identity, like the kimono, is just another aesthetic feature that enhances her personal brand of universal style.

In stark contrast to Song's taste for the polished and appropriate, Yambao is "obsessed" with "everything colourful and embellished."[44] In a style story published on May 1, 2014, he asserts: "My roots are firmly planted in the land of all things shiny and excessive. I love a good bling!"[45] Yambao is referring to his style of dress, but he might just as well be talking about his style of communication and embodiment. Reading through his style stories, especially the earlier ones, readers quickly get a sense of his bombastic (but not loud, as I will explain in chapter 4) sartorial style, his affected vulgarity, his obnoxious—sometimes caustic—humor, and his seemingly reflexive but clearly self-conscious tendency to exaggerate.

While personal style bloggers generally represent themselves as "real people" (as opposed to airbrushed models), Yambao revels in artifice and shallowness. In fact, one of his blog posts is titled "Everything about Me Is Fake and I'm Perfect." He is deliberately superficial, ostentatious, and self-contradictory. In another post, in which he pleads to his readers to send him an Anya Hindmarch tote bag that is not for sale in the Philippines "because I live in the cesspit of Asia. My country doesn't exist according to the people at Anya Hindmarch," he ends with a self-aware statement about his materialism: "There really is no excuse for you people not to get me one. Do it for the poor. Do it for the whales. Do it for the seals. Do it for the third world kids. Do it for me because I'm preeeeettttty!! Hahaha. Ok. Over and out. This obsession is silly. Silly, I tell you!"[46]

While Yambao's obsession may be silly—even to him—it would be a mistake to disregard his style stories as just silly. In fact, they are quintessential examples of what Susan Gubar terms "racial camp." Building on Andrew Ross's understanding of camp as "contain[ing] an explicit commentary on feats of *survival* in a world dominated by the taste, interests, and definitions of others," Gubar argues that "racial camp hints that feats of survival occur through inauthentic mimicry that affronts the blatantly suspect arbiters of good taste."[47] In Yambao's style stories, the pretentiousness, classism, and affective responses associated with luxury fashion are amplified to the point of humor and sometimes way beyond. Yambao does not just like something, he's obsessed with it, and the latest "must-have" fashion accessory becomes something he really must have at any cost—including prostituting himself.

However, in exaggerating the language and behavior of the fashion elite, Yambao is not simply mocking them. He is coping with his exclusion from the fashion elite and surviving through camp until he is included. As Christopher Isherwood has observed, "you can't camp about something you don't take seriously. You're not making fun of it; you're making fun out of it. You're expressing what's basically serious to you in terms of fun and artifice and elegance."[48] Yambao's camp-inflected strategies facilitate the survival of his self-image as a queer global superstar in "the cesspit of Asia" as well as the survival of his love for fashion in spite of the Western fashion industry's racist imaginary (in which the Philippines and, by extension, Filipinos do not exist).

Yambao's style stories are camping taste on two fronts. One is the homophobic Catholic tastes of mainstream Filipino society. Because of his nonnormative gender presentations of identity through both men's and women's clothes and accessories and feminine consumer practices, he is often subject to verbal and nonverbal gay bashing. He experiences this so frequently in Manila that he has become acutely aware of even subtle forms of discrimination. As he puts it, his "entire body is covered with invisible 'You're-Staring-At-Me-And-Giving-Me-Crappy-Looks' sensors." So too is his women's luxury handbag: "Heck, even my [Hermès] Birkin bag, which I used today, is covered with such detectors." In the same post, he gets back at those who go "all hoity toitty on me" by writing (in neon pink bold text), "Punk kid my ass when my Birkin bag is DEFINITELY more than their third world annual income."[49] This remark exemplifies Yambao's camp-inflected practices of taste work. It is an obnoxiously self-aggrandizing display of Western materialism and classism even as it is a clearly pained expression of alienation.

Yambao's attempts to distance himself from other citizens of the Philippines (which he regularly refers to in his excessively pretentious fake French as "the land of the brown, l'exotique and the natives"[50]) may be one reason he is more popular in North America and Europe than in the Philippines. In 2006, less than 4 percent of his readers were from the Philippines: "The number of people who read my site outside the shithole I call home easily outnumbers my fellow brown ricers." What does this mean? According to Yambao, "Well, geography is no boundary when it comes to Bryanboy's faggotry and at this point, the world is my fucking oyster."[51] In 2009, the composition of his readers had not changed. In one blog post, Yambao calls readers from Germany, Italy, and Canada his "target audience" since "not even [popular retailers] Shoemart (or Rustan's) in the Philippines probably doesn't even know I exist!!!"[52]

Yambao's tendency to assert his status with Western expressions and forms of material culture does not mean that the Western fashion elite is spared from the blogger's critical camp aesthetic strategies. In his use of obscene language and his discussions of obscene behaviors that almost always have to do with Western fashion commodities, his style stories are affronts to the social etiquette and cultural norms of luxury fashion even as they are testaments to his desire to belong to this world. Yambao once blogged "screw Anna Wintour"—a blasphemous if not professionally suicidal statement against the doyenne of the fashion world.[53] In an open letter to Riccardo Tisci, creative director of the French luxury fashion house Givenchy, Yambao embraces the title of the "fashion whore" by offering the Italian designer sexual favors in exchange for free clothes.[54] He also describes his "obsession" with new fashion garments and his excitement about the opening of a new luxury fashion retail store in terms of highly graphic, painstakingly detailed bodily functions—all those his body is capable of and some it is not (such as menstruation).

Perhaps even more offensive to the Western fashion establishment than his vulgar language is the vulgar truths Yambao tells about it. As he points out in his style stories, he is a citizen of a country that "doesn't exist" for Western fashion companies. He also recognizes that the menswear designers he covets do not have him in mind as their ideal consumer. On June 16, 2014, he wrote on his blog: "I'm sure you are aware that I'm on the opposite end of the Raf Simons target demographic spectrum. I'm not a tall and gangly, post-pubescent Aryan situation."[55] This is not the first time Yambao has noted the racial homogeneity of men's fashion media imagery. While the racial problem on women's fashion runways and in magazines has constantly been a topic in the fashion media in recent years, little has been said about men's fashion runways. Yambao's observation on his blog that the world of menswear as embodied by male models "is actually more aryan nation compared to women's wear" is astute.[56]

I do not want to idealize Yambao, though. His flagrant classism, racism, sizism, and misogyny have attracted a lot of criticism that he undoubtedly deserves.[57] One of his critics has gone so far as to hack his website. The permalinks, or permanent URLs, for a significant number of his blog posts are now nonoperational. If you attempt to read these posts (the older ones seem most affected), you are automatically redirected to a website with the address ihatebryanboy.com. If that website ever had original content, it no longer does. As of this writing, the site only shows information about its hosting provider, a company called Bluehost, which is based in Provo, Utah. While Yambao's readers have complained about the redirecting, the blogger hasn't responded to them publicly or, it seems, been able to resolve the problem.

The bulk of the criticism against Yambao takes the form of a tabloid-style exposé whose intent was to uncover some astonishing or dirty truth about the blogger who in the inaugural days of his blog anointed himself "Planet Earth's Favourite Third World Fag."[58] Like the attacks on bloggers discussed in the previous chapter, the personal attacks against Yambao also emphasize his cheapness or fakeness. But unlike the previously attacks, these are concerned with Yambao's cheap moral character as a person, not just as a fashion blogger.

In September 2012, a Philippines-based arts and culture magazine called *Rogue* published a lengthy investigative story titled "Will the Real BryanBoy Please Stand Up?" The article paints Yambao as a petty, insecure, and immature person who kicked his sick friend out of their hotel room in freezing weather with no money so that he could have sex with three French men he just picked up, and who spent his day planning an outfit for a blogger awards ceremony while his mother was in the hospital undergoing major surgery. But the real focus of the article, as the title suggests, is Yambao's deceitfulness. The article accuses the blogger of a long list of lies, crimes, and moral ambiguities. The article says that he has "an album full of credit cards—with different variations of his name"; that the exclusive private school he supposedly attended has no record of him at either of its campuses; that the home he lived in with his parents was actually in a lower-income town outside of Manila, rather than the tony Manila neighborhood he claims to be from, and that although the house was "tiny" and "makeshift," his room was oddly crowded with Fendi, Gucci, Prada, and Louis Vuitton clothes, shoes, and luggage; and that the man he introduces as his driver is actually his long-suffering father.[59] Rumors like these have followed Yambao since the early days of his blog, but to focus on discovering what is true and false about the blogger who once admitted, "I can totally picture myself as a nasty, catty, bitchy, self-centered, delusional, egotistical, so-full-of-me-me-me-and-no-one-but-me **Mean Girls (Regina George)** queen bee-type of person" is to miss the strategic aspect of his taste work.[60]

As I've been suggesting, style stories are strategies by which Asian superbloggers work their identities to negotiate their fraught position as a legitimate difference. Song's style stories legitimize and make legible her difference through written and sartorial constructions of a familiar style of gendered Asian embodiment. Like the kimono-style garments she favors, her racial identity is an aesthetic feature of her personal style that is fashioned to adjust to and be appropriate in any context. No longer understood as a historical category of social difference, racial identity is expressed and enacted in her style stories as a style of embodiment that is distinctive (and thus value adding) but within the bounds of Western legibility and legitimacy.

Yambao's written taste work also expresses race as an individual characteristic rather than a social category, but unlike Song, Yambao imagines his racial identity to be transcendent rather than contained. His use of prestige brands and his brand name–dropping—expressed in his excessively pretentious and theatrical mode of camp—construct an identity plastered with the markers of Western style and status. These designer brands are intended to make legible the distinctiveness of his Filipino or Third World difference. In the terms of Carbado and Gulati's identity work strategies, Yambao employs a tactic of partial passing by racial distancing, as if he is saying: "I may be from the Third World but I'm not like them; as my fashion tastes illustrate, I'm like you."

We see this taste practice of racial distancing in a recent style story in which Yambao recalls browsing in a Chanel store. He tells his readers about a pair of "major" white Chanel sneakers that he loved but ultimately did not buy: "I realized I can't have a multi-logo-a-gogo situation, with what, a Rolex watch, Louis Vuitton trolley and Goyard tote—the lewk [look] screamed Asian at Duty Free."[61] For all his trenchant criticism of the Western fashion industry's racial hierarchies, Yambao has not only internalized but is also reproducing a prevailing racial stereotype about Asian tastes as cheap, tacky, and unsophisticated (less evolved than Western and, tacitly, white tastes). By fashioning himself in and through Western fashion descriptions and fashion choices (including the choices not to buy), his style stories are intended to demonstrate the legitimate difference of his racial body. The message of this style story is that he is not like those other Asians "at duty free" who are cheap foreigners touring the world of luxury fashion; he belongs in this world. By not succumbing to "a multi-logo-a-gogo situation," he unmarks his body of particularly racialized codes of Asian taste (though he is still wholly ensconced in nonlogo forms of sartorial excess like the Rolex watch and the Louis Vuitton trolley).

Through his style stories and his conscious play with the aesthetic modes of camp sensibility (artifice, exaggeration, pretentiousness, and so on), Yambao brings forth "a vision of the world in terms of style" as well as a vision of his rightful place in it.[62] He uses his style stories and outfit posts to fashion a public image of himself as the queer global superstar that he has long privately believed himself to be. Less than two years after Yambao published his first outfit post (before there was even a word for that kind of post), what had been dismissed by others and sometimes by the blogger himself as fantasies and self-delusions had become real.[63] With Fendi's appropriation of Yambao's signature pose and Jacobs's many public displays of affection for him, it is clear that the self-titled "Le Superstar Fabuleux" is now widely acknowledged, if not universally accepted, in the Western fashion industry.

# Chapter 3.

## "So Many and All the Same" (but Not Quite): Outfit Photos and the Codes of Asian Eliteness

In January 2011, Franca Sozzani, the outspoken editor in chief of *Vogue Italia*, slammed personal style bloggers for their practice of producing and publishing photos of themselves wearing clothes in public: "They . . . only talk about themselves, take their own pictures wearing absurd outfits. What's the point? I don't even know who they are except a few names because they are so many and all the same, they are so worried about what to wear to get noticed that my eyes only see a crowd in the end."[1] Sozzani does not mention who the exceptions are, but we can assume that at least two of the names she knows are the bloggers who go by the monikers Susie Bubble (Susanna Lau) and BryanBoy (Bryan Grey Yambao). Lau has been prominently featured in Sozzani's magazine a number of times, most notably in its October 2009 roundup of best blogs. And in September 2010, Sozzani invited Yambao, whom the magazine described as "one of the world's most famous fashion bloggers," to shadow her for a day.[2] But whomever Sozzani was thinking about when she wrote the remarks above, her characterization of bloggers as "so many and all the same" is only partially accurate. By her own account, there are exceptional differences. So while there may be so many, they are not quite all the same.

This chapter takes Sozzani's description of bloggers and their outfit photos as a valuable provocation to analyze both the work that outfit photos do to construct sameness, difference, and distinction and the cultural economy in which such meanings are produced and valued. Specifically, I am concerned with what outfit photos' aesthetic forms and technocultural structures might tell us about how racialized eliteness is constructed in the personal style blogosphere. If personal style bloggers and their outfit photos are generally all the same, as Sozzani and others contend, what makes some bloggers and outfit photos more elite than others? That is, what accounts for Asian superbloggers' standout status in a visual field of outfit photos whose forms and practices are nearly unvarying? How do outfit photos facilitate Asian superbloggers' pursuit of legitimate difference—of embodying a status of distinction that stands out but does not stick out in the crowded blogosphere? And what does this tell us about the kind of Asianness that sells in the top tiers of fashion media (as opposed to other industries) when it is attached to eliteness?

One of the first things to say about personal style bloggers' outfit photos is that Sozzani's estimation of them is mostly right. As a whole, they have a highly consistent formal framework and they all perform the same function. Their purported purpose is to directly and transparently reflect the genuine day-to-day style of the blogger. As Yambao has said, "blogs should reflect what goes on in your life as opposed to you creating something specifically for the blog." He also insists that, with regard to his outfit photos, "everything is really organic, and I don't plan shoots."[3] The idea that blogs and their defining features, outfit photos, are nonmediated media that transmit direct messages about personal style is echoed throughout the personal style blogosphere. Erika Marie de Palol, who *Teen Vogue* once spotlighted as its "Blogger of the Moment," writes on the "About Me" page of her blog Fashion Chalet: "Blogging is an outlet for me to be able to express in more depth why I love Fashion so much. Clothing isn't something you just wear, it's a lifestyle and expression of who you are."[4]

Despite bloggers' claims of authentic and immediate representations, it is generally known that outfit photos are not the spontaneously created and published snapshots of personal style they are made to seem. Increasingly, they are highly crafted productions of the blogger's taste and image that use a fairly stable set of formal and aesthetic strategies. For example, the presentation of outfit photos in personal style blogs and other social media spaces almost always begins with at least one head-to-toe shot, with the blogger centered in the photograph.

In the early days of the personal style blog, the head-to-toe shot was captured with the aid of a full-length mirror. So-called mirror shots and the outfit photo genre itself are widely credited to Lau.[5] While outfit photos have been part of the personal style blogosphere since its beginnings, appearing sporadically in early blogs like the African American blogger Kathryn Finney's The Budget Fashionista (founded in 2003) and Yambao's Bryan-Boy (founded in 2004), Lau's practice of regularly documenting her outfits on her blog—with a camera positioned in front of her face and pointed at a full-length mirror—established and popularized outfit photography as a cultural norm and everyday practice in the blogosphere.

In March 2006, when Lau began creating her outfit photos, they had an amateur quality to them that was highly appealing as a representation of authentic style her audience could relate to.[6] They provided an immediate and stark contrast to the unrelatably hyperslick fashion photos that are found in magazines and that she ingeniously collaged into the background of her early outfit photos.[7] In a short time, Lau's mirror-shot technique had become a common practice of fashion-minded Internet users. Photos of individuals posing in their favorite outfits with a point-and-shoot camera or camera phone pointed to a mirror permeated personal style blogs and appeared in popular online fashion community forums like the Fashion Spot's now-defunct WAYWT ("What are you wearing today?") and Flickr's Wardrobe Remix (sites in which Lau was or is a favorite source of inspiration).[8] By 2012 the mirror shot could be seen in traditional mainstream publications like the Wall Street Journal. An article that pronounced digital self-portraiture an important new professional skill in the digital age included a prominently placed mirror shot (featuring another Asian superblogger, Tina Craig of Bag Snob). It also included a litany of instructions for achieving the best self-portrait that is so precise it comes across as persnickety: "Cock your hip—on the side where you're holding the camera—and jut the other shoulder forward. Your free arm can dangle against your body—unless you are wearing a sleeveless shirt, in which case the hand should be placed on the hip."[9]

Mirror shots are still popular, but many bloggers have incorporated other means of self-portraiture, such as using a tripod and the camera's self-timer or a remote shutter release device. Other bloggers, including Lau, now work with a photographer friend or family member to create

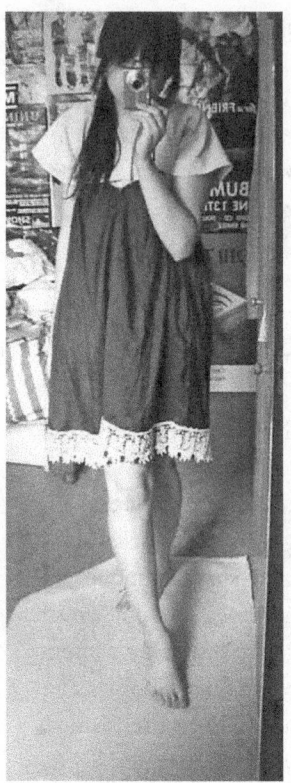

3.1 (*left*) Lau in "DIY Dress Day," Style Bubble, May 29, 2006.
3.2 (*right*) Lau in "Summer Black," Style Bubble, July 23, 2006.

outfit photos. A recent article on Fashionista.com identifies a new "beau-tographer" trend, in which "a man is fully employed by his girlfriend to be her full-time photographer." The article credits Asian superblogger Rumi Neely for starting this trend: "While Neely, the muse, would gallivant around southern California in her outfits—simple, chic and edgy—[her then-boyfriend, Colin] Sokol would be her shadow, snapping her every move with a Canon 5D. They didn't know it then, but they would be the creators of a new business model that others would emulate."[10]

It is never easy to definitively determine when a trend (in fashion or otherwise) begins. It is especially difficult to pinpoint the origins of trends that begin on the Internet, where distinctions between the original and the copy are blurred to the point of being meaningless. The first outfit photo

3.3 Craig in Katherine Rosman, "Super 'Selfies': The Art of the Phone Portrait," *Wall Street Journal*, June 28, 2012.

Lau created on her computer is as much a digital simulation as the same outfit photo when it is read, sent, saved, or shared to other computers. What's more, her first outfit photos cannot be understood as original in the traditional sense of the word since they were composites of print fashion photographs and other digital images and texts (through hyperlinks). Still, it is unlikely that Neely was the first blogger to have her boyfriend photograph her. Lau's longtime boyfriend Steve Salter, a fashion blogger in his own right (Style Salvage), has been taking her outfit photos since at least 2008, when Sokol began photographing Neely. Yambao has described "photographer boyfriends" as a "big mistake," but he also told *Teen Vogue* that "I'll get whoever I'm with to do it," suggesting that a boyfriend may have taken a picture of him in the past.[11] If we cannot know for sure who invented outfit photography, it is clear that Asian superbloggers are valued and recognized for their roles in developing this core practice of personal style blogging.

The development of outfit photography gave rise to more varied and sophisticated camera angles and distances that could not easily be captured using a mirror. For example, close-ups are now a standard outfit photo shot that almost unfailingly always follows the head-to-toe shot or shots. Close-ups do important taste work. They allow bloggers to identify and direct the viewer's attention to their favorite sartorial details like a particular design embellishment, the texture of the material, or a subtle pattern in the fabric. Which details are emphasized accord with individual bloggers' tastes, but some shots like the "shoe shot"—widely attributed to and unreservedly claimed by the Vietnamese Canadian street style blogger Tommy Ton (Jak & Jil)[12]—have become standard close-up shots.

While the Internet is rife with photographs of women (especially Asian women not wearing clothes), the outfit photos that Asian superbloggers developed and popularized have helped make images of women (and men) wearing clothes in public one of the most dynamic and diverse parts of the Internet mediasphere. Today, countless outfit photos circulate online. What's more, the massive appeal that the still relatively new social media technology and practice of outfit photography has for people as a way to construct and share images of themselves, their unique fashion tastes, and their personal styles of daily living and embodiment has helped move outfit photos beyond the personal style blogosphere. Even people who are not personal style bloggers participate in this activity.

Marlene, a Southeast Asian blogger from New Zealand who is based in London, regularly posts outfit photos to her travel and lifestyle blog called Chocolate, Cookies, and Candies, but she states: "Now bear this in mind that 1) I'm not a personal style blogger. . . . 2) I'm not a professional blogger."[13] Another blogger named Lana Lou, a white American woman whose blog is part lifestyle blog and part cancer awareness blog, parodies personal style bloggers but also creates and posts her own outfit photos. One of her personal style blogger caricatures reads: "Hey look, some professional photographer just caught me walking around on my lunch break from my job at Target. I love my Michael Kors shoes, Marc Jacobs bag, and Chanel dress. See how easy it is to be beautiful? Just spend all of your money and you'll be happy."[14] Just below this, she posts outfit photos along with the requisite inventory of garment descriptions, prices, and shopping links. Anecdotally, I've seen (and enjoyed) a considerable number of outfit photos on my Facebook, Instagram, and Twitter feeds—social networks that are predominantly made up of my academic friends and colleagues.

Lou's caricature is suggestive of another constant formal characteristic of personal style blogs. "Some professional photographer just caught me walking around" exemplifies what is perhaps the most striking and consistent feature of outfit photos: their "snapshot aesthetics." Snapshot aesthetics—the term was coined in 1966 by the longtime and now late director of photography at New York's Museum of Modern Art John Szarkowski—borrow the amateur visual style of late nineteenth-century snapshot photography associated with Kodak cameras to lend a sense of authenticity to photos.[15] Because early snapshots were created for and marketed to nonprofessionals (Kodak's slogan was "you press the button, we do the rest"), the photographs often lacked technical expertise. But it was precisely the unskillful nature of these photos that gave them so much emotional meaning and value. Family snapshots, baby snapshots, birthday snapshots, and so on are understood to be artless portrayals of private and intimate moments—authentic glimpses of real life because they are taken spontaneously (in a snap). Distinct from art photography, snapshots don't feel technically or artistically manipulated; they appear to be genuine, serendipitous moments happily caught by the camera.

With regard to bloggers' outfit photos, snapshot aesthetics are produced by formal, visual, and discursive means that work together to give viewers the feeling they are looking at a style moment that is immediate and spontaneous rather than premeditated or choreographed. Formal attributes of outfit photos might include odd angles, bad lighting, and blurring. Commonplace visual features of outfit photos include out-of-place hair, vernacular postures that can look off-kilter, awkward, or in situ (for example, walking across the street, sitting in a café, or texting on a smartphone). The primary discursive component of outfit photos—style stories—also does important aesthetic work to add snapshot value to the image. Much like snapshot photos kept in scrapbooks or shoeboxes that have writing scribbled on the back or as a caption on a scrapbook page, outfit photos are not only visual forms. The text or style stories that accompany these images function to construct and establish the temporal spontaneity or snapshot quality of the outfit photo in much the same way that a picture blurred by motion or with wisps of hair covering a face do.

Lou's parody supports a point I made above that blog audiences are not fooled by outfit photos' snapshot aesthetics. While some bloggers insist (as Yambao has) that their outfit photos are unstaged, many others in the personal style blogosphere openly admit that their photos are the results of choreographed spontaneity. Neely's former "beau-tographer" discusses in detail how he and Neely prepared for their outfit photo shoots.[16] As he explains, a typical shoot begins with bloggers scouting photographic sites, planning outfits, and evaluating ideas about the composition and concept of the outfit photos (sometimes with the help of semiprofessional photographer boyfriends). Arguably, bloggers have always choreographed outfit photos to some degree—choosing what to wear, where to pose, and how.

For detractors, the choreographed spontaneity of superbloggers' outfit photos makes them inauthentic or fake portraits of taste, style, and fashion subjectivity. The judgment that the outfit photo or blogger is fake is implied in Lou's caricature. But the temporal construction of snapshot spontaneity is not a phenomenon that began with outfit photography and personal style bloggers. It has been a part of the development of the snapshot since its invention at the beginning of the twentieth century.

In Nancy West's highly engaging history of Kodak, she mentions that the company largely credited with inventing snapshot photography was also the first to stage snapshot photographs for the purposes of creating the appearance of spontaneity. Between 1900 and 1915, "the majority of [Kodak's] advertising photos were produced by professional photographers working with models, who would often spend an entire day taking pictures in order to get one 'unsophisticated' photograph."[17] Kodak's snapshots that appeared to represent, in the words of a photography writer of the time, "happy spontaneity" were in fact the products of work that sometimes lasted hours or even days.[18]

The nontechnical construction of snapshot photography by Kodak and by women's photography clubs and women's magazines at the time effectively deskilled and feminized early snapshot photography. Rather than an art practice that required technical knowledge and skill, the technological aspects of snapshot photography were downplayed, and snapshot photography was marketed to middle-class white women—especially mothers—

as a respectable hobby.[19] Even women who were highly skillful photographers publicly insisted on their amateur status for fear of masculinizing themselves.[20] The gendered construction of snapshot photography as an amateur practice (so easy that even a woman could do it, as Kodak ads used to imply or state outright) concealed the skill, expertise, and work often involved in creating snapshot photos.[21]

Similarly, the discursive and aesthetic construction of outfit photos (by bloggers and nonbloggers) as amateurish, whether in the sense of a self-indulgent and frivolous hobby (for example, as Sozzani argues) or as nontechnical and not complex (as in Yambao's description of outfit photography as "organic"), renders invisible the actual work and work conditions involved in this core practice of personal style blogging. As I will elaborate in chapter 5, for superbloggers the deskilling of personal style blogging is itself a taste work practice that is designed to construct their identities as creative workers.

Now more than ever, a considerable amount of time and work goes into creating outfit photos. As well as the preproduction activities I noted above, superbloggers and many hobbyist bloggers apply at least basic processes of digital photo enhancing (such as color adjustments, cropping, and reframing) to their photos before posting them online. What is designed to look like a spontaneously made image using an odd camera angle or an in situ pose, for example, is more often than not the result of extended pre- and postproduction time. In other words, while Lou is right that outfit photos may be created on breaks from a paid job, they are not breaks from work in toto.

## The Work Outfit Photos Do

Some iteration of the snapshot scenario Lou satirizes seems to be performed in every outfit photo: the blogger seems to be saying, "Oh, hey look! I just happen to be walking around looking fabulous here" (and here and here and here . . . ). "Looking fabulous here" is an idea that bloggers rarely state outright but that readers like Lou assume follows from bloggers' decisions to publicly broadcast their daily outfits. The seemingly endless repetition of form and style inherent in snapshot photography is intensified with regard to outfit photos because they are digital images. Unlike the audiences for analog snapshots, digital snapshot audiences are not limited to close friends and family members. The open-source platforms that host most personal style blogs (notably, WordPress, Blogger, and Tumblr, for example) enable and encourage blog audiences to reproduce—to "share," in the language of social media—other people's outfit photos in their own networks, immeasurably extending the outfit photo's audience to casual acquaintances and strangers. Most bloggers add social sharing buttons to their websites and individual blog posts that make it easy for readers to share an outfit post on Facebook, Twitter, and other popular social media sites. Effectively, the technocultural structure supporting outfit photography distributes the work of reproducing outfit photos to countless others besides the blogger.

The production of new outfit photos and the potentially viral repurposing and circulation of existing ones multiply the distribution of snapshot aesthetics. If outfit photos are outlets for sartorial self- and social expressions, then they share a common formal, visual, discursive, and temporal aesthetic grammar that makes them seem like "so many and all the same." For critics like Sozzani, the standardized formal aspects and procedures of outfit photos suggest a cookie-cutter approach to personal style that damages bloggers' claims to sartorial individuality and authenticity. Again, this critique is not entirely wrong. Outfit photos are an inherently redundant medium. They are exemplary works of art in the age of mechanical reproduction, what Walter Benjamin presciently identified as works of art "designed for reproducibility."[22]

The digital composition and storage of outfit photos on open-source blog platforms as well as the mimetic culture of the personal style blogosphere—in which skills, techniques, and material and nonmaterial commodities are mostly openly shared, exchanged, and appropriated—intensify the quality of reproducibility that Benjamin identifies as intrinsic in mechanically reproduced works of art. Yet digital reproductions, like earlier mechanically reproduced art works, are never exactly the same. While digital reproductions and what Jos de Mul usefully terms "digital recombinations"[23] do not suffer any loss in visual quality or visual information as a result of reproduction in the way that facsimiles or photocopies do, each repeated production results in outfit photos that are almost the same but not quite. When outfit photos are shared to different media sites (such as Twitter, Facebook, or another blog), their contexts and so their meanings are changed. An outfit photo posted to one's own blog is an expression of personal style. Reposted to a different site by another user, the photo expresses an idea about shared tastes or a message of sartorial inspiration.

When bloggers produce additional outfit photos or when others are inspired by personal style bloggers to create their own outfit photos, they typically re-create the formal and aesthetic features that give outfit photos their recognizable and, importantly, their relatable appearance (for example, the initial head-to-toe shot and the subsequent close-ups as well as the formal, visual, and discursive snapshot aesthetic features). But each outfit photo is different in some way, whether in terms of the clothes worn, the photographic setting, the individual featured, or the exact posture of the body. Other differences might result from variations in the camera angle (a camera held in front of the face or at chest level and pointed at a mirror versus a camera attached to a tripod), the picture quality (a photo taken from a camera phone—with or without the forward-facing feature—or from a digital single-lens reflex camera), and the size dimensions of the outfit photo (different blog platforms have different image size specifications and limitations).

Like other practices of bloggers' taste work already discussed in this book, outfit photography exemplifies the blurred distinctions between material and digital labors. The digital recombinations of outfit photography begin with the physical interfaces of the body, the clothes, the camera, and the mirror, well before any interactions with, within, or between computers take place. Lau's outfit photos, in particular, are digital recombinations of earlier photographic and theatrical poses (discussed further in chapter 4) and of traditional fashion photographs cut out by hand and scanned into her computer, then re-placed in the context of her blog and her personal style.

The "so many and [mostly] all the same"—or, as I want to rearticulate the phrase, the "almost the same but not quite"—quality of outfit photos sums up critics' main problem with the genre. But this misunderstands the character and value of, and the potential implication for, social agency that acts of repetition with a difference suggest. As we know from Benjamin, the value of classic art lies in its singularity, in its "unique existence at the place where it happens to be."[24] The uniqueness of its existence in time and place is what gives classic art its "aura." In a footnote elaborating on the aura, Benjamin writes: "the aura [is] a 'unique phenomenon of a distance however close it may be.' . . . The essentially distant object is the unapproachable one. Unapproachability is indeed a major quality of the cult image."[25] In contrast, the value of digital art, and specifically outfit photos, lies not in its unapproachability but in its relatability. Outfit photos showing what are referred to as real people in real clothes allow us to see our self-images, tastes, and styles reflected in those of others. Outfit photos are not aspirational but inspirational, as blog audiences often note in their reader comments. Blog audiences are inspired and in fact able to follow bloggers' sartorial examples (for example, pairing unconventional colors and different print patterns, or adopting a new trend that was unappealing on the rack but came alive when worn by their favorite blogger), their consumer examples (such as learning where and when to shop for the best bargains or how to spot a counterfeit garment or accessory), and their authorial examples (such as by starting their own personal style blog).

Even when celebrities and fashion models create and post outfit photos, the repetitive and familiarizing qualities of outfit photos and their intimate communication function (of self-expression and of creating taste communities) help make their outfit photos more relatable. Outfit photos of celebrities and fashion models supposedly off duty suggest that they are just like us. As I discussed in chapter 1, in the age of social commerce and reality advertising, the quality of relatability is both a highly prioritized consumer value and a highly prized nonmaterial commodity that generates value.[26] And as we saw in the construction and popular reception of Sarah Palin's image as a plainspoken down-home hockey mom during the 2008 presidential campaign, a "just like us" relatability also carries a significant amount of cachet in political spheres.

When outfit photos are copied, shared, or turned into memes so that they appear in a wide range of contexts; are reproduced by a vast array of users; and are indexed under a multiplicity of search terms, their value increases rather than decreases. As de Mul explains, "in the age of digital recombination, the value of an object depends on the extent of its openness for manipulation."[27] "Manipulation" in this context includes all the ways a digital object is adapted and changed, as well as handled and used. The ad for the online retailer Moxsie that I discussed in chapter 1 serves as an example of the value attached to and embedded in recombination or manipulation. The ad, which featured a model posed and styled to look like Lau, did not harm the Asian superblogger's status in the blogosphere.

Instead, it was widely interpreted as an homage and an indication of her high standing. The retailer's act of copying Lau's style of dress and embodiment actually enhanced her prestige as an influencer.

While Lau did nothing to encourage the media attention related to the ad's significance or to generate value from the Moxsie ad itself, Yambao is one of the foremost experts at spinning digital gold from hay. As early as 2006, when the luxury fashion behemoth Fendi appropriated his signature BryanBoy pose for its international ad campaign (without notice, compensation, or credit), Yambao demonstrated his deftness for turning his unpaid labors into value-producing activities. As I discuss in greater detail in chapter 4, Yambao seized on Fendi's appropriation of his style and made it into a rich opportunity for self-publicity and the accumulation of precious cultural and social capital.

## Asian Superbloggers ahead of the Fashion Curve

Asian superbloggers' elite status is suggestive of new social relations of time between Asian fashion workers and Western fashion's cultural and labor economies. In contrast to the colonialist representations of culturally and politically backward or historically frozen Asian subjectivities, cultures, and societies that are common in Western fashion media,[28] Asian superbloggers represent themselves and are recognized by their readers as being ahead of the fashion curve. In the examples above, Lau's and Yambao's outfit photos and the tastes these photos make visible serve as the cultural referent of two Western fashion companies' style mimicry. I use the term mimicry—like the "almost but not quite" structure of sameness and difference—to invoke Homi Bhabha's famous model of colonial mimicry. As examples of style mimicry, though, the Moxsie and Fendi ads represent an inside-out inversion of Bhabha's colonial framework.

In "Of Mimicry and Man," Bhabha argues that the colonizer-colonized relationship is discursively constructed by repetition and ambivalence. The reproduction of colonial power operates through the colonized Other's mimicking of colonial representations and discourses. But the repetition or mimicry contains an implicit paradox: "mimicry emerges as the representation of a difference that is itself a process of disavowal" of " 'normalized' knowledges and disciplinary powers."[29] What Bhabha means is that the necessary reproduction of colonial power by colonized Others reveals the constructed or unnatural state of colonial knowledges, specifically colonial ways of knowing and seeing difference. The slippage between Western signs of difference and the constructedness of their significations or meanings, Bhabha explains, produces a double and discursively self-defeating articulation: "The excess or slippage produced by the *ambivalence* of mimicry (almost the same, *but not quite*) does not merely 'rupture' the discourse, but becomes transformed into an uncertainty . . . so that mimicry is at once resemblance and menace."[30] What is menaced or threatened is colonial authority and "its power to be a model" of representation, to be the privileged referent of normativity.[31]

Bhabha's theoretical model of mimicry is premised on an asynchronous relationship—as well as nonequivalent racial and gender relationship—between colonized and colonizer: the colonized are structurally positioned to mimic what the colonizer has already done. Bhabha's framework of power and difference points to a long-standing analytic and discursive tendency in the West to imagine itself as belonging to a different (and faster) historical time and trajectory than the rest. So as well as embodying a racial and gender difference, the colonized are discursively constructed as embodying a temporal difference and distance from the colonizer. Historically, the "almost the same, *but not quite*" difference of colonized others has been coded in temporal terms like "undeveloped" or "developing," "primitive," "backward," and "unsophisticated."

Bhabha's theory of colonial mimicry has been an incredibly valuable framework in shaping the thinking about the cultural politics of power and difference. But the almost-the-same-but-not-quite world of outfit photography and the personal style blogosphere suggests far more complicated processes and relations of differentiation. More than a simple reversal, Asian superbloggers' cultural representations indicate a striking inversion of Bhabha's colonial mimicry. Asian superbloggers are in the position of the style referent being mimicked rather than that of the mimicker. They are representational models of imitable (and relatable) styles of dress, embodiment, and representation. What's more, the repetition of Asian superbloggers' style references produces not a difference that is subversive, but one that is instead constitutive of a new formation of racialized eliteness.

As scholars like Lydia Liu and Anne McClintock have pointed out,[32] Bhabha's model for understanding relations of power and difference fails to account for subject positions that fall outside of the conventional binaries of oppressor/oppressed, dominance/resistance, and margins/center. As these scholars suggest, not all mimicry is subversive, and not all oppressions are the same. Today—especially in the context of social media, in which self-expression, community making, and pleasure are thoroughly enmeshed in corporate logics and goals of capital accumulation—acts of agency and structures of oppression no longer fit neatly, if they ever did, into these categories of power relations.

As I have been trying to make clear throughout this book, the phenomenon of Asian superbloggers represents one of the "messier questions of historical change and social activism" that McClintock argues challenge the limits of Bhabha's binary framework of differentiation.[33] The bloggers' fraught position as a racial and numerical minority in the top tiers of the fashion blogosphere and broader fashion media has made them vulnerable to racial and economic stereotyping and its overt and subtle effects (such as being singled out for special scrutiny and racialized criticism). Yet given the vast reserves of cultural, social, informational, and material resources at their disposal, Asian superbloggers do not fit into any traditional definition of the *oppressed*. They also occupy a fraught position as digital workers whose labors are embodied in myriad ways, and for whom work opportunities and rewards are conditioned to a great extent by the cultural economic value of their Asian bodies in this Asian moment of fashion. Additionally, and more specifically to this discussion, the leading roles Asian superbloggers played and continue to play in building and developing what are now the essential practices of personal style blogging like outfit photography complicate any easy assumptions about the position they occupy in the framework of colonial mimicry or about the relations and meanings of the margins and the center.

In the section that follows, I consider what outfit photos tell us about how Asianness is defined and asserted in the blogosphere, paying particular attention to the temporal dynamics of new constructions of Asian eliteness. Specifically, I examine the ways in which the choreographed spontaneity of outfit photos is a device of taste identity work that marks a new, and highly valuable, temporal relation of Asians to fashion capitalism.

## Styles of Asian Eliteness

In recent years, images of Asian eliteness have gained attention around the world. In 2012, the Korean rapper Park Jaesang—globally known as Psy—created the anthem to Asian eliteness with his (mostly) Korean song and music video, "Gangnam Style." The song refers to a wealthy district of Seoul, South Korea. The people who live there, it has been said, are not just "Silicon Valley self-made millionaires. They're overwhelmingly trust-fund babies and princelings."[34] Psy's YouTube video achieved an unprecedented billion views several months after it debuted, surpassing the record held by Justin Bieber for a most-watched video on YouTube.[35] This is the second YouTube record it broke. About two months earlier, "Gangnam Style" made Internet history when it became the most-"liked" YouTube video ever, beating out the American electronic dance music and rap group LMFAO.[36] As of this writing, the video has been viewed just over 2.1 billion times and has earned the South Korean singer music awards from countries all over the world, including Germany, Brazil, France, the United States, and South Korea. His signature horse-dance move has been imitated by a wide variety of people, from U.S. President Barack Obama and UN Secretary General Ban Ki-moon to winners of the reality TV cooking competition show *Chopped*.[37] The song has been played and/or performed at countless events, including international music awards shows and a baseball game at Los Angeles's Dodger Stadium.[38]

The song satirizes the materialism of the Gangnam "one percent" and the Gangnam style of conspicuous consumption and ostentatious wealth emerging across Korea and other parts of Asia. The music video is a spectacular display of material excess: flashy cars, sexy women, big shiny jewelry, spas, and a stable of horses. But the display of Asian eliteness is so over the top that it is rendered ridiculous. This is the point Psy is making. He has said: "Human society is so hollow, and even while filming I felt pathetic. Each frame by frame was hollow."[39] So even without understanding Korean, the video's visual narrative (with its silly horse dance and its references to delusions of grandeur, in which a beach resort scene turns out to be set in a playground sandbox and a swanky nightclub turns out to be a bus full of elderly tourists) suggests that Gangnam style is not a type of Asian eliteness that should be taken seriously. In fact, the image of Asian eliteness that Psy portrays corresponds with many of the prevailing stereotypes circulating today about newly moneyed, logo-driven, gaudy Asian luxury consumers.

The excesses of Asian eliteness that "Gangnam Style" represents is mirrored in Kevin Kwan's award-winning novel *Crazy Rich Asians*, which is centered on three Chinese Singaporean families who are part of the billionaire class. Like the people satirized in "Gangnam Style," Kwan's characters are all trust-fund babies, princelings, aristocratic socialites, and heirs to the British commonwealth's biggest business fortunes in Singapore, Australia, Canada, and elsewhere. While the book takes place mostly in Singapore, its main characters have homes in California, Vancouver, Hong Kong, London, and Sydney; they are educated in top schools in the United Kingdom, France, and the United States; and they vacation in Switzerland. They hobnob with global superstars as well as Asian, European, and African royalty; shop in Paris for couture dresses that cost $200,000 each (and are often from the *next* season); don "lychee-sized rubies"[40] while traveling on personal jets to party in Shanghai and private island resorts in Indonesia; work in Hong Kong, California, Australia, and elsewhere; and have individually climate-controlled closets for their fur, cashmere, and leather clothing.[41] Never wearing an outfit twice is considered a matter of morals, and standing in line at Louis Vuitton is deemed as degrading as the food lines in Japanese-occupied China. (One character says: "Reminds me of the Japanese occupation, when they forced all the Chinese to wait in line for scraps of rotten food."[42]) It is in moments like these that Kwan's satire of Asia's ostentatiously wealthy is most evident.

As well as having staggering wealth, the characters' social and political connections are vast and their physical beauty is extraordinary. Kwan's descriptions of characters' appearances are as outrageous and excessive as his descriptions of their wealth. A minor character, Jacqueline Ling, is described as "a Chinese Catherine Deneuve, only more beautiful."[43] Also beyond beautiful is "Astrid [Leong, who] wasn't attractive in the typical almond-eyed Hong Kong starlet sort of way." Kwan depicts her as "an inexplicably alluring vision. She was always that girl stopped on the street by modeling scouts, though her mother fended them off brusquely. Astrid was not going to be modeling for anyone, and certainly not for money. Such things were far beneath her."[44] Just as outside-the-box-gorgeous is Nick Young, the only son and scion of the most powerful family in Singapore (and Astrid's cousin): "Even from afar, he stood out in high relief.

Unlike the other fellows with their regulation Indian barbershop haircuts, Nicholas had perfectly tousled black hair, chiseled Cantonese pop-idol features, and impossibly thick eyelashes. He was the cutest, dreamiest guy she'd ever seen."[45]

In both Psy's and Kwan's popular representations, Asian eliteness is constructed by extravagance and excess that renders it tacky and gaudy. From the eye-popping displays of material wealth (including Psy's flashy cars and shiny diamonds and Kwan's "lychee-sized rubies" and a "massive four-tiered marble fountain with a golden swan spouting water from its long upturned beak"[46]) to the outrageous displays of asinine behavior (Psy's horse dance and the incessant and petty gossiping and fighting in Kwan's novel, as when a character says: "Parker, put down those Pierre Hardy flats or I'll poke your eyes out with these Nicholas Kirkwood stilettos!"[47]) Asian eliteness is vulgar and unlikable. And this may be why "Gangnam Style" and *Crazy Rich Asians* are so popular.

Given *Crazy Rich Asians'* almost nonstop torrent of designer name dropping, it is not surprising that U.S. fashion magazines including *Vogue*, *Elle*, *Glamour*, and *Vanity Fair* have reviewed Kwan's book. Their overall assessment is that it makes for a fun, trashy summer read. *Elle* describes it as "a juicy, close anthropological read of Singapore high society" and says that "Kwan's satirical portrayal rings so true."[48] A *Vanity Fair* interview with the author includes a comment by the reporter that the novel is "a precise rendering of Asian upper-crust society," although Kwan insists: "I want to emphasize: this book is fiction." Kwan also clarifies that "people do have exquisite taste there; it's not just these stereotypical Asians wearing head-to-toe brand names just for the sake of it."[49] The crossover appeal of Psy's music video and Kwan's novel indicates the rising interest among Western audiences in Asia's economic boom and its social and cultural effects. But it also suggests a much more ambivalent response.

"Gangnam Style" and *Crazy Rich Asians* confirm prevailing stereotypes about the new Asian elite. As the above-mentioned reviews of Kwan's novel demonstrate, for some Western audiences the representations of Asian eliteness may be over the top, but they are not out of the realms of reality. Such constructions of Asian eliteness sell in Western popular culture because they are entertaining and easy to consume. They do not challenge dominant ways of seeing and knowing racialized difference or racialized eliteness. In fact, they prove Valentine Fillol-Cordier's point (discussed in chapter 1) about the essential cheapness of Asian consumers, whatever their social and economic status: "You can't pretend to have lots of taste if you're simply buying all that shit and spending tons of money."[50]

At the same time, Psy's and Kwan's satirical portraits of Asian eliteness provide Western audiences with opportunities to laugh at the gaudiness of Asian elites. They serve as coping strategies for anxious Western audiences worried that Asia's rising economy will tip the racial and geographical economic balance of the global order (as we have seen, some of the most anxious among these Westerners are economically, professionally, and emotionally invested in the U.S. and European fashion industries). Laughing at and laughing off racial Others as a means of dealing with racial anxiety are as old as the nineteenth-century traditions of Black minstrelsy in the United States and the United Kingdom. But no matter why outrageous and ostentatious constructions of Asian eliteness sell, it is clear by the success of these two items that such expressions of racialized eliteness do in fact sell well in the spheres of popular music and fiction.

The almost-the-same-but-not-quite visual economy of the personal style blogosphere sets the conditions for a different type of racialized eliteness that is relatable. Rather than the over-the-top displays of material wealth and abundance seen in popular constructions of Asian eliteness, Asian superbloggers' eliteness is made up of a set of familiar aesthetic forms and a technological and cultural structure of collaboration and communication. Certainly, the possession of luxury material goods and valuable economic resources plays a role in advantaging some bloggers over others, but owning a lot of fancy stuff is not the sole or even the main criterion for blog eliteness. After all, Asian superbloggers dress in and promote a wide spectrum of luxury, mass-market, and fast-fashion brands (think of Neely's partnership with Forever 21 and Lau's ad campaign with Gap, for example). Contrast this with the socialite and villain in Kwan's novel who "tossed back her long, wavy black locks and sniffed, 'You know I only wear six designers: Chanel, Dior, Valentino, Etro, my dear friend Stella McCartney, and Brunello Cucinelli for country weekends."[51] Asian superbloggers' commitment to mixes of high and low fashion labels is just one of the ways they make their racial bodies relatable as a legitimate difference.

More significant than the sartorial content of outfit photos are their formal aesthetic features. Their formal qualities serve as forms of recognition, as structural means of establishing and communicating sameness to and among audiences and bloggers. What critics dismiss as redundant formal elements are aesthetic structures that facilitate community making by offsetting a multitude of differences in the visual content of the outfit photo and the social status of the blogger. The effects of recurring camera angles, camera distances, and associated snapshot aesthetics provide a standardizing frame of visibility that brings familiarity to strangers, to people whose styles of dress and embodiment are not like ours. The repeating aesthetic structure of outfit photos, seen across elite and nonelite personal style blogs, makes outfit photos recognizable as outfit photos, distinguishing them from a constellation of other media images. It also makes bloggers recognizable as personal style bloggers to each other and their audiences. Outfit photos' recognizable aesthetic forms index bloggers' cultural literacy in the visual and formal grammar of outfit photography, signifying their membership in this aesthetic community.

For Asians whose temporal relationship to Western fashion capitalism has been historically asynchronous and asymmetric, the outfit photo's aesthetic structure operates as a form of recognition in another way. While critics disparage outfit photos' snapshot aesthetics as fake representations of self, style, and taste, the aesthetics' temporal construction of in the moment–ness actually provides a truer portrait of racial subjectivity than most fashion media images.

In fashion media's visual economy, Asians and Asianness are conventionally marked as temporally distant and different from white Western people and culture. In their dress and their tastes, Asians are routinely represented in fashion media as lagging behind the West. We see this in Karl Lagerfeld's 2009 fashion film, *Paris-Shanghai: A Fantasy*, in which Chinese characters (played by white European models like Freja Beha and Baptiste Giabiconi in yellowface makeup) are portrayed wearing Mao-style suits. Their ethnic clothes function as material signs of how far they are behind Western fashion time signified by the Chanel clothing in the film, as well as in the runway show in Shanghai at which this film debuted.[52] The popular discussions of rising Asian economies and the new class of Asian luxury consumers also rest on the temporalization of Asianness and a discourse of developmentalism. Asian luxury consumers are either criticized for having tastes that are in need of "maturing" or are congratulated for their "fast-maturing" tastes.[53] In both cases, the racialization of Asian consumers is premised on assumptions about Asian taste as almost the same but not quite in sync with Western fashion tastes.

The formal conventions of outfit photography's snapshot aesthetics provide a different frame of temporal racial representation that is controlled by individual bloggers and has been strongly shaped by Asian superbloggers. Snapshot aesthetics—in all their redundancy—condition the possibility for a repetition with a difference. They make it possible for Asian bloggers to craft images—not often visible in traditional fashion media—of Asian bodies, subjectivities, and tastes that are synchronous with, if not slightly ahead of, the greater fashion community. Constructions of Asian eliteness in the personal style blogosphere follow a different temporal trajectory than in its contemporary counterparts. Even while Kwan's characters are dressed in the latest fashions—sometimes wearing impossible-to-get next-season items—they are not represented as fashion forward or as leading fashion trends. Represented as socially and sartorially gaudy, they correspond to stereotypes of Asian cheapness. Their style of Asian eliteness, despite or rather because of their obsession with brand names and their compulsive tendency to drop those names, runs counter to the blogosphere's value of relatability. Thus, it has little value in this popular cultural space.

It is worth noting that the do-it-yourself (or do-it-with-others) approach to outfit photography facilitates a new relation between Asians and fashion time that differs significantly from the normative social relations of time that structure the work and living conditions imposed on Asian industrial fashion workers. Analyzing the gendered time politics of globalization, Barbara Adam points out that capitalist discourses combine ideas of economic and social progress with the logics and values of "clock time": "To be 'modern' and 'progressive' means to embrace the industrial approach to time. Therefore, it was not only ruthlessly prescribed as the norm for colonial subjects but also self-imposed by a number of societies who [sic] saw it as a precondition to becoming fully fledged industrial nations."[54] Asian garment workers who are depicted in racial and gendered terms as people socially and culturally asynchronous with the fashion companies and fashion consumers whose clothes they make are brought up to speed by clocks, quota counters, and a regime of highly controlled schedules for working and not working (eating, talking, going to the bathroom, and sleeping). As Adam incisively puts it, to work for a transnational corporation is to be subject to a process of "colonization with time."⁵⁵

To return to my previous point, the construction of Asian eliteness in the personal style blogosphere is based less on the possession and display of luxury material goods and more on the production and exchange of nonmaterial services and value. While many superbloggers' outfit photos demonstrate their possession of a substantial wardrobe of luxury clothing (and better-than-average skills as·photographers and models), what ultimately distinguishes elite from nonelite outfit photos is neither sartorial nor visual. In the personal style blogosphere, status depends on the frequency and extent to which audiences view, "like," share, comment on, and reappropriate bloggers' outfit photos. The greater the interactivity that outfit photos attract and sustain, the greater the status of the blog and blogger.

The outfit photo phenomenon creates a new expression of eliteness based on the production and exchange of information. I explained in chapter 1 how Asian superbloggers are structurally advantaged in multiple ways in fashion's new media economy. Here, I suggest that their elite status is also structurally linked to outfit photography's technological and cultural architecture of collaboration and communication. Elite subjectivities in the blogosphere are the embodiment of myriad related cultural, social, geographic, and informational mobilities enacted in and by outfit photos. Outfit photos that are viewed, shared, and circulated by audiences outside the blogger's local community and beyond the original purpose and context of the blog (for example, when an actual outfit photo or an image inspired by an actual outfit photo is used in a fashion ad) can generate all-important cultural buzz for blogs and increase the social status of bloggers. Outfit photos also mobilize the socioeconomic status of bloggers when their circulation creates a path into modeling and marketing agencies, giving elite bloggers opportunities to generate cultural as well as financial capital. Unlike previous expressions of racialized eliteness that have been constructed in terms of biological or cultural differences (such as the model minority discourse), racialized eliteness in the personal style blogosphere is constituted through technological and cultural processes and practices.

The technologization of subjectivity and social status—and the phenomenon of Asian superbloggers, in particular—would seem to support the popular and persistent belief that the personal style blogosphere and Internet more generally are postracial meritocratic spaces. The idea that the best outfit photos—no matter who the blogger is or where he or she comes from—will enable a blog or blogger to rise to the top of search results, blogrolls, and social media web or RSS (rich site summary) feeds is at the core of the discourse about the fashion blog's democratization of fashion media.

Rather than evidence of the fashion media's postracism, the personal style blog's technological and cultural formation of Asian eliteness exemplifies the shift in the ways that race and racism are represented, produced, and consumed in digital media economies. As the pathbreaking scholarship of Peter Chow-White, Wendy Hui Kyong Chun, Jesse Daniels, Shoshana Magnet, Tara McPherson, Lisa Nakamura, and others has amply demonstrated,[56] race is embedded in and wedded to digital technologies and practices—sometimes in ways that are invisible to human perception, and sometimes in ways that escape our notice. With the advent of digital and virtual technologies, racial logics and its operations have moved— perhaps *expanded* is a better word—from overt to covert registers. They exist at the level of code and computational operations,[57] they emerge not as representational forms but as techniques of representation (Chun's insistence on a shift in critical focus "from the *what* of race to the *how* of race"[58] has never been more important), and they appear as mechanical failures that seem nonsubjective and unintentional. It is against this backdrop of the changing meanings and locations of race that Nakamura and Chow-White (following McPherson) urge "media critics [to] force themselves to do more than read what's visible in new media interfaces, for this work may distract us from the working of race within code itself."[59] My discussion of outfit photography and personal style blogging builds on the insights of this research. As I hope is clear by now, in the personal style blogosphere race, difference, and distinction also operate through codes—both codes that activate and organize computational procedures (for example, algorithms that determine search result rankings) and codes of conduct and taste that govern social norms and behaviors.

Technological constructions of blogger eliteness are not postracial. They are constructed through technical processes that express and extend cultural and social norms of taste, race, gender, and class. In the personal style blogosphere, Asian eliteness is carefully crafted via practices of taste work and stereotype management to make difference relatable, legible, and imitable. Recall that Yambao stops himself from buying the white Chanel sneakers he loves because he fears embodying the gaudy Asian stereotype ("the lewk screamed Asian at Duty Free"[60]). Only a certain style of Asian eliteness is a valuable commodity in the fashion media economy; other styles are considered to be quite cheap. Eliteness that is loud and showy (that screams "Asian at Duty Free") exceeds the bounds of legitimate difference and leaves a racial aftertaste.

Achieving eliteness in the personal style blogosphere is not simply a matter of doing good work or demonstrating the will to work hard. It is fundamentally a practice of taste and identity work. For nonwhite bloggers, this work invariably involves an extra dimension of racial and gendered modes of impression management that contain difference. Karen Shimakawa observes about Asian American theatrical performers that they "never walk onto an empty stage . . . that space is always already densely populated with phantasms of orientalness through and against which an Asian American performer must struggle to be seen."[61] The same struggle to disidentify oneself from stereotypes of gaudy and cheap tastes—in other words, to be seen and recognized as not too Asian—is central to the work of personal style blogging for Asians. A white blogger might have bought those Chanel sneakers—and even if he or she did pass on them, it would not have been because the blogger was worried about having a look that would "scream Asian at Duty Free."

# Chapter 4.
# The Racial and Gendered Job Performances
# of Fashion Blogger Poses

Spend any amount of time looking at the variety of fashion blogs, and a set of recurring poses becomes apparent. While there is no one definitive pose, there is a loosely bound, idiosyncratic set of gestures, postures, and glances that characterize fashion blog subjects. Some of these poses include standing with legs crossed or feet turned inward (pigeon-toed stances); far-away gazes; oblique glances; and clavicle-enhancing shoulder rolls, often with a single hand on the hip (the teapot) or both hands on hips (the sugar bowl).

Fashion blogger poses pervade contemporary fashion media and social commerce spaces. They permeate social media platforms, from Facebook to Instagram and Pinterest. They also appear on e-commerce and online auction websites like eBay and Etsy (an auction site focused on handmade or do-it-yourself arts and crafts)—sites on which amateur fashion models are the norm. In recent years, fashion blogger poses have joined the mainstream. They appear in traditional media sites such as billboards, magazines, and the style sections of major newspapers.

As omnipresent as these poses are, however, few analyses of them exist. If they are discussed at all, such poses are usually dismissed as the silly things girls do. A Google search I did for "fashion blogger poses" returned 31,500 results. The first two were lampoons of fashion blogger poses. Seven of the top ten results included links to sites that gently or harshly poked

4.1–4.4 Representative sample of fashion blogger poses.

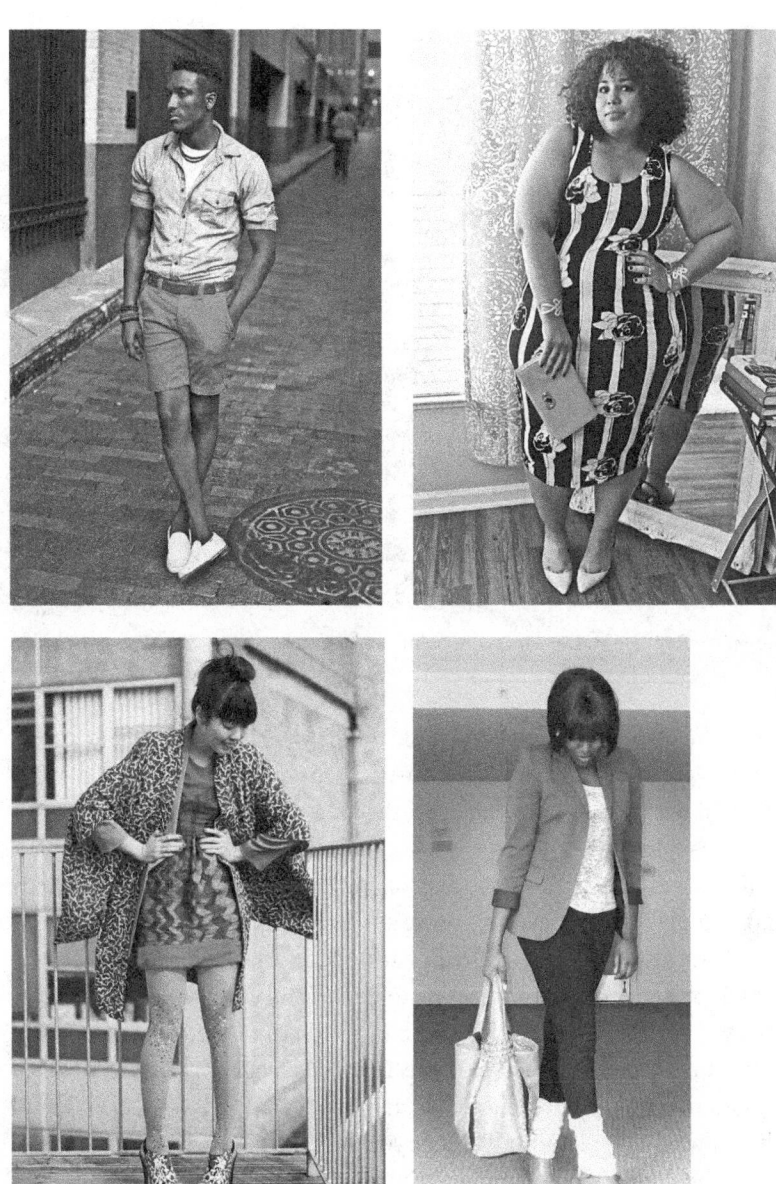

4.5–4.8 Representative sample of fashion blogger poses.

4.9–4.10 Representative sample of fashion blogger poses.

fun of the poses. The remaining three results were links to or about a short essay I wrote for *Hyphen*, an Asian American arts, culture, and politics magazine, about fashion blogger poses (the essay draws on an earlier version of this chapter).

In each of the parody sites, fashion blogger poses are overtly or tacitly and textually and/or visually associated with women and femininity. A white blogger named Stuart Bradley asks, "Can anyone explain to me why girls do this?" His blog post goes on to describe in exaggerated and slightly annoyed language a set of fashion blogger poses. He attaches photos of himself performing each pose. "The Tilt," he suggests, is either the result of feminine frailty or stupidity: "I can never decide what's happening in photos when people pose like this. Maybe their heads have become too heavy for their necks to hold up? Unlikely, given that their heads are full of fluff."[1]

Such judgments say more about the critic than about the poses. Fashion blogger poses are not just performed by "girls"; corporate employees like those behind the professional basketball team Brooklyn Nets and the e-commerce entrepreneurs pictured in a recent *Wall Street Journal* article about executive dressing are also striking the poses that fashion bloggers popularized.[2] The traditional power stance of authority—a wide masculine posture that takes up a lot of space and implies control and dominance—is giving way to more narrow feminine stances that leave room for communication and collaboration. As I will show in this chapter, fashion blogger poses are reflective of the changing values and gendered attitudes related to knowledge, expertise, and authority under late capitalism in the digital age. For personal style bloggers, they are also value-producing activities— job performances that can accrue a significant amount of cultural, social, and financial capital.

In this chapter, I examine fashion blogger poses as job performances, taste-identity work practices that demonstrate and heighten bloggers' leading roles in the blogosphere and larger fashion media. For Asian superbloggers, like many other minoritized workers, their job performances have an added racial and gendered dimension of managing the impressions others have of them in ways that contradict prevailing stereotypes. How fashion blogger poses both establish Asian superbloggers' valuable role in this digital media economy and how the poses help the bloggers negotiate dominant relations of race, labor, and capitalism are the primary questions this chapter answers.

## Identity Work in Blogs

In examining fashion blogger poses as job performances, my discussion builds on as well as provides a new direction for studies of race, gender, and workplace that include distributed work spaces and nonwaged social media practices. Workplace studies show that postures, mannerisms, and other bodily practices function as nonverbal strategies of impression management that can shape perceptions about a worker's personality, competence, and authority. For minoritized people, nonverbal impression management—the work of managing others' racial and gendered assumptions, which workplace studies call *identity work*—is also crucial for negotiating negative racial, gender, and sexual assumptions that coworkers and superiors may hold, assumptions that can adversely affect work opportunities and advancement.

Devon Carbado and Mitu Gulati, whose work I briefly discussed in chapter 2, are two of the foremost legal scholars investigating the subtle dynamics of workplace discrimination. In their individual and joint research, they identify several strategies of nonverbal identity work. These include "signaling hard work" by keeping a jacket in the office or a light on after business hours to suggest late-night work. They also observe workers cultivating a harried, tired look to suggest that their focus is on work rather than appearance. Other nonverbal strategies of identity work are "racial comforting" (for example, laughing off racist or sexist jokes to prove themselves to be team players) and "racial passing" (that is, actively or passively assuming a different racial identity).[3] Additional examples of racial and gendered impression management include making temporary adjustments to one's physical appearance such as wearing one's hair or makeup differently, or taking more dramatic measures such as cosmetic surgery.

The pressure on minority employees to "work" both their own sense of identity and their "attributal identity" (the racially gendered attributes that shape how others define and perceive them) are subtle forms of workplace discrimination.[4] They compel minorities to do extra work to achieve equitable levels of treatment. How well minority workers comply with stated and unstated institutional expectations about professionalism can have a bearing on whether they are hired and equitably promoted, trained, and compensated.

Similar identity work burdens exist in the virtual world. Natasha Martin observes that online communications have changed the nature of professionalism by introducing a playful element to professional interactions (for example, the friendly and informal tenor of instant messages and the silly graphical designs of avatars). Virtual workplaces "tolerate (and even expect) a certain level of casualness and frivolity," which loosens workplace cultures.[5] This loosening could promote openness and tolerance for difference. Yet minority workers face the same, if not greater, racial and gendered pressures in virtual workplaces as they do in physical ones. Martin gives the example of a white and a Black employee each creating an avatar that wears a gold chain medallion. Co-workers and superiors may find the white employee's avatar humorous and ironic, while perceiving the same avatar created by the Black employee to be "too racial." Thus, Martin finds that minority employees are compelled, even in virtual reality, to engage in identity work to influence others' racial and gendered responses. She suggests that the pressure minority workers feel to cover up aspects of their identity or to engage in impression management can "heighten their sense of isolation."[6]

In another study of virtual workplace discrimination, Miriam Cherry finds that race, gender, and age frame work-related virtual interactions. Cherry interviewed a human resources professional who conducts job interviews on Second Life, a virtual world customizable for online users. The human resources professional and the prospective employee interact as avatars. Second Life has the potential to provide an unbiased job interview setting, since hiring decisions are ostensibly based on qualifications rather than real physical appearance, but Cherry's informant reveals that she circumvents Second Life's pseudonymity by asking questions aimed at uncovering "what's behind the avatar"—"if it's a man or a woman, if they're young or old."[7] While these questions may not be necessary in traditional interview settings, as interviewers can read the interviewee's body in front of them and make assumptions, they are always irrelevant and against existing laws banning racial, gender, and age discrimination. Cherry's research shows that virtual workspaces still demand racial passing or racial comforting identity work. Scholars like Carbado and Gulati, Martin, and Cherry are leading the charge to expand the interpretation of racial discrimination in Title VII of the Civil Rights Act of 1964 to go beyond what the act calls "intentional racial animus" and include implicit bias.

The work spaces that social media users forge and inhabit differ from the more formally organized work environments usually studied, such as corporate law firms, academic departments of universities, and financial institutions. Many flexible workers are turning airports, train stations, hotels, and homes into temporary and makeshift work spaces. Any place can be transformed into a work space, and such spaces are often not places at all but the "transit points and temporary abodes" that Marc Augé calls the "non-places" of supermodernity.[8] I contend that these temporary, nontraditional work spaces also include the nonplaces of blog interfaces, web browsers, and other web service platforms.

Unlike traditional, privatized work spaces, the work spaces of personal style bloggers are distinctively public: sidewalks, street corners, open fields, alleys, and boulevards are some of the popular settings in which bloggers do the work of posing and photographing. As well as being work spaces without walls, bloggers' online work spaces are also without clear structures for hiring and advancement. For bloggers, there is no assessment rubric for job qualifications, promotions, or raises. There is a broad set of job performances that characterize personal style blogging (including outfit photography, fashion blogger posing, and responding to readers' comments) but these are not exactly work responsibilities that are linked to promotions and financial incentives. And unlike many other Internet practices from professional blogging to updating one's profile on a business-related social networking service like LinkedIn, much of personal style blogging is not considered work at all. Bloggers as well as detractors have expressed this opinion. Recall that Bryan Grey Yambao (aka BryanBoy) describes blogging as an "organic" practice as opposed to one that is a result of learned skills and knowledge.[9]

Despite the structural differences in work conditions and work space arrangements between personal style blogging and traditional work modes, minority workers in both cases face disparities in terms of expectations, experiences, and behaviors. For minority workers across many different types of occupations, identity work is part and parcel of their job performances and job opportunities even when they are not working (perhaps especially when they are not working, in cases of after-work socializing). And as Carbado and Gulati's examples suggest, such identity work is often embodied. Minority workers signal knowledge, expertise, and professionalism by styling their clothes, hair, makeup, and physical comportment in ways that accord with their work culture's dominant values and norms.

Asian superbloggers perform as their core work practices the kinds of racial and gendered image management that constitutes extra identity work for other workers. In other words, identity work is the bloggers' work. Through the embodied job performances of posing, bloggers exhibit their style knowledge and self-fashioning competencies as well as manage the racially gendered assumptions that the Western fashion public has about them. A 2009 memo prepared for the Council of Fashion Designers of America exemplifies a widespread attitude held by U.S. and European fashion companies and consumers that Asian tastes lag behind Western standards. Although the memo focuses on Chinese consumers, similar attitudes have been expressed about other rising Asian markets. The memo observes that "most Chinese do not yet fully understand or appreciate the lifestyle associated with luxury goods. . . . The China market will require . . . efforts aimed at educating Chinese consumers about a sustainable luxury lifestyle and culture."[10] So while fashion industry insiders and financial journalists champion Asian luxury markets as the next big thing, the rise in power and significance of these new markets has also reinvigorated some old stereotypes about Asians' cheapness ("do not yet fully understand or appreciate the lifestyle associated with luxury goods") and backwardness ("the China market will require . . . educating"). As I discussed in previous chapters, dominant fashion discourses seem unable or unwilling to imagine that Asians might lead fashion's creative and business trends.

Fashion-forward Asian subjectivities are sorely underrepresented in fashion print media. While we have seen a huge demand for Asian commodities (such as Hello Kitty and Pokémon), Asian bodies are seldom represented as being in the vanguard of fashion and style. In fact, the global phenomena of cute culture may be taken to confirm racial and temporal stereotypes of Asian lag. Critics of cute culture regularly refer to and repeat the judgment of Takeo Doi, a Japanese psychologist, that cute culture encourages a form of "willful immaturity or childishness."[11] To indulge in Hello Kitty and other cute commodities is to desire childhood or the childlike qualities and experiences associated with cute culture. Even prominent Asian American designers who have experienced their own wave of media attention and industry recognition in recent years are not exempt from racial and temporal constructions of their identity and their work practices. Media discourses regularly invoke their Asian roots to explain their creative and business decisions.

As I discussed in chapter 1, fashion's global economic center of gravity is shifting toward Asia. U.S. and European fashion designers and companies have instituted new business plans aimed at courting Asian luxury consumers that include launching initial public offerings in Asian stock markets, opening retail stores in Asia's major cities, and creating and debuting fashion collections in Asia (sometimes exclusively made for Asian consumers). Yet when Asian American designers adopt this model, their creative and economic vision is regularly characterized as glances backward to their Asian roots, even as one of the most repeated truisms in fashion discourse is that Asia is the site of fashion's future.

Asian American fashion designers are not naïve about the racial and temporal context in which their bodies and work are perceived. Recent moves by designers like Phillip Lim (in his spring 2011 collections) and

Jason Wu (in his fall–winter 2012 collection) to incorporate Asian design elements into their collections and debut them in Asia suggest that they, like their contemporaries, see the latest Asian chic wave as a business opportunity. (John Galliano, Karl Lagerfeld, Marc Jacobs, and Ralph Lauren did the same in their collections for spring 2007, prefall 2010, spring 2011, and fall 2011, respectively.) However, racial and temporal assumptions about Asian American designers' cultural and emotional bonds with Asia put them in a unique position relative to white American and European designers. Seen as insiders with special instincts about and insights into Asian culture, tastes, and history, some Asian American designers are using this position to play with and disrupt stereotypes from within. For example, Wu, whose most notable fan is First Lady Michelle Obama, has acknowledged that his fall–winter 2012 collection was intended "to poke fun at [these racial expectations] a little bit by interpreting [them] through stereotypes."[12] But not everyone recognizes the irony. Missing the costume-y overtones of the designs (Wu has described them as "inauthentic"[13]), one observer commented that "his current collection . . . plays off his Asian roots."[14] A headline for a video in the *Globe and Mail* reads: "Latest Collection by Jason Wu Show [sic] Chinese roots."[15]

We see the same kind of racial and temporal framework structuring Asian editions of fashion magazines created to target the new Asian luxury consumer class. The reason European and U.S. fashion companies launched these magazines was to capture the attention and disposable income of Asian luxury consumers. The companies hoped these magazines would help them gain a foothold in the all-important new Asian markets. But while the fashion news has repeatedly indicated that the consumers of the moment are Asian, the look and embodiment of the current fashion moment—exemplified by fashion magazine covers—remain white.

The significance of the fashion magazine cover is difficult to overstate. Who is featured on the cover is the lead story not only of that particular magazine issue but also in the public discussions about that issue. Being a cover girl is considered an honor among those in the fashion industry and fashion public. She is the embodiment of the look of the moment.

Yet of the eighty-eight *Vogue China* covers between 2005 (the year the publication was launched) and 2012, forty-seven featured white models or actors, and only thirty-four featured Asian models or actors (often Maggie Cheung or Du Juan). Five featured a group of Asian and white models, and one featured a Black model (Naomi Campbell, on the January 2009 cover). Only one of these covers featured an Asian American (Lucy Liu, April 2009). The racial disparity between white and nonwhite covers for Elle Thailand is worse. Of that magazine's thirty covers between 2010 (its launch year) and 2012, twenty-six featured white models or actors. The Black Barbadian singer Rihanna (August 2010), the Brazilian Portuguese model Adriana Lima (November 2011), the white-Asian British model Alexa Chung[16] (June 2012), and the Mexican-Italian singer Selena Gomez (August 2012) appeared on the four remaining covers. These covers make it visually explicit that whiteness is still leading the world of fashion (even in the Asian moment) in terms of ideals of beauty and body image.

Asian superbloggers are presenting new Asian embodiments of fashion-forwardness. The fashion blogger poses known as the Susie Bubble and BryanBoy poses (named after their respective inventors, Susanna Lau and Yambao) are two of only a small number of brand-name fashion blogger poses. This distinction underscores both the exceptional prominence of the two Asian superbloggers who created the poses but also the function of fashion blogger poses as job performances that can elevate a blogger's standing in fashion's new economy of images, information, and communication.

Before discussing these brand-name poses, it is important to understand what fashion blogger poses generally are. I described above what the poses look like. In the following section, I explain their cultural significance in the age of participatory media and information economies.

### The Look and Meanings of Fashion Blogger Poses

Broadly, fashion blogger poses are a set of photographic poses circulating in the fashion blogosphere (and beyond) that emphasize vernacular styles of fashionable embodiment. They are antithetical to the dramatic, often exaggerated poses that characterize fashion model poses in print editorials and runways (see figures 4.11 and 4.12). In professional modeling arenas, traditional photographic poses operate as an "aesthetics of exclusion"[17] that reproduce notions of "unrealizable beauty."[18] The images and practices of professional modeling reinforce fashion's aspirational culture: consumers are meant to admire but never attain fashion models' high

4.11 and 4.12  Liye Kebede in the "Float On" editorial for American *Vogue*, April 2010.

glamour. This is the work of fashion models. Their job is to embody the aspirational looks and fantasies that drive consumer desire and spending.

The April 2010 issue of American *Vogue* included a gravity-defying editorial called "Float On," featuring the Ethiopia-born top model Liya Kebede.[19] In the six-page spread, Kebede embodies over and over again the impossibly high bar of beauty, cool, and style that distinguish professional fashion model poses from fashion blogger poses. The aesthetics of Kebede's body, posture, face, and hair demonstrate a unique mix of playfulness and control. Her dress billows out, but her facial expression is unflappable. Her body (like the Chloé dress retailing for $4,295 that she wears in one image) seems to float off the ground, yet her hair is exquisite and restrained. The caption describes the dress as "whisper weight,"[20] but, as is the case with all elite models, that description might also be aptly applied to her body. In short, everything about Kebede's look represents "unrealizable beauty" for the vast majority of women of any race. Even the clothes she promotes are generally unattainable, especially by women of color who constitute the numerical majority of the working class and working poor in the United States and globally.[21]

The captions, unlike bloggers' style stories, aren't personal narratives or customized shopping and style guides. Rather than connecting the clothes to the actual body and life of the person wearing them, the text floats on the page and, written without reference to Kebede or any other person, its meaningfulness is ungrounded in subjective particularities. The captions' claims to universality are most obviously expressed in pronouncements like this: "light as air romantic dresses give *any silhouette* momentum for spring" (emphasis added). In these implicit as well as literal claims to a universal beauty and style—one based on impossibly high standards—the captions promote an aesthetics of exclusion.

In contrast, fashion bloggers' embodied vernacular styles are aesthetics of inclusion, compatible with the digital media economy's social character. Fashion blogger poses are vernacular styles of embodiment that are used to indicate a genuinely fashionable subject. Set in everyday spaces and public nonplaces, fashion blogger poses are in situ poses that suggest fashion's embeddedness in individuals' everyday life rather than its being sequestered in corporate fashion's highly guarded spaces. The snapshot aesthetics of fashion blogger poses give the impression of spontaneity— of the camera's capturing an arbitrary moment in the blogger's everyday (but always fashionable) life. Correspondingly, clothing, hair, and photographic styles appear natural, or at least not belabored.[22]

Fashion blogger poses exemplify and animate the principle of effortless style, a core value in the fashion blogosphere. The idea of sartorial effortlessness can be traced back to the sixteenth-century Italian concept of *sprezzatura*. In Baldassare Castiglione's famous etiquette manual *The Book of the Courtier* (1528), he advised Renaissance Italians to "practice in all things a certain nonchalance [sprezzatura] which conceals all artistry and makes whatever one says or does seem uncontrived and effortless."[23] As an expressive and cultural form of sprezzatura, or effortless style, fashion blogger poses challenge institutional notions of style and fashionability that are based on one's access to highly guarded and controlled systems of exclusivity and privilege. The effortlessness—some would call it the amateurishness—of fashion blogger poses suggests that style is open and unique to everyone.

4.13 and 4.14 Personal style blogger Natalie Live of The Tiny Closet photographed with her feet firmly on the ground and in everyday, if nondescript, places on September 27, 2012, and July 17, 2013.

Fashion blogger poses are the bodily performances of the democratization of fashion discourse.

At the same time, fashion blogger poses' allure of effortlessness (the seeming easiness of performing these poses) invokes deep-seated ideas about feminine practices as not real work and thus in opposition to productive processes. Femininity itself is characterized by such discourses of effortlessness. In her song "Flawless," Beyoncé insists that she "woke up like this." Sampling Chimamanda Ngozi Adichie's TED talk on the unfair gendered expectations she experienced as a Nigerian girl and woman,[24] Beyoncé's song is meant to be a feminist declaration that women are "flawless" the way they are. But the flood of "bedstagram" photos it triggered—photographs created for and posted to the popular photo-sharing site

Instagram of celebrity and noncelebrity women waking up with perfectly tousled hair and exquisitely made-up faces—demonstrates the slipperiness of this concept.[25] Beyoncé's notion of flawlessness, much like the effortless stylishness of fashion blogger poses, can easily veer into older and powerful gendered expectations that women both look beautiful and make it seem easy—in fact, effortless—to look beautiful by concealing the actual time and work such practices of femininity demand. The discursive tendency to deskill women's cultural and economic practices has a long and multisited history.

New expressions of mainstream feminism, including fashion blogger poses, are fraught with the dangers of capitulating to or enacting hegemonic constructions of femininity even as they indicate new modalities and meanings of feminine knowledge and skills. While fashion blogger poses may recall more traditional postures of feminine passivity and submissiveness, I argue that the poses also challenge masculinist ideas of what the proper authoritative body looks like.

In their many variations, fashion blogger poses differ from the traditional power stances described in career advice manuals like Carol Kinsey Goman's The Silent Language of Leaders. Within the large and growing career guidance field, Goman stands out as a top executive coach. She runs her own consulting business and has written numerous books and blog posts for Forbes and the Washington Post. On the power stance, Goman writes: "Feet . . . say a lot about your self-confidence. When you stand with your feet close together, you can seem timid or hesitant. But when you widen your stance, relax your knees, and center your weight in your lower body, you look more 'solid' and sure of yourself."[26] Later in her book, she offers this advice to women in particular: "Females can compensate [for a smaller stature] by standing straight, broadening their stance . . . and even putting their hands on their hips in order to take up more physical space."[27]

Goman describes body arrangements that outwardly express internal qualities of self-assuredness, authority, and competence. These qualities, she implies, come more naturally to men through their larger stature. And indeed, the power stance is visible in many male-dominated sites from the boardroom to the boxing ring. According to Goman, women can compensate for their gender difference (rendered in her books as a professional liability) by appearing big rather than small, and solid rather than soft. In other words, they can compensate by embodying the heteronormative masculinist ideas about power, knowledge, and expertise that are encoded in the traditional power stance.

Fashion blogger poses are diametrically opposed to traditional power stances. Bloggers effect pigeon-toed postures and stand with their legs crossed or close together, accompanied by one hand on a hip or both hands on the hips. There are also shoulder rolls that effectively reduce the body in form and space. In traditional career manuals, fashion blogger poses are characterized as diminished postures, physical displays of feminine submissiveness. But such interpretations of fashion blogger poses do not take into account the new gender dynamics of labor markets and skill sets.

Fashion bloggers' bodily techniques symbolically invert economic power, illustrating the contemporary feminization of labor that is characteristic of information and knowledge economies.[28] With the popularization of personal computers and online communication and commerce technologies since the 1990s, information and knowledge economies demand a highly skilled and flexible casual labor force that possesses skills traditionally associated with femininity, including communication, cultural production, and self-care. Such skills characterize what the social media consultant Gary Vaynerchuk calls a "thank you economy," in which "the ability to digitally listen, respond and nurture a one-to-one relationship with the consumer is going to transform the way companies do business. Success will come through 'outcaring everyone.' "[29] In the service-based "thank you economy," the accumulation of financial capital relies on flexible social, cultural, informational, and affective competencies. Women and girls have been positioned as the ideal flexible subjects. Valerie Walkerdine, Helen Lucey, and June Melody explain in *Growing Up Girl* that flexibility is a historically feminine characteristic: "It is women, of course, who have faced reinvention so obviously. The transition from mother and housewife in a long-term monogamous marriage to a working woman often bringing up children alone is a large one. If we also add that women have long been invited constantly to remake themselves as the (changing) object of male desire, then it becomes clear that women have long had to face the recognition that the unitary subject is a fraud and that constant and perpetual self-invention is necessary."[30] Walkerdine, Lucey, and Melody also argue that "the economic man of liberalism . . . is now female."[31] Girls and women who have historically been positioned on the margins of market and labor policies and structures are now central to them.

However, an analysis of fashion blogger poses as a bodily discursive system suggests instead that the economic man is feminine. In other words, it is not just that actual (embodied and identified) women and girls have replaced actual men as centers of economic production, but rather that positions and postures ascribed with femininity instead of masculinity are key to economic structures. These positions and postures are bodily and cultural performances of care, communication, and collaboration that—while historically associated with women and girls—can be and are performed by people of various identities.

Goman's advice that women approximate men's solid, wide posture to appear powerful may be unsatisfying, but it does highlight the fact that bodily discourses are focused on gender, not sex. After all, women can also perform the traditional masculine power stance (albeit in uneven ways). In contrast to Goman's advice, however, style bloggers reject this authoritative pose altogether. In doing so, the bloggers perform and popularize poses—we might call them counterposes—that reflect labor's feminization and traditionally feminine skills and services. To reiterate, just as some women can and do perform masculine poses to increase their cultural capital in business settings, some men can and do perform feminine blogger poses for the same purpose. To develop this point further, I now turn to a closer look at some of the basic techniques of fashion blogger poses.

One of the basic movements of these poses is a tapered feminine stance, often pigeon-toed or with legs crossed. Wide, solid stances are less common even among male fashion bloggers and fashion blog subjects. More typically, men stand with their legs crossed or their feet closely paralleling each other. The tapered stance is often accompanied by "the teapot" or "the sugar bowl" pose, which may recall but certainly do not replicate the masculine squaring-off posture. By placing their hands on their hips, fashion bloggers do not create the illusion of a bigger body taking up more space. Instead, when fashion bloggers and fashion blog subjects place their hands in front of—rather than squarely on—the hips, they highlight their triceps and accentuate their clavicles to produce the visual effect of slender arms and a thinner body. The teapot and sugar bowl stances create the illusion of a smaller body. In this way, fashion blogger poses fetishize feminine smallness in the same way that the fashion industry long has.

As the body is made to look smaller, more toned, and—tacitly—younger, fashion blog subjects align their bodies with the dominant standards of feminine beauty that shape the globalized fashion system. Numerous scholars and media critics have addressed the psychological, health, and sociocultural dangers caused by fashion's relentless pursuit of unrealistically thin bodies.[32] One of the leading researchers in this field is Susan Bordo, who has written extensively on the subject. In *Unbearable Weight*, she explains the historical context of "the slender body" as a bourgeois fashion signifier that began in the late nineteenth century: "Corpulence went out of middle-class vogue at the end of the century. . . . Social power had come to be less dependent on the sheer accumulation of material wealth and more connected to the ability to control and manage the labor and resources of others."[33]

Today, body weight is read less as one's ability to control and manage others and more as one's ability to manage oneself. Bordo explains: "The firm, developed body has become a symbol of correct *attitude*; it means that one 'cares' about oneself and how one appears to others, suggesting willpower, energy, control over infantile impulse, the ability to 'shape your life.' "[34] Popular reality television fitness contests like *The Biggest Loser* and *Celebrity Fit Club* and countless daytime talk show segments devoted to weight loss repeatedly link smaller bodies to one's control not only of one's diet, but also of one's psychological, social, professional, and economic worlds. The enormous pressure to control and manage one's body and image is especially intense in this age of ubiquitous self, state, and social surveillance, in which one's image is both everything and everywhere, from CCTV security monitors to Facebook pages that we create and are tagged in.

Although fashion blogger poses comply with traditional beauty standards of thinness, they are not simply submissive postures. Fashion blogger poses offer a different body language of expertise that challenges the masculinist power stance's normative gender logic. Fashion blogger poses create social, ideological, and discursive dialogue spaces that are crucial in the "thank you economy." When fashion bloggers pose with their hands on their hips, they do not cut intimidating figures. On the contrary, their bodies lean forward, toward the camera, suggesting interest and engagement. Rather than claiming and holding ground, the blogger leans in, encouraging the digital dialogue that is crucial to information and knowledge economies. Fashion designers, bloggers, and journalists often describe social media's significance in the fashion business in these terms. As the fashion journalist Suzy Menkes puts it, "the world changed when fashion instead of being a monologue, became a conversation."[35] Menkes's formulation of fashion capitalism as an information-sharing or communication economy is suggestive of the new gender dynamics of production processes that, as I have argued throughout this book, have made the Asian superblogger phenomenon possible. If monologue-style speech like dictation and instruction are masculine modes of communication—off-limits to women who do not want to be perceived as bitchy or bossy—then dialogue-style speech, from chitchat to gossip, is a feminine mode of communication. Once devalued as nonproductive communication, these and other modes of social and collaborative interactions—with all the components and behaviors of etiquette that social conventions entail (that is, the "thank you economy")—are, as Walkerdine, Lucey, and Melody and Menkes suggest, valuable and valued skills in the new information-sharing economy.

In this context, cultural stereotypes about women being natural communicators may in fact advantage women in information economy labor markets. What's more, racially specific stereotypes about Asian women as exemplary embodiments of feminine characteristics like accommodation, agreeableness, and service goes some way toward explaining why some Asian superbloggers are so highly sought out as brand ambassadors and corporate marketing partners—even as racist discourses such as stereotypes about Asian cheapness limit opportunities for all Asian bloggers.

Fashion blogger poses are at once sites of both exploitation and empowerment. They are aligned with traditional ideals about feminine smallness and cuteness shaping dominant norms of behavior and expectations that have historically served to reproduce and secure women's diminishment. But they are also value-producing job performances, new modes of labor that generate cultural, social, and financial capital. They demonstrate currently valued professional skills that even a staid media outlet like the Wall Street Journal recognizes.[36]

The fashion blogger lean-in pose can be as subtle or as bold as the more traditional feminine leaning in that communicates romantic interest. What is distinct about the fashion blogger pose, however, is that bloggers do not position their bodies to attract masculine attention or the male gaze but to establish a multidirectional dialogue in which feminine (though not necessarily women's) concerns and feminine (though not necessarily female) actors are central. It is in this way that the fashion blogger's lean-in pose is neither aligned with nor operates alongside Sheryl Sandberg's better-known conceptualization of leaning in.

Sandberg, Facebook's chief operating officer, wrote a best-selling book called *Lean In* that advised women to "lean in" to their careers. The book has prompted important mainstream conversations about gender and labor. But Sandberg's "lean in" prescribes a very differently positioned approach to gendered labor. As feminist—especially women of color feminist—critics of *Lean In* have discussed at great length, Sandberg's book depoliticizes women's empowerment by focusing on the actions of individual women rather than the institutional structures of sexism, classism, and racism that shape and limit advancement in labor markets for different women.[37] The collective message delivered by these critics is that Sandberg's position as a wealthy white woman grants her privileges, including particular forms of insulation from classist and racist attitudes, that have enabled her to "lean in" to and benefit from the values, goals, standards, and environments of corporate labor markets.

The fashion blogger lean-in pose, in contrast, is not primarily aimed at gaining entry into the corporate world and advancing up the ladder. Personal style bloggers, especially hobbyists who are as versed in fashion blogger poses as superbloggers are, do not expect or necessarily even want to participate in the corporate sites of the dominant fashion industry, much less advance within these sites. As a vernacular mode of embodied communication, the fashion blogger lean-in pose emphasizes social and interpersonal interactions that draw on traditionally feminine knowledge, skills, and interests. The art and skill of communication, so crucial to knowledge economies, is manifest in this popular blogger pose.

By leaning into the digital conversation, the fashion blogger pose tacitly invites interaction, asking others to participate by commenting on the blog post, creating their own blogs, and reproducing the fashion blogger pose. The lean-in pose creates casual discourse spaces that begin outside fashion's institutional borders but unfold into the centers of fashion. What has long been a cool, aloof, and unapproachable culture and industry is made accessible and inviting by fashion bloggers' vernacular embodiment.

While Sandberg's lean in puts the onus on individual women to transform themselves by bending toward the culture and expectations of corporate capitalism, the fashion blogger's lean-in pose has effected a reverse movement. It is no longer uncommon to see fashion media industry lumi-

4.15 (left) Lau on her apartment balcony, "Party Shirt Time," Style Bubble, December 30, 2011.
4.16 (right) Lanphear at an Australia Fashion Foundation event, July 18, 2013. Courtesy Billy Farrell/BFAnyc.com.

naries like Anna Dello Russo (editor-at-large for *Vogue Japan*) and Kate Lanphear (style director for U.S. *Elle*) adopting the vernacular body language of fashion bloggers. Indeed, fashion blogger poses have become a kind of corporeal lingua franca that reflects social commerce's contemporary values—specifically, communication, collaboration, and interactivity. For professional arbiters of style and consumption, fashion blogger poses are also job performances that convey shared values to consumers.

Critics of personal style bloggers argue that fashion blogger poses—like the formal aesthetics of the outfit photos that frame them—are awkward and fake. On one of the many forums dedicated to bashing personal style bloggers hosted by the site Get Off My Internets, one detractor articulates the rhetorical question that almost all critics ask in one form or another.

An anonymous user asks: "Like who stands like this?" Fashion blogger poses look awkward in comparison to professional modeling poses, and deliberately so. The nonaesthetic aesthetic of fashion blogger poses—like the snapshot aesthetics of outfit photos—is designed to look spontaneous, improvisational, and natural. Unlike professional fashion models whose bodily movements express a sure-footed and graceful agility (the "cats" of the catwalk), bloggers' movements include the natural awkwardness and clumsiness of human physicality (such as the pigeon-toed stance or the lean-in that Bradley refers to as "The Tilt") and the occasional moments of spacing out (for example, the elsewhere gaze). Bloggers' style and taste as expressed through fashion blogger poses are embodied knowledges innately held in the blogger's body, rather than in the fashion industry, and transmitted directly through that body to blog audiences in ways that seem unmediated and genuine.

### Race, Resistance, and the Susie Bubble Pose

Fashion blogger poses provide some insight into the effects of the fashion industry's enduring racial bias even as they reflect changing relations of gender and expertise. The Susie Bubble pose, a stance that characteristically involves at least the elsewhere gaze and a pigeon-toed posture, is an exemplary performance of racialized identity work in the personal style blogosphere. As I will explain below, it is a tactic of impression management that subtly but significantly negotiates racial barriers that can limit Lau's participation in the personal style blogosphere. And as job performances go, it is a highly successful one.

The Susie Bubble pose is the most emulated, and therefore most influential, fashion blogger pose. In fact, it has achieved brand status. The Susie Bubble pose makes literal the term *identity work*. As practices of personal branding, performances of identity enable and sustain capitalist accumulation. In neoliberalism's enterprise culture, personal branding is increasingly ubiquitous. The business magazine *Fast Company* insists that "we are CEOs of our own companies: Me Inc. To be in business today, our most important job is to be head marketer for the brand called You."[38] However, few bloggers' personal brands are as widely recognizable as Lau's and Yambao's. The Susie Bubble and BryanBoy poses have helped make these bloggers the epitomes of success in fashion's new labor market. Thus, these poses are not only products of a corporatized identity but also emblems of knowledge and expertise. The Susie Bubble and BryanBoy poses establish Lau and Yambao as distinguished experts with critical competencies in fashioning and managing the body and self-image—two skills that are highly valued in networked capitalism.

As I mentioned in the introduction, nonwhite fashion workers in both the formal and informal labor sectors face a myriad of economic and social constraints. While fashion workers are disproportionately women of color from the working poor or mostly white gay men, the manufacturing, education, design, retail, and media sectors of the fashion industry have not escaped the problems of racism or sexism. In a study of creative industries (including the fashion industry), Colette Henry found that social barriers still limit women's advancement. Male designers receive more media attention and win more industry awards than female designers.[39] Furthermore, male-led fashion companies are more financially successful than female-led ones. According to the 2012 list of billionaires in Forbes, thirteen of the top fifteen wealthiest people in the fashion industry were men, and only two were women—all were white Europeans or Americans.[40] Whites don't just happen to dominate the highest rungs of the fashion ladder. Fashion labor's stratifications are designed to secure whites' position as the arbiters of luxury lifestyle and culture—a sensibility that, as the Council of Fashion Designers of America memo analyzed above indicates, Asians are not imagined to possess.

The Susie Bubble pose is an innovative and instinctive tactic for negotiating the racial dynamics of Western fashion and beauty culture. This pose and, as I discuss below, the BryanBoy pose have moved Lau and Yambao into positions of high status typically dominated by whites. The bloggers' achievement is not merely occupational but cultural and social as well, given that the highest rungs of fashion are not only dominated by white people but also defined through the bodies and values of whiteness.

Scattered throughout Lau's blog, but most prevalently in her earlier posts, are brief and casual remarks in which Lau admits to feeling ugly. In a 2007 blog post that connotes her racial ambivalence as an Asian personal style blogger, she observes: "Let's just say me and my looks aren't exactly best friends. Being taunted for being ugly at school didn't help."[41] In a post that pokes fun at fashion blogger poses, Lau explains that the elsewhere gaze she has come to be identified with "works particularly well for me and my not so model-esque mug."[42] The racial significance of these statements become clearer in later blog posts in which her eyes and most of her face are crossed out. In fact, her eyes are still mostly hidden in her outfit photos. This is particularly significant, given how central eyes have been to Asian racialization in the United States. As Lau explains it, her blog is "an open invite to view my love of fashion and how I express that in my style but . . . 'Look at the outfit . . . not the face.' "[43]

As I mentioned in chapter 3, Lau's earliest outfit photos were taken using the "mirror shot" technique. She aimed a small point-and-click camera toward a full-length mirror and captured her reflection. The mirror shot enabled her to achieve two paradoxical goals: She could photograph herself from head to toe to show her entire outfit as well as block her face from view. While other "mirror shooters" like Yambao positioned their cameras at chest level, leaving the face fully visible, Lau always held the camera directly in front of her face. When Lau began using a tripod rather than a mirror, she continued to hide her face. In these outfit photos, Lau draws thick black Xs over her face and eyes, an editorial mark that highlights her face and eyes as problems or mistakes in the image. More drastic examples of Lau's self-editorialization are the photos in which her head is entirely cropped out of the frame. She admits in one headless outfit post to feeling like a fashion failure from the neck up, compared to the "overwhelming amounts of fashion straight A*'s." She writes, "I had given into feeling ickle and rubbish."[44]

By 2007, when Lau's boyfriend and fellow fashion blogger Steve Salter (Style Salvage) began photographing her, she found more creative ways to hide her face with hair, hair accessories, and the elsewhere gaze. Lau's strategic positioning of these style objects along with her head and eye positioning reinforce her demand that we "look at the outfit . . . not the face." Today, Lau's elsewhere gaze—an aesthetic convention born out of racial ambivalence—is a hallmark of her personal style.

This is not to say that Lau invented the elsewhere gaze. It was a well-established photographic pose long before Lau popularized it in the fashion blogosphere. In the late nineteenth century, illustrations in fashion magazines and the so-called live mannequins of Charles Fredrick Worth (widely recognized as the first fashion designer) served as technologies of communication and knowledge that conveyed messages about beauty,

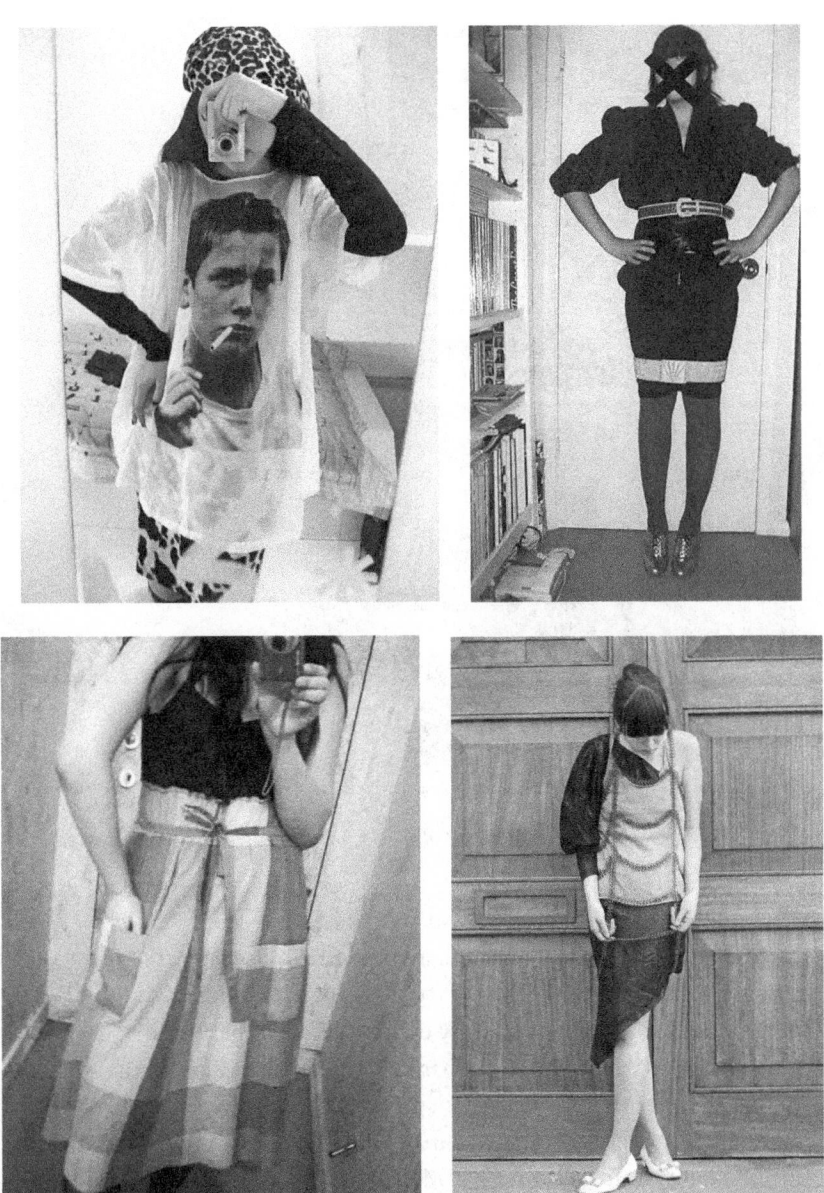

4.17–4.20 The evolution of Lau's elsewhere gaze.

4.21 The evolution of Lau's elsewhere gaze.

femininity, and aspirational lifestyles. These messages were expressed through a set of bodily practices that included the elsewhere gaze.

Then, as now, fashion poses are consistent with prevailing ideas about heteronormative femininity. In the early period of fashion media, the popular "Victorian prudishness," as Daniel Harris explains, meant that shame "about the propriety of women displaying themselves as objects of envy and desire" played a central role in shaping ideas and looks of feminine fashionability. Harris continues: "Models avoided frontal contact with the viewer and maintained the pretense that they were utterly unaware of our presence, an obliviousness that quickly became a convention of posing, a mannerism that shielded them from accusations of immodesty and exhibitionism."[45] This posing convention also reflected and reinforced women's historical position as the object rather than subject of the gaze. Making oneself available to being looked at and photographed from the perspective of men (the photographer) while not returning the gaze was constructed as a normative mark of good taste. The personal style blogger's elsewhere gaze is also an expression of modesty, but its meaning is closer to the etymological roots of the word *modesty*: freedom from exaggeration. The elsewhere gaze marks the style moment as a snapshot moment that is genuine. The pose is unassuming. It suggests that the blogger is either unaware of the camera or unprepared for the shot.

In the age of social commerce in which real people's real style is so widely valued, such modesty is less sharply gendered than earlier iterations of the elsewhere gaze, but homophobic attitudes and anxieties even in the fashion industry add another social dimension to our understanding of the pose. The elsewhere gaze of male fashion models is shaped by differently gendered pressures related to respectability. In the 1960s, male models began appearing in larger numbers in magazines and runways, partially due to gay liberationist challenges to normative sexuality. Sexualized male imagery became more acceptable.[46] In fact, the first retail companies to pursue gay male consumers were those selling clothing or alcohol. While retailers and advertisers may have wanted to attract these consumers, male models were not then and are not now necessarily gay. Joanne Entwistle and Ashley Mears, following Sean Nixon and William Scott, describe the elsewhere gaze of male models, or "[the tendency] to look off into the distance," as a strategy for "avoiding a direct, homoerotic gaze."[47] In other words, male models used the elsewhere gaze to maintain respectable or normative heteromasculinity in the fashion modeling's feminized labor market. Models' notoriously short career spans may have also encouraged some male models to strike a heteromasculine pose to protect future work opportunities outside the fashion industry.

From the very beginning, racial ideologies have been embedded in the gendered elsewhere gaze. White middle-class women could signify feminine respectability by the elsewhere gaze. As a bodily expression of Asian femininity, though, it signifies a racially pronounced shyness or coyness. Theatrical and cinematic performances of archetypal Orientalist female stereotypes (for example, Lotus Blossom, China Doll, and the geisha) routinely employ the elsewhere gaze to signal Oriental feminine embodiment. Sometimes performed by white actors (men or women) in yellowface or under the direction of a white producer, the elsewhere gaze in these performances are not expressions of Asian feminine respectability but of white mainstream perceptions of and desires for acceptable Asian femininity.

The parameters of feminine respectability or acceptability did not extend to many other nonwhite women at all. Popular human exhibitions throughout the nineteenth and twentieth centuries that especially focused on the body parts of Black, Indigenous, and Asian women from the Hottentot Venus to the Cordilleran women (then called Igorots) of the Philippines Exhibition at the 1904 St. Louis World's Fair did not grant these women any degree of respectability. The photographic camera, which shot these women from all angles and distances for the alleged purposes of anthropology, science, and medicine, served as a tool for visually authenticating the popular view of nonwhite women as both exotically and repulsively primitive.[48]

Lau's elsewhere gaze bears the traces of its gendered and racial history. But in the social, cultural, political-economic, and technological context of the personal style blogosphere, her pose is more than a self-representational performance of portraiture: it is a job performance that produces material and nonmaterial benefits. The Susie Bubble pose—like the BryanBoy pose, as I discuss below—allows Lau to participate in a new fashion labor market that continues to be racially stratified. Nonwhite bloggers use these job performances to negotiate implicit racial boundaries of beauty and style that may exclude or limit their participation in the blogosphere.

## Racial and Queer Appropriations through the BryanBoy Pose

Yambao's BryanBoy pose is another example of identity work that aestheticizes race. In the BryanBoy pose, the performer bends forward from the waist, puts one hand on a hip, and stretches out the other arm to clutch a luxury handbag (in the photo below it is the Louis Vuitton Monogram Denim Neo Speedy Satchel).

When Yambao introduced the pose on his blog in July 2005 (not long after its launch in October 2004), his readers immediately embraced it. Yambao solicited as well as received numerous photos of his readers striking the BryanBoy pose. These are still viewable on his blog. Each one of these photos is a visual fan letter. Viewed together, they show the di-

4.22  The actual BryanBoy pose in "Holy Fucking Shiyet Fendi," BryanBoy, May 4, 2006, and "Fendi: Stop the Fucking Press!," BryanBoy, August 15, 2006.

verse range of his audience—from a multiracial group of undergraduates at Sarah Lawrence College and a white soldier named Erick stationed at California's Vandenberg Air Force Base to Asian fans around the world—as well as their high level of engagement with Yambao and the blog. A Google search for "BryanBoy pose" returns hundreds of photographs on Flickr, Photobucket, and other fashion-themed blogs and websites. The wide adoption of the pose demonstrates the success of Yambao's aestheticization processes. As Lau did with the Susie Bubble pose, Yambao used the Bryan-Boy pose to transform his racial embodiment into a style of embodiment that is seemingly universal. The rapid adoption and circulation of these poses among multiracial audiences and across social media publics indicate the far-reaching influence of these two bloggers.

4.23 Angela Lindvall striking the BryanBoy pose for Fendi.

LOUIS VUITTON

4.24 Scarlett Johansson striking the BryanBoy pose for Louis Vuitton.

While the blogosphere was introduced to the BryanBoy pose through Yambao and his blog, the larger fashion public was unaware of it until the luxury fashion company Fendi (helmed by iconic designer Karl Lagerfeld) launched its spring–summer 2006 ad campaign. On its billboard ads, Angela Lindvall, a white model who was born and raised in the American Midwest, performs the BryanBoy pose. It was the appearance of this pose in a traditional fashion media site (and enacted through the body of a professional white model) that led Yambao to claim and coin the BryanBoy pose.

After BryanBoy fans alerted the blogger to the Fendi ad, Yambao reacted immediately and effusively. In a blog post titled "Holy Fucking Shiyet Fendi," Yambao writes: "IT'S MY POSE!!!! IT'S MY HAND ON THE HIP POSE! IT'S THE BAG HANGING ON THE AIR POSE! THE BEAUTIFUL ANGELA LINDVALL DID THE INFAMOUS BRYANBOY POSE!!!" He includes a link to the original BryanBoy pose. And he hints that Fendi may have committed a legal misstep by copying his pose without offering him credit or compensation: "SOMEONE PLEASE CALL THE PRESS OFFICES OF FENDI AND KARL LAGERFELD AND TELL THEM I LOVE THEM SOOOO MUCH (AND THEY SHOULD GIVE ME FREE BAGS FOR COPYING MY POSE!!! HAHAHA)."[49] Yambao's excitement about being recognized by this iconic fashion company outweighs the monetary and legal issues he notes. Clearly he understands the power dynamics of the fashion industry well enough to know that he stands to gain more by interpreting the ad as a "tribute"[50] (his words) than a legal trespass.

Three months later, Fendi reprised the BryanBoy pose in another ad campaign—this time with the blogger's implicit permission.[51] Over the course of several more months, the BryanBoy pose appeared in an array of media sites, from an Apple billboard in San Francisco (in which an iPod replaced the handbag) to the Louis Vuitton spring–summer 2007 campaign featuring Scarlett Johansson.

In the mainstream production and circulation of the BryanBoy pose, the materiality of Yambao's Asian body and his identity as a racial and sexual minority are subsumed by his style of embodiment. To be sure, Yambao also reduces race to style when he encourages his multiracial and multinational fans to strike the BryanBoy pose. In his fans' adoption of the pose, the racial particularity of his embodiment is made malleable and flexible so that it can be embodied by anyone. In Fendi's and Louis Vuitton's appropriation of the pose, its racial origins are erased altogether. The popularization of Yambao's brand-name pose (as with the Susie Bubble pose) rests on the aestheticization of racial particularity and Yambao's ability to transform racialized embodiment into universalized style.

Fendi's and Louis Vuitton's unauthorized use of Yambao's pose is not surprising in some ways. Fashion has a long history of misappropriating minority cultural forms. Examples from fashion's recent history include Dolce and Gabbana's spring 2013 fashion show at Milan Fashion Week in which models walked the runway wearing "mammy" figurine earrings, Victoria's Secret's use of native headdresses in its 2012 show, and Givenchy's presentation of harem pants and burqa-style head garments at its fall 2009 show at Paris Fashion Week. The contradiction in which such head coverings signify high fashion when worn by white models on the runway and oppressive ethnic garb when worn by observant Muslim women (who, if they lived in France and other countries that have criminalized the burqa, might be arrested for this sartorial choice) exemplify the cultural logic of global capitalism. Racial differences are acceptable and even laudable when they are commodified for corporate profit.[52] Yambao's BryanBoy pose is remarkable as a practice of identity taste work because it strategically rearticulates the minority-dominant power relationship on which global capitalism has been based.

Reacting to the Fendi ad campaign, Yambao blogs, "2006 IS THE INTERNATONAL [sic] YEAR OF BRYANBOY & FENDI."[53] In so doing, he claims these ads as evidence of his social and cultural capital, placed on a par with Fendi's. Moreover, he uses Fendi's own ads to accrue even more capital to himself and his blog. In this practice, Yambao's physical body is not the primary site of his identity work. Still, his blog post is an example of embodied identity work insofar as personal blogs are the technological embodiment of the blogger. This is reflected in the cliché "I blog, therefore I am." Yambao uses his BryanBoy blog—his digital double—to reclaim credit and assert his visible agency in the fashion's public sphere. Yambao's blog posts make visible what Fendi erases: his racially and sexually minoritized body. In Yambao's blog posts, this body is not a sign of racialized inferiority but a personal brand. In effect, Yambao succeeds in positioning himself within fashion's mainstream discourse and imagery.

Without the social media platform and the worldwide blog audience that Yambao had already acquired, Fendi's visual quotation would have almost certainly remained uncredited—something Fendi may have been counting on. The blog enables Yambao to announce that he is the inspiration behind the Fendi ad (a diplomatic way of describing the ad as a knockoff), and achieve both intentional and unintentional outcomes.

First, Yambao's blog post allows him to successfully reclaim the pose as his own entrepreneurial creation, exposing Fendi's false claims to authenticity. Second, the post enables Yambao to capitalize on Fendi's own ads, positioning himself and his blog at the center of luxury fashion's cultural economy. When read against capitalism's history and continued use of racialized labor, Yambao's personal branding efforts uncover the labor that too often remains hidden behind luxury fashion's labels. Not only does the blogger bring into public light the hidden labors of his body and blog, but he also insists that his labors share space in the luxury object's sign system. What might be otherwise devalued as free Asian labor is now imbued with status and prestige, precious social capital in the value system that luxury handbags emblematize and instrumentalize.

Third, in claiming the pose as his own—in effect, revealing the queer Asian body beneath the aesthetic surface of the ad and Lindvall's pose— Yambao does more than replace the Fendi brand with his personal brand. Reversing fashion's popular authenticity discourse in which white Europeans and Americans are imagined as fashion, style, and beauty innovators, Yambao proclaims himself the pose's original creator: "NOTHING CAN BEAT THE ORIGINAL, THE LEGENDARY AND THE INFAMOUS BRYANBOY POST."[54] Challenging the popular notion that Asian people and places embody cheap, fake style, Yambao locates the center of style originality and innovation at his queer Filipino body. Here, the Asian superblogger flips the cheap knockoff Asian stereotype around, so that the marginalized Asian body becomes haute couture while Fendi is the cheap knockoff.

But as is the condition of art in the age of digital reproduction, distinctions between the original and the copy are blurred. The BryanBoy pose, with its emphatic thrusting out of the chest and behind, is itself a visual citation of gay male performances of femininity (many of which draw from straight women's performances). So when Lindvall and Johansson perform the BryanBoy pose, what we see is a straight white woman performing a queer Asian man performing straight white women. Fashion and fashion media are "knockoff economies," as Kal Raustiala and Christopher Sprigman write.[55] Yet racial and economic stereotypes overwhelmingly associate Asians with cheap fashion practices and sensibilities.

Yambao's blog post exposes and troubles those stereotypes through the exaggeration of queer racial camp sensibilities. His use of capital letters in these and many other blog posts constructs a "loud" personality. But just as humor has long been a strategy for softening or taking the sting out of racial discourse, Yambao's characteristic irony and wit effectively softens racial difference and the counter racial pose that is the BryanBoy pose.

A fourth outcome of Yambao's branding efforts is his queering of an iconic feminine accessory's social history. This outcome is unintentional but no less significant. The luxury handbag has long been the emblem of white bourgeois femininity. As Susan Hiner[56] notes in her wonderful history of this exemplary feminine status symbol, the handbag emblematizes modern concepts of femininity. It signals women's financial independence, because the handbag is an instrument of shopping. It also marks women's social autonomy: as a portable accessory, the handbag allows women mobility in public spaces while still concealing personal contents and thus maintaining a respectable femininity. Fendi's replacement of Yambao's queer body of color with a (presumably) straight, white female body reproduces the luxury handbag's traditional symbolic meaning as a status accessory signifying white bourgeois femininity.

Ironically, though, it is the BryanBoy pose that evokes the handbag's original queer sign system. The handbag has been an iconic feminine fashion accessory since the nineteenth century, but initial reactions to the reticule (an early form of the handbag held with the hand or arm by a cord) were predominantly negative: the item was considered "objectionable in large part because it blurs gender lines." Hiner explains: "The reticule is distinctly classed down and, even more scandalously, masculinized. What had been invisible as undergarments in the form of pockets, 'happily' if obscurely placed under paniers and yards of silk, has now been externalized in the reticule; it is carried in plain sight and passed promiscuously 'from hand to hand' . . . mak[ing] visible a relationship with money that propriety dictated was the sphere of men, not women."[57] The handbag's queer erotic and economic origin is reanimated in the unlikely site of Yambao's BryanBoy pose. The pose (with the body bent forward from the hips, chest thrust outward, butt thrust upward, and lips pursed in sassy attitude, with one hand placed high on the hip and the other clutching a luxury handbag) queerly eroticizes the fashion object. In performing the pose, Yambao accesses the privileges of white bourgeois femininity (notably, the privileges associated with ideal embodiment) while also queering this ideal. In Yambao's production and performance of a highly stylized queer Asian identity, he links Asian embodiment and queer sexuality with luxury consumption.

## The Bodily Work of Taste and Race

The close association of race and taste—exemplified in the cheap Asian stereotype, in which Asianness is read as a strong indicator of cheap tastes—suggests that racial identity work and taste work are linked practices. The awareness of their interconnectedness is born out in studies of race and taste that demonstrate how individuals create taste cues from the clothes they wear, the music they listen to, and the construction of their social network profiles.[58] Such taste cues are deployed as strategies for signaling social position. Taste also reflects, as Pierre Bourdieu has famously argued, the social conditions that shape taste patterns.[59] Thus, individual and institutional taste patterns are mutually constituted. We choose to watch particular kinds of television shows that affirm our sense of social identity, but television networks also create programming and styles of presentation that are designed to target audiences based on racialized taste patterns.

The Susie Bubble pose and the BryanBoy pose demonstrate a reverse movement of taste work. Rather than styling the self through self-fashioning and consumer practices and choices, fashion blogger poses enact and enable a process of turning the racial self (along with associated racial stigmas) into a personal style. The Susie Bubble and BryanBoy poses take a group identity—Asianness—and individualize it as a personal style. In these fashion blogger poses, styling the self is first and foremost a bodily practice, not a consumer practice. The body is the means, not just the site, of identity work. To some degree, contemporary white artists like Madonna, Gwen Stefani, Justin Bieber, Miley Cyrus, Iggy Azalea, and many others are examples of turning the self into style through the bodily work of changing speech and bodily movements. But these artists' identity work does not transform the white self into individual style but rather into familiar, unimaginative gendered and racial stereotypes—caricatures that draw from and bank on historically rooted ideas about race and difference.

The Susie Bubble and BryanBoy poses are bodily modes of an identity work that rearticulates race, changing it from a group identity to an individual style. As a practice of taste work, the poses have enabled these two Asian superbloggers to advance in a new labor market that, to a large degree, they created: the elite personal style blogger market. These related but distinct fashion blogger poses are examples of identity work that effectively aestheticize Asianness, turning it into personal style and legitimate difference. The poses are means by which Lau and Yambao align themselves and the public perceptions of them with the postracial culture of the personal style blogosphere and the larger fashion media complex. Postracial ideology is characterized by an understanding of the new flexibility of racial or ethnic categories—a belief played out painfully in Tyra Banks's reality television modeling competition *America's Next Top Model*, in which one of the modeling challenges involves racial masquerade and ventriloquism (see seasons four and thirteen).[60]

As racialized fashion workers, Lau, Yambao, and other Asian superbloggers rearticulate their racial and ethnic identities in ways that mesh with the values and norms of the personal style blog culture to gain strategic advantages. We have already seen this strategy at work in a number of ways, from Aimee Song's discursive construction of her style of dress and embodiment as ethnic but neutral to Yambao's sartorial self-regulation to avoid embodying a look that screams cheap, foreign Asian (see chapters 2 and 3). In each of these examples, Asian superbloggers do not disidentify from their racial background but instead rearticulate Asianness through or as aesthetics. Rather than looks that scream Asian, their taste work creates softer Asian styles of embodiment that have a particular value and can create value in the new fashion economy.

Lau's elsewhere gaze is an example of the aestheticization of Asianness through identity work practices of body and image management. The Susie Bubble pose effectively aestheticizes Lau's racial ambivalence about the ugliness of her eyes and face by turning it into personal style. In so doing, the pose rearticulates racial shame as individual distinction, a personal brand. Lau's bodily identity work of aestheticizing race as personal style enables her economic, cultural, and social participation in fashion media. In fact, the Susie Bubble pose has not simply opened doors to established fashion media labor markets that have been historically closed to Asians, but it has also created doors and spaces that have led to the formation of an entirely new fashion labor market.

In the aestheticization of race, race is repurposed as a consumable good as well as a renewable resource for social, economic, and cultural capital that enables Lau to build broad social influence. The more the Susie Bubble pose circulates—creating ever larger networks of social interactivity and connectivity—the more social and financial capital Lau accrues as an influential personal style blogger or superblogger.

By aestheticizing race, bloggers render racial identification as individuating taste performances. In this way, they present racial identification as unfixed, dynamic, and contingent. Rather than a predetermined cultural inheritance, race is constituted through the enacted performances of personal vernacular style. Bloggers use self-branding to open up space in participatory media's crowded image culture and economy where they can be seen as individuals. Consider Yambao's often repeated brand tagline, "Planet Earth's Favourite Third World Fag."[61] His identity and the terms of his visibility are premised on categories of social difference (Third World and fag) that are rearticulated as a unique individual brand.

Lau's aestheticization of race is quite similar. For example, in a blog post I discussed in chapter 2 about chinoiserie's resurgence on runways, she acknowledges that the trend "might not sit all that well with actual Chinese women" but that she "on the other hand was . . . dazzled" by the collections.[62] Lau links her exceptional perspective to her racialized difference as a British-born Chinese person—an exceptionalism that has gotten her into some trouble in the past with diasporic Chinese readers.[63] Here again, her difference—this time from "actual Chinese women"—is rebranded as exceptional individuality.[64] Whereas the claiming of racial identities has traditionally signaled collective solidarity in the face of systematic patterns of racialized exclusion and subjugation, the aestheticization of race integrates race into capitalist processes and practices of personal branding.

Asian bodies, particularly those that are female or queer, have been incorporated into commerce through both fashion economies and transnational service economies, including cultural and sexual tourism, domestic labor, commercial surrogacy, and bride trafficking. Commodified in an uneven exchange between powerful and disempowered nations and people, female and queer Asian bodies have been key contributors to, but not beneficiaries of, global capitalism. Indeed, it is the racist devaluation of their bodies as cheap commodities that conditions their economic participation.

In a way, Yambao's bowed BryanBoy body raises the specter of Oriental service-based sexuality, except that his significant social and cultural capital restructures the erotic and economic frame surrounding the images and desires attached to Asian bodies. Here, the erotic and economic desires signified by the luxury handbag are owned by a queer Filipino man, not imposed on him. The BryanBoy pose, a personal brand, marks this queer Asian male Third World body as self-possessed.

Historically, stylized poses, postures, and gaits have been dynamic sites where minoritized people struggle against others' values of and meanings for bodies.[65] With fashion blogger poses we see that the struggle over the values and meanings of Asian bodies—even those with situated privilege—has extended into sites too often interpreted as spaces of nonproductive recreation and leisure. Although Lau's and Yambao's embodiment styles are limited as cultural or political strategies, they nonetheless have cultural, political, and (for their creators) economic effects. Specifically, they advance what Dick Hebdige identifies as style's most dangerous power: the presence of difference.[66] The Susie Bubble and BryanBoy poses offer countervisions to the ways fashion has perceived Asian bodies and performances of Asian fashion labor.

# Chapter 5.
## Invisible Labor and Racial Visibilities in Outfit Posts

"We all know that fashion bloggers are some of the batshit craziest little shopping addicts around."[1] This indictment of fashion bloggers as irrational consumers comes from a blogger called Lancelle, who runs a blog dedicated to skewering all forms of lifestyle blogging. By opening her statement with "we all know," Lancelle suggests that fashion bloggers' shopping addiction is common knowledge. And Lancelle is not wrong. Her characterization epitomizes one of the primary reasons critics give for their negative perceptions of personal style blogging.

Some bloggers even share this opinion. In October 2013, the online community site Independent Fashion Bloggers hosted a public forum titled "Does Fashion Blogging Make You a Shopping Addict?"[2] While forum responses were mixed, those who answered yes rehashed common stereotypes about bloggers, including themselves. In both joking and reflective tones, a number of bloggers admitted behaviors that correlate with implicitly gendered stereotypes of shopping addiction and fashion victimization. Another blogger, Catherine Everett, who did not participate in the forum but who wrote a blog post on the same topic for *Teen Vogue*, provides a more measured response: "I don't know, there's even times where I'm actually a bit disgusted in [sic] the consumptive habits of fellow bloggers. . . . [A]t its core, I guess fashion blogging is materialistic."[3]

These judgments suggest that personal style bloggers' relationship to fashion consumption is excessive, even rising to the level of addiction. Personal style bloggers are perceived as fashion victims whose compulsion to shop and style themselves have, in the words of John Fairchild, "carried them off to the wilder shores of fashion."[4] Fairchild founded W magazine and claims credit for coining the term *fashion victim*, but the idea of the fashion victim precedes him. The feminized figure of irrational overconsumption can be found most notably in the work of Thorstein Veblen[5] and Georg Simmel.[6] In fact, Fairchild's description of fashion victims echoes Simmel's observation that the fashion victim shows "excesses in the tendencies of fashion, crossing the limit observed by others of his epoch."[7] According to Bjorn Schiermer, who traces the fashion victim's history and stereotypes to the Middle Ages, the "essential trait of fashion victimization" is the "display of excess."[8]

Yet if displays of excessive spending and excessive styling are the defining characteristics of fashion victimization, then personal style blogging cannot be an example of fashion victimization. If we look a little closer at the technological and aesthetic conventions of personal style blog posting, we see that very little shopping is actually included in the visual and textual content of personal style blogs.

The technological and aesthetic conventions of outfit posting (or how outfit posts look on a screen) make invisible the many and sometimes tedious physical, emotional, consumerist, and biopolitical processes and procedures of self-fashioning that constitute personal style blogs. Instead, what outfit posts highlight are the results of self-fashioning. In one blog post after another, bloggers provide photos of and information about complete looks or outfits. All but nonexistent are visual or textual representations of bloggers navigating their way through busy retail districts; looking for a parking space; waiting for a dressing room while juggling a handbag, a cell phone, and a small mountain of clothes in multiple sizes and colors; trying on clothes in a hot and cramped dressing room (or clothes from their closets); vying for time at one of the few mirrors in a dressing room area; or queuing at the cash register.

Outfit posts are the individual units of a personal style blog. Each outfit post typically includes a style story and a number of outfit photos. This primary mode of blogging in the personal style blogosphere does not depict the work of consumption and self-fashioning. The technological and aesthetic conventions of outfit posts represent personal style blogging as a mostly effortless activity. In outfit posts, bloggers' style is represented as thoroughly integrated into and coextensive with their everyday life. Outfit posts suggest that bloggers come by their stylishness easily and effortlessly, reaffirming the idea of the personal style blogosphere as a site of real people and real style.

To find discussions of the actual labors of consumption and self-fashioning, we have to look at a distinct but related site of social commerce called the haul vlogosphere. Haul vloggers video record their shopping "hauls," in which they purchase copious amounts of apparel, accessories, cosmetics, and personal grooming products, often from a mass-market retailer. While unloading their hauls, vloggers provide detailed accounts of the brand, price, retailer, and use of each purchased item. They emphasize the work of consumption—the effort of accumulating the haul—rendering haul vlogging as a kind of manual labor, with all the class-based norms and expectations that the word haul implies.

Personal style bloggers and haul vloggers' different approaches to online fashion media represent a wider tension in mainstream Western fashion culture, which wants to hold together fashion as fantasy and fashion as reality culture. The social media phenomenon of haul vlogging—of highlighting, sometimes in great detail, fashion consumer labors—is related to a phenomenon in traditional fashion media. In recent years, pressure from feminist activists, the American Medical Association, and others concerned with the rising levels of eating disorders among both adults and children have convinced some fashion magazine editors, photographers, and models to begin stripping away fashion's glossy façades of manufactured glamour. There is a growing push from various sectors of the public, Hollywood, and within the fashion industry to make the industry more transparent about the amount of technical and physical work that goes into making the people in fashion magazines look so flawless. A number of fashion models and actors have publicly criticized magazines' excessive use of digital alteration and have openly acknowledged that they do not look like their images in magazines.[9] In its April 2009 issue, the French version of Elle magazine[10] ran a series of covers in which the models wore no makeup and the images were published unaltered. The images inside the magazine underwent all of the usual applications of digital manipulation. More so than the cover alone, the juxtaposition (whether or not this was the editors' intention) brings into stark relief the amount of physical and digital labor that goes into making the fashionable body.

Some fashion industry stalwarts have defended fashion's use of very thin and very photoshopped models. Fashion writer Lisa Hilton argues that "fashion is about fantasy."[11] Echoing Hilton, British *Vogue* editor-in-chief Alexandra Shulman insists, *"Vogue* is a magazine that's about fantasy to some extent and dreams, and an escape from real life. People don't want to buy a magazine like *Vogue* to see what they see when they look in the mirror. They can do that for free."[12] Even Lena Dunham, who has made a name for herself as a feminist and so-called body-positive actor, does not think that digital alteration is necessarily a bad thing. When fans condemned *Vogue* for digitally retouching Dunham's cover image in the February 2014 issue, the actor defended the magazine: "A fashion magazine is like a beautiful fantasy. *Vogue* isn't the place that we go to look at realistic women, *Vogue* is the place that we go to look at beautiful clothes and fancy places and escapism."[13] The fantasy feeds into and increases the aspirational quality of fashion media imagery that is a driving force of fashion consumerism. If fashion is about fantasy, then it is because fantasy generally sells.

While fashion magazines and personal style blogs both conceal the bodily and technical labors that go into creating their images, personal style blogs are not simply online fashion magazines. Personal style blogs are in fact where fashion audiences go to look at real people and real style. In this way, the blogosphere is a paradoxical fashion media site. The technological and aesthetic conventions that conceal self-styling and con-sumer labors actually facilitate bloggers' construction of their real style as an unbelabored or effortless style.

The notion of fashion consumption as an effortless activity is not a new one. Since at least the end of the nineteenth century, with the publication of Veblen's classic study *The Theory of the Leisure Class*, fashion consumer-ism and self-fashioning have been understood as "not work," as nonpro-ductive feminine activities. Delineating the consumption and production activities in gendered terms, Veblen asserts: "While one group produces goods another group, usually headed by the wife or chief wife, consumes for him [her husband] in conspicuous leisure; thereby putting in evidence his ability to sustain large pecuniary damage without impairing his supe-rior opulence."[14] French high heels, skirts, hair accessories, and corsets all figure into Veblen's theory as significations of women's unproductive consumerist predispositions: "The wearer cannot when so attired bear a hand in any employment that is directly and immediately of any human use."[15] Self-fashioning practices, according to Veblen, are antithetical to work practices.

Yet as I have argued throughout this book, the activities that bloggers—and, indeed, all fashion consumers—are engaged in every day are productive activities that create value and accumulate capital. What's more, the practices of fashion consumerism and self-fashioning are today recognized as value-adding skills that can give individuals a competitive edge in the arenas of work, self-worth, and romantic love. If consumption is still viewed as a feminine activity, it is also one that is at the center of productive economies.

More salient to this discussion is Veblen's influential theory of conspicuous consumption. Throughout his study, Veblen underscores the fact that conspicuous consumption is the result not only of the visual display of decorative clothing and personal commodities but also of visible consumption. He contends that "propriety requires respectable women to . . . [make] . . . a show of leisure."[16] Accordingly, a "diligent application of effort and expenditure" go hand in hand.[17] He insists furthermore that "the well mannered" should demonstrate "a conscious effort . . . to show that much time has been spent in acquiring" luxury goods.[18] The haul vlogosphere is rife with representations of labor-demanding (though not necessarily labor-intensive) shows of consumption. In the personal style blogosphere, though, consumer labor—not to mention the retail labor of stockists, salespeople, and shippers—is rendered invisible. The result is that bloggers' styles of dress and embodiment appear effortless and natural.

A fundamental aspect of the work of personal style blogging, then, is to make consumer and self-styling labors invisible. In so doing, bloggers create images of their styles of dress and embodiment as styles that don't break a sweat. But more crucially, as I argue in this chapter, their effortless style also facilitates the construction of their labor identity as fashion workers whose labors are not sweated. What outfit posts' technological and aesthetic conventions conceal is not simply the labors of self-styling and consumerism but also, and just as importantly, the porousness of the boundaries between material and digital labor.

## Invisible Labor and Flexible Capitalism

The erasure of personal style blogging labor began well before the invention of the personal style blog, with the restructuring of capitalism and the reorganization of work toward a greater emphasis on flexibility. The shift in capitalist societies in the 1970s and 1980s toward a post-Fordist organization of labor gave rise to increased flexibility in where and when people worked, workers' skills and knowledges, and accumulation strategies (for example, outsourcing and casual or informal labor). It also provided for some, as Aihwa Ong has shown us, flexible citizenship.[19] Such flexibility, now central to labor processes and labor markets, has increased with the widespread distribution of new communication and information technologies in the 1990s.[20] Today, economies are driven by activities that were not traditionally and still are not generally recognized as work, such as unwaged and voluntary social media activities.

The personal style blogosphere is an exemplary model of a flexible production system. Personal style bloggers participate in flexible productions of content (such as image, text, audio, and video) and services (for example, those provided by marketers, broadcasters, fashion models, and fashion experts); flexible consumption of information, goods, and style; and flexible employment, involving irregular and itinerant work hours and spaces). Personal style bloggers work from home, in hotel rooms, on streets and sidewalks, and in open fields—at all hours of the day and night. They are mostly self-directed and self-employed, otherwise employed, and/or unemployed. Bryan Grey Yambao began blogging while living in his parents' home in Manila. Susanna Lau began blogging as a distraction from her full-time job as a digital advertising account manager. Aimee Song is an interior designer by "day" and blogger by "night." Blogging's flexible structures afford bloggers enormous creative freedom and freedom to create their own work environments; the same is true for people working in other networked economies. Bloggers do not need to endure any formal oversight, and they control all of the social, cultural, and financial capital they generate through their blogs.

Furthermore, barriers to entry into this flexible, informal labor market are relatively low, making it possible for amateurs and hobbyists to participate. Personal style blogs require only a modest amount of financial investment. The primary tools of a personal style blogger—a computer, digital camera, and high-speed Internet connection—are by now common middle-class household items rather than specialized equipment. Maintaining a personal style blog does not require a significant amount of disposable income, either. Popular blogging services like Wordpress and Blogger are free and relatively easy to set up and use.

Informational capitalism's emphasis on part-time work, temporary work, and home work has obscured labor and economic relations. In the personal style blogosphere, the dissolution of boundaries between home and work make it difficult to distinguish what is work and what is play. All personal style blogging takes place beyond the parameters of traditional office spaces and office hours (for example, it is not uncommon for a blogger to illicitly write or edit a blog post during work hours). Daily personal style blogging, like Internet surfing, self-fashioning, commenting, and social networking, is a personal and leisure activity that can be potentially appropriated by capital—with or without the blogger's consent. These and other social consumption practices once seemed outside of economics, but as we know from digital labor scholarship, they are now highly efficient sources of value production.

Informational capitalism's technological and social infrastructure enables consumers to voluntarily cocreate value. But the positive services and experiences that informational capitalist structures provide also make it possible for telecommunication and fashion corporations to justify radically uneven wealth distribution. While expert fashion consumers like superbloggers reappropriate a bit of the value their labor creates, this value is negligible compared to the value that corporations acquire from consumers' free and casual labors.

In addition to the restructuring of labor and economies that make work like personal style blogging invisible as work, bloggers' own technological and aesthetic practices contribute to the invisibilization of their labor by concealing the time, effort, and skills involved in creating personal style blogs.

## The Spatiotemporal Dimensions of Personal Style Blog Labor

Although I contest claims that personal style bloggers are shopping addicts or fashion victims (these terms are inherently misogynist, and personal style blogging does not meet their definitions), it is nevertheless true that bloggers' wardrobes are often large. There are several reasons for this. First, personal style bloggers love clothes, or they would not participate in this blogosphere. Just as music lovers collect music and book lovers collect books, personal style bloggers collect clothes. Second, blogging typically requires a constant stream of new posts portraying different outfits for a range of seasons, occasions, and moods. An extensive wardrobe is instrumental (though not essential) to personal style blogging.

Personal style bloggers seldom mention how they acquire their clothes. A 2009 Federal Trade Commission (FTC) mandate, though, requires that bloggers disclose the products they receive for free as well as what, if any, financial relationships they have with the companies whose products are featured on their blog. The rule is intended to help readers distinguish bloggers' paid endorsements from their voluntary ones. In 2014, the FTC updated its guidelines and required bloggers to include disclosures in their short-form blog posts on sites such as Twitter and Instagram. The FTC rule does not apply to print fashion media journalists, who regularly receive free products and services to review. Bloggers have noted and protested this disparity, but as of this writing, print fashion media journalists are still exempt. However, because of this rule, we can assume that all the clothes featured in a blog are shopped for or gifts from family and friends unless noted otherwise.

Whatever the method used for acquiring clothes, the public rarely sees personal style bloggers' wardrobes in anything but a finished state. Even in the fashion media genre called closet confessionals—which has its roots in television programs like Robin Leach's 1980s *Lifestyles of the Rich and Famous*—the clothes, shoes, and accessories offered up to our touristic gaze are shown neatly hung, folded, and otherwise stored. Song's closet confessional, as seen in *Glamour*, *Teen Vogue*, and *Lucky* magazines, features a closet that is roughly the size of a small bedroom.[21] Its design and organization are evidence of her interior design training. Lau's closet confessional for the e-commerce website Bluefly (a former sponsor of the reality television competition *Project Runway*) takes place while she is traveling during the spring 2011 Fashion Week season.[22] The site of her confessional is a well-appointed hotel room and includes a small hotel closet crowded with designer clothes.

Blog audiences know, of course, that clothes do not just appear in bloggers' wardrobes or on their bodies. Yet the labor of consumption is not within the temporal, visual, or cultural purview of the personal style blogosphere. In other words, outfit posting's technological and aesthetic conventions hide the foundational work of personal style blogging. This is a striking discrepancy for a media practice committed to journalistically and fastidiously documenting the sartorial everyday. Thus, the outfit posts that are the primary form of blogging media content are not portraits of consumption but of having consumed. The temporal distinction is significant.

As we know from labor theorists, the logic, order, and management of time and space define labor categories: agrarian labor is defined by the fluctuations of seasonal time, while industrial labor is defined by linear and standardized "clock time."[23] Industrial labor also embodies spatiotemporal and gendered distinctions between the workday and the weekend, the home and the workplace, and leisure and labor. Informational capitalism's postindustrial, post-Fordist labor, as I noted above, is arranged around individualized flexible time. As we will see with the personal style blogosphere, flexible time can also be nonlinear, nonsequential, and discontinuous.

Spatiotemporal structures do more than define work environments; they also signal and secure labor hierarchies. The degrees of control that workers have to manage their work time and spaces constitute the differences between free labor, subjugated labor, and/or surplus labor (an informal labor force whose work time is temporary, insecure, and irregular). Ideologies of racial difference are embedded in these labor structures. Historically, free labor and whiteness have been mutually constitutive. That is, free labor has not only been the preserve of white workers, but whiteness has been a defining characteristic of free labor.[24]

As I discussed in chapter 1, the garment factory and sweatshop have been key historical scenes of women's subjugated labor since the late nineteenth century. Over the past forty years, globalization has added to this economic category of gendered labor a decidedly racial register. Asian female garment workers are imagined to be biologically predisposed (with their nimble fingers) to the semiskilled tedious and repetitive work of apparel mass production. Perceived as a docile and easily controllable work force, Asian fashion labor is characterized by high levels of control over workers' spatiotemporal experiences, including the micromanagement of their lunch breaks, bathroom breaks, and personal conversations. Asian fashion workers are also punished for speaking out about their labor conditions, as they face termination and even death (as in the case of Bangladeshi labor activist Aminul Islam in April 2012). The categories of free labor and the various forms of subjugated labor—including slave labor, indentured labor, and sweated labor—are economic expressions of racial and gendered logics.

The personal style blogosphere's twenty-first-century labor structure is markedly different from earlier forms. Rather than the top-down control of work time and spaces that condition apparel manufacturing, personal style blogging labor is organized around flexible and what appear to be shape-shifting arrangements of space and time. As readers scroll through outfit posts, they see the blogger take quantum leaps from one spatiotemporal site to another, and from one outfit to another: one photo might be set in an unidentified park, while the next one is set in an unidentified alley. There is no temporal flow between outfit posts, no sense of duration or continuity. The erasure of intermediary flows of time and space between outfit posts creates a sense of constant presentness, or what I call untimeliness. Untimeliness describes not a sense of apunctuality (arriving too early or too late) but of a noncontinuous instantaneity. Outfit posts designate an always different and self-contained here and now. A full webpage of outfit posts—usually containing about five or six compressed posts—depicts a range of disconnected spatial systems, in which each outfit post represents a totally autonomous spatiotemporal unit that neither continues the post before it nor anticipates the post after it. Much like David Harvey's notion of postmodern time, outfit posts' untimeliness shortens time horizons "to the point where the present is all there is."[25] Outfit posts produce a similar spatiotemporal experience for blog readers. Readers' experiences of time and space are not necessarily grounded in their real-time geographic locations but are instead generated from individualized and distinct streams of information, knowledge, and communication.

How bloggers came to be at the place and time of a particular outfit post, or how they came to be wearing the outfit featured, is not the concern of personal style bloggers or their audiences. Bloggers instead aim to document the outfit event or, rather, the outfit nonevent. They intend to chronicle the everyday social life of their outfit and their own lives as lived through clothing.

What is important in outfit posts is not the outfit's "commodity state"[26] but rather, to adapt Igor Kopytoff and Arjun Appadurai's formulation,[27] the outfit's biographical indexicality to the blogger—the outfit's social life and the social life of the blogger it refers to. The post's function is to re-cord these lives. Outfit posts emphasize the social and cultural routes of clothing's trajectory—what happens to clothes after they are produced, distributed, and purchased. As Appadurai indicates, the meaningfulness of objects is not exhausted by their commodity state as an object of capital-ist exchange. For personal style bloggers, the outfit as object is much less important than the outfit as a personal tool for narrating personal taste, a style of personhood, and sartorial life. The outfit in an outfit post is a means of creative individualism, self-expression, self-actualization, and self-enrichment. Much of the scholarship about style blogs emphasizes the personal motivations and benefits underpinning outfit posting.[28] Al-though bloggers' personal narratives are important, creative practices do not happen in a vacuum. Outfit posting is mediated by impersonal tech-nological and corporate infrastructures that enable but also manage and shape bloggers' creative practices.

### The No-Sweat Style of Fashion Toast's Rumi Neely

Bloggers may experience outfit posting as creative self-expression, but the conditions for creating the outfit post express capitalist logics and values. Popular and critical understandings of outfit posting as a primarily self-expressive activity gloss over bloggers' actual work practices and work conditions. In so doing, these interpretations obscure the economic power relations that sustain the personal style blogosphere and that inform su-perbloggers' creative decisions. In this section I want to take a closer look at the work conditions of outfit posting by examining the spatiotemporal arrangements of Rumi Neely's outfit posts. A single webpage of Neely's blog Fashion Toast provides a representative picture of what a successive series of outfit posts in the personal style blogosphere look like.

Neely's first post on her webpage on the day of this writing is dated July 2, 2012. It is titled "oasis"[29] (her titles are never capitalized). Neely is rep-resented somewhere in "the Beverly Hills Hotel circa yesterday," wearing Céline sunglasses and a Helmut Lang top. No other part of her outfit is visible or mentioned. This is a rare (but not unique) exception to the gen-eral convention that outfit posts have at least one head-to-toe shot. The next post, dated June 29, 2012, is titled "casual friday."[30] Here, Neely poses with Yambao on an unmarked sidewalk that we can only assume is in Los

Angeles, based on the posts before and after it. She wears an Isabel Marant hoodie, Ksubi shorts, and Chloé sandals and carries a Proenza Schouler PS11 handbag. If we keep scrolling down on the page, we get to June 28, 2012. The blogger is now "at the flower shoppe"[31] wearing a Reformation dress; Ray-Ban sunglasses; Céline wedge heels; and bracelets by Hortense, Pascale Monvoisin, and Jennifer Zeuner; she holds a Balenciaga clutch. The last post on the page is titled "pink in beverly hills."[32] Neely poses near a large rosebush, presumably in Beverly Hills, wearing a Reformation Hemlock dress and 3.1 Phillip Lim heels.

In the minute or so it takes to scroll through a single *Fashion Toast* webpage (across four to five outfit posts), Neely not only jumps from one space to another (hotel, sidewalk, and flower shop), but she also goes through quick changes into completely different outfits that, given their labels, were undoubtedly purchased across a wide range of times and store locations. Yet the considerable labors of outfit posting—traveling to stores, trying on clothes, standing in line, putting together the outfit, planning and composing the outfit photo, writing the blog post, and uploading the images— are not visible anywhere. Outfit posts by Neely and other elite fashion bloggers depict personal style blogging not as labor but as the ordinary, spontaneous activities that many young women do. Bloggers' technological and aesthetic practices make it seem as if outfit posting happens in no time and with no effort at all. Outfit posting's production cycle is accelerated to the point of seeming instantaneous. And of course the distribution cycle of outfit posts—the transmission from the blogger's computer to blog audiences—is more or less instantaneous.

Because outfit posts make looking stylish seem easy and ordinary, the blogging labor of outfit posting is rendered as an easy, leisurely activity. The work of acquiring new clothes or maintaining existing clothes (such as having clothes altered or dry-cleaned) is largely absent in the mainstream fashion blogosphere. The slapdash and sometimes disheveled looks that are associated with laundry days or bad hair days are also missing in the personal style blogosphere. Stylishness—in terms of appearance and feeling—seems like a constant and universal feature of bloggers' everyday worlds. This is not to say bloggers never dress down or let their hair down. On the contrary, faux casual styles like the model off-duty look—an especially popular style right now—are ubiquitous. These casual looks, however, also emblematize the core principle of effortless chic.

It is worth noting that Neely does not mention the retail value of her clothes, though we are expected to infer from the labels that her wardrobe was expensive. The absence of any price discussion demonstrates again the class-based difference between haul vlogs and personal style blogs. Personal style bloggers follow the bourgeois taboo against money talk, whereas haul vloggers unreservedly discuss prices, especially discounts, deals, and rebates. One of the primary services that haul vloggers provide to viewers is to report on and compare prices. Not mentioning price tags helps personal style bloggers maintain their middle-class position and their status as creative people whose expressive activities are untainted by commercial matters.[33]

By making self-fashioning's time and labor invisible—as though it takes place in no time and with no effort at all—outfit posting serves two important representational functions. First, it allows personal style bloggers to position themselves in contrast to haul vloggers and similar laboring bodies. Second, it allows them to distinguish their status from people considered to have tacky tastes, those whose styles of dress, consumption, and embodiment are often stereotyped as overwrought and belabored (people who look like they are trying too hard).

Race shapes these class formations in particular ways. For Asian superbloggers, the intersection of race and class in the outfit post's construction of effortless style creates opportunities for claiming racialized elite tastes and subjectivities. Representations of Asian superbloggers' effortless blogging and self-fashioning labors counter the deep-seated perceptions of cheap Asianness discussed in previous chapters. Bloggers' practices of making labor invisible actually enable new racially classed visibilities. They provide a new visibility of Asian fashion consumers whose styles of dress and embodiment are effortless—a style of dress that is not tacky because it is not trying too hard by using a lot of logos, for example. The practices also make visible a new and elite sector of Asian fashion work that is not sweated labor (more on this below). For Asian superbloggers, making their labors invisible is a means of controlling and managing their own racialized and class-based visibility.

Taste and class distinctions are important identity markers in the personal style blogosphere, where race is ostensibly not a factor that shapes the quality of or potential for participation. When the popular magazine *Time Out London* mistook Lau for another Asian woman seen in a Google advertisement,[34] Lau seemed especially incensed that the other woman was a haul vlogger. Lau describes her as a "female 'blogger' . . . raving about . . . satchels in a YouTube haul video-esque set-up."[35] She also refers to the racial undertones of the mistake: "I remember all y'all faces and would never make a piss-poor gaffe like that." The implications of Lau's words, especially her use of scare quotes around blogger, are both that all Asians do not look alike and that they do not work alike. The class and labor distinction is an important one in the blogosphere.

As well as making visible new racialized eliteness in terms of their labor and taste identities, outfit posts' technological and aesthetic conventions are effective tools for staging bloggers' cosmopolitan mobility. In chapter 3, I argued that racialized eliteness in the blogosphere is less about the possession of luxury goods and more about the embodiment of informational mobilities (such as the extent and methods of an outfit photo's circulation and viral repurposing). Eliteness is also embodied in bloggers' cosmopolitan mobility over geographic and social spaces. From outfit post to outfit post, we see the superblogger at work or play against an adventurous, fast-moving backdrop of exotic and hip locations, at all hours of the night and day. Bloggers further emphasize their cosmopolitan subjectivity by highlighting (when possible) their relationships with fashion industry people from around the world. Outfit posts are more than expressions of personal identity. They are identity-making practices that cultivate and display bloggers' self-image, status, taste identity, and, as I discuss below, their labor identity. The spatiotemporal structure of outfit posting and its invisibilization of labor elevates bloggers' standing in fashion's labor hierarchies and its divisions of race and class.

For Asians, whose relationship to the Western fashion industry has been characterized by various temporal regimes of dominance, the shape-shifting arrangements of time and space in outfit posts offer potentially transformative methods of labor identity construction. If the work environments associated with Asian fashion labor have historically been characterized by the rigid top-down control of time, space, and worker movements, then outfit posts' individually created and controlled spatiotemporal systems provide a new context for seeing and knowing Asian fashion labor. The outfit posts by Lau, Song, Wendy Nguyen, and others portray an Asian fashion labor force that is individuated, dynamic, self-enterprising, and highly mobile.

These bloggers' outfit posts position them on the side of innovative rather than instrumental fashion work.

## For the Love of Blogging

Outfit posts provide a global media platform for new ways of seeing Asian bodies. In this still relatively new but already wildly popular and very public domain of fashion media, Asians are defining the contexts and terms of their visibility. While we saw an uptick in the numbers of Asian models represented in leading fashion magazines and runways in 2012 and 2013 (those numbers declined in 2014), even the most recognizable models are subject to the racial attitudes and whims of fashion designers, advertisers, and casting agents. Outfit posting depicts fashionable Asian bodies and style authorities we have not seen before in mainstream fashion media. In this way, Asian personal style blogs constitute a kind of alternative media sphere in which Asian cultural productions, modes of production and distribution, and the terms of audience relation are controlled in greater measure by Asian consumers.

The high status and visibility of an albeit small number of Asian superbloggers seem to demonstrate the realization of informational capitalism's promise that new technologies enhance professional and personal opportunities to take control of and shape our lives, bodies, and images. But this is a technological and aesthetic illusion created by outfit posts' spatiotemporal structure. In glossing over the actual work and work conditions, as well as the breakneck pace with which information work is now rendered, outfit posts mask the real power relations underpinning and conditioning digital labor work environments and practices. While outfit posting has transformative possibilities for presenting new cultural and labor identities for Asians in fashion contexts, it does not fundamentally alter the deeply stratified labor regimes sustaining the personal style blogosphere. Indeed, the outfit post's invisibilization of labor may be particularly problematic for Asian bloggers.

The same technological and aesthetic conventions that elevate personal style bloggers' socioeconomic status also make blogging labor unrecognizable as work—sometimes even to bloggers themselves. Superbloggers and hobbyist bloggers regularly assure readers that they are not paid to create their blogs, that their featured products are not corporate gifts, and that their sole motivation for blogging is their love of fashion and their love of sharing fashion knowledge—not the hope that blogging will lead to wage-earning, gainful employment. Bloggers' and audiences' emphasis on the importance of bloggers' love of blogging (a criterion for measuring the authenticity of bloggers' textual, sartorial, and visual expressions) has the dangerous effect of detaching work from compensation.

"I could just set up a blog myself and I could write about whatever I wanted. It was just me, doing my own thing. And I found that to be really liberating," says Jennine Jacob, founder of the personal style blog The Coveted and of Independent Fashion Bloggers, a community website for fashion bloggers.[36] Slight variations on this sentiment can be found throughout the blogosphere and in media stories about bloggers. For bloggers and their audiences, including many scholarly readers, the personal style blogosphere is fundamentally a site of self-expression, self-presentation, and self-determination. Bloggers routinely emphasize that blogging is an exercise in personal and consumer agency—the two processes are intertwined in the neoliberal era of social commerce. Blogging is fun and rewarding in large part because it "accommodates consumers' needs for recognition, freedom, and agency."[37] Outfit posting's technological and aesthetic practices reinforce this celebratory message by making blogging's actual work invisible. In the personal style blogosphere, many bloggers consider it the expression, not the construction of personal style, that matters.

But online expressions of personal style matter in sharply unequal ways. While top bloggers have millions of highly engaged, monthly visitors (who write comments, share posts, and click on links), most bloggers have little to no online traffic. Bloggers who want to build and/or maintain their audience size are pressed to meet ever-higher productivity levels at increasing speeds to accommodate the growing demands of readers who, with accelerated fashion cycles and the twenty-four-hour availability of the Internet, have come to expect a constant flow of new information. In addition, the implicit competition with other bloggers for new readers and increased traffic to their blogs also pushes bloggers to publish regularly and frequently.

This exemplifies the paradox of informational capitalism. As work conditions have become more flexible, work hours have lengthened. Rather than improving the quality of work life, informational capitalism has increased working hours for global laborers, especially middle-class workers.[38] (The working class, on the other hand, has seen an overall drop in work hours as under- and unemployment rises.) A 2007 study by the International Labor Organization found that the once-standard forty-hour workweek is fast becoming a relic of the industrial era: "About one in five—22 percent or 614.2 million workers—around the world are working more than 48 hours per week."[39]

Checking and responding to work e-mail and voice mail messages from home or while on vacation are routine activities under networked capitalism. Today, being electronically on call for work is both a self- and externally imposed job expectation for many people—including personal style bloggers. So while workers who have the luxury of individually organizing their work space and work time are hypothetically able to compress the traditional work week, work time is expanding—creeping into family, leisure, commuting, and sleeping time.

In the era of social commerce, it is not only waged workers whose productivity has risen. Largely unpaid consumers are increasingly taking part in productive processes by providing ideas, information, and marketing through social media, which is then used to create new products and services. Personal style blogging and other related digital activities do not represent the end but the culmination of capitalist production that increasingly relies on consumers' knowledge and activities for value creation, or what Alvin Toffler and George Ritzer and Nathan Jurgenson have called "prosumption."[40] Since the invention of automatic telephones and fast-food restaurants, consumers have been recruited to work in the name of increased freedom: placing our own phone calls without a switchboard operator's assistance, or filling our cups with as much or as little ice as we want at the soda machine. Today, personal style blogs and other digital fashion technologies also promise consumers increased freedom, happiness, and "swagger" (a promise one virtual fitting room makes)[41] in exchange for their personal information, time, creative activity, and emotional energy. Indeed, the internalized and external expectations that bloggers produce media content as a kind of surplus value—just out of love for blogging and fashion, rather than for payment—transforms personal style blogging into highly gendered and racialized forms of "emotion work."[42]

Emotion work and emotion management are significant aspects of personal style blogging labor. Based on blogging's highly social and personal character, superbloggers especially must repeatedly demonstrate their public engagement, openness, and approachability. Bloggers' familiarity with readers means that they are equally exposed to readers' admiration and criticism. Readers are equally as comfortable extolling bloggers' style and rising status as they are with needling them about blogging slowdowns. After the U.S. fast-fashion retailer Forever 21 released its ad campaign featuring Neely, her readers inundated her blog with congratulatory notes that suggested a level of intimacy with the Asian superblogger that is rarely offered to professional models: "to see how far u come is inspiring"; "you deserve it Rumi!"; "Rumi I'm soooo happy for you!!"; and "You have worked hard and come a long way from when you started your blog hun."[43] At the same time, if readers are unsatisfied, they are equally not shy about publicly voicing their opinions in the comments section of the blog, on Twitter, or on some other social media platform. Just as often, readers simply stop checking stagnant blogs, turning instead to other more active blogs. For superbloggers, a decline in online traffic and audience engagement jeopardizes their prominent side projects and high-profile media attention. Andrew Ross has pointed out that precarious employment is the predominant condition of labor under contemporary capitalism.[44] In some ways, successful bloggers experience greater levels of precariousness than hobbyist bloggers because they have more to lose in the way of readers, corporate sponsorships, and collaborations.

Personal style blogging's precarious conditions contribute to bloggers' anxiety-fueled compulsion to work. Consider this blog post by Susanna Lau, published on August 4, 2009: " 'Damned if you do, damned if you don't' has been running through my head for a while now ever since I received an email pointing out quite rightly so that I seem to be writing less on the blog. More specifically, volume of words is at an all time low. . . . [M]y full time job at *Dazed* [an online arts magazine] has been taking up the bulk of my time and I'd like to devote as much time to [*Dazed*] as possible because it's something that I'm driven by and want to succeed [at]." Rather than expressing irritation at the reader's demand for more of her unpaid labor, Lau is contrite. She continues: "I guess I felt I owed [an apology] to readers . . . [ellipsis in original] it does feel like a lot of the time, I'm letting people down."[45] Lau's post is notable for several reasons. First, it demonstrates the high level of audience engagement and interaction that her blog fosters. Because most personal style blogs do not attract an audience of any significant size, a slowdown or speedup in productivity will likely go unnoticed. Audience interactivity is a privilege but it is also a burden. Lau's self-monitoring and her readers' informal oversight provide some indication of the labor conditions that outfit posting techniques hide: although produced by casual and unpaid labor, personal style blogs are not outside of capitalist forces and modes of work. Like so many other knowledge and information economies, the personal style blogosphere is underpinned by what Mark Deuze has aptly described as a "hypercapitalist culture of flexible yet never-ending productivity."[46]

In fact, the personal style blogosphere's economic work ethos is embedded in the very architecture of blogs: in the counters displaying the number of times a post has been read, shared, and linked to by users; in the counters showing the numbers of comments each post receives; in the types and quality of the banner ads the blog attracts; and in the time and date stamps tracking a blogger's labor output. These architectural features embody capitalist ideologies without violating the blogosphere's principle of effortlessness, since representations of work time and effort are computer-generated rather than blogger-generated.

In addition to displaying productivity, standard design features such as time and date stamps regulate blogger productivity. Blog posts are published on an irregular schedule, but bloggers and their audiences are nevertheless concerned with publishing pace (as we saw with Lau's readers). Some blogs carefully record time down to the day, while others record it down to the minute (for example, 10:32 PM or 5:13 AM, as measured by the local time on the blogger's computer, which may differ from the local time of the reader). Precise or general, the blog post's time stamp is a standardizing managerial system that naturalizes industrial-age productivity norms and their associated values of punctuality and accumulation (of cultural and social capital in the form of blog posts, reader comments, tweets, "likes," "shares," and so on). The time stamp, more than any other blogging design feature, demonstrates that industrial-age capitalist values are embedded in networked social media sites and practices. The time stamp shows, in Aleena Chia's words, that "participation in social media is not about free-flowing creativity but about the solicitation of productivity within prescribed sociotechnical frameworks."[47]

For personal style bloggers, moreover, calls to work on the blog are implicitly calls to work on one's body and image. Blogging's technological and aesthetic practices reproduce informational capitalism's logics of continuous self-fashioning. Good citizenship under informational capitalism requires individuals to assume responsibilities for their health and welfare that the state once fulfilled (for example, by using the Internet to research, compare, and buy health insurance or to constantly update and promote one's professional profile and employability). Under informational capitalism, individuals are incited to undertake endless self-optimization procedures not only for their own good but also as a matter of social good. Popular social media forms, practices, and technologies have intensified the self-optimization imperative. They allow users to create, manage, and broadcast their public identities, reputations, and personal brands. Social media status updates facilitate self-optimization since they necessarily involve the continuous updating of visual, social, cultural, and professional identities.

For personal style bloggers, the outfit post offers both self-optimization and innovation, since blog work and self- or identity work are inextricably intertwined. Continually producing fresh new outfit posts is the defining practice through which people legitimize themselves as personal style bloggers, as individuals with informed, up-to-date sartorial knowledge. But by making invisible the processes of their knowledge work—the labor that goes into gaining sartorial knowledge and know-how and the labor of presenting them—outfit posting's technological and aesthetic conventions effectively deskill feminine knowledge and competencies at a time when they are starting to be recognized as value-creating resources in some contexts. As much as they exemplify labor's feminization, then, outfit posting and personal style blogging are also examples of women's work: those hidden socially reproductive labors that have long underpinned capitalist production.

Personal style blogging overlaps with women's work in almost every way. Just as women's work is traditionally associated with the unpaid and social labors related to liberalism's private sphere—domestic labor, child care, and reproductive labor—so personal style blogging is typically unwaged and related to the private sphere of self-fashioning. Conventionally understood as unskilled work, women's work—housekeeping, child care, sewing, cooking, and self-styling—is thought to be the natural domain of women and girls. The technological, aesthetic, and ideological construction of bloggers' real style serves at once to reinforce the naturalization of feminine skills and knowledge and to rationalize their devaluation. Indeed, a persistent theme in women's work throughout history is that it is paid and valued very little, if at all.

Women's work is also defined by its focus on the production and management of emotions. Bloggers' relationships to their audiences are characterized not by social distance (as is the case between fashion models and fashion consumers) but by what Jennifer Terry describes as remote intimacies—social and affective links sustained through media communication technologies and networks.[48] For fashion bloggers to be popular, they must produce, cultivate, and maintain remote intimacies. Audiences have to feel a connection with the bloggers' style of writing, photography, posing, and dress. These affective and technological connections constitute the blogger-reader relationships that are the basis for the personal style blogosphere—a public space in which disparately located people are tied together through their shared consumption of fashion conversations, information, images, and objects. Comments sections in even moderately active blogs are replete with grateful, admiring, and often adoring thanks to bloggers for providing inspiration and enjoyment. Readers choose personal style blogs that inspire them to freely express themselves through their sartorial style, to take risks in their fashion choices, and to seek out new and sometimes nonmainstream designers and labels. A slowdown in blog productivity, to return to the previous example of Lau, means that bloggers are producing less inspiration and less enjoyment. Tellingly, Lau responded to her fan's disappointment through more emotional labor; in the e-mail message that prompted the post, in Lau's blog post, and her readers' response to her post, she engaged in exchanges of guilt, reassurance, and support with her readers.

Since I began reading and researching personal style blogs in 2008, I have never come across a case in which a male blogger—of any sexuality—apologized for his productivity. Recall that when Yambao's readers begin pressuring him for more and more frequent content, rather than apologizing to his readers, he chastises them: "[I] sometimes feel like packing up and calling it a day because of the horrible, unreasonable demands by [blog] audiences." Continuing this line of thought, Yambao clearly identifies the blogger-reader relationship he is interested in: "My blog is my ship. I'm the captain and my readers are my passengers. Thank you for joining me aboard but nonetheless, the ship will still go on whether there are passengers or not. . . . Want to go to another place outside my itinerary? Then pack your spring/summer 2011 Dior, your Karlie Kloss barbie doll and take the Royal Caribbean cruise line instead."[49] Male bloggers sometimes explain blogging slowdowns or hiatuses, informing readers of them ahead of time. Usually, these notices are accompanied with the promise that regular blogging will resume on a set date. But male bloggers do not apologize for their absence, much less express guilt, shame, or anxiety about it. To be sure, not all female bloggers articulate an emotional obligation to their work either, but it is only female bloggers who express regret about their productivity levels. Affective labor is an essential component of all personal style blogging, but gendered expectations that women care for others also places higher demands on female bloggers.

Like the more traditional modes of women's work, personal style blogging's economic relations are also obscured. Whether or not blogging yields financial benefits, personal style blogging first and foremost involves processes of social reproduction that appear to operate outside of capitalism. The personal style blogosphere's primary activities include the production of taste identities, communities, and relationships through visual, textual, formal, and sartorial expressions about personal style, fashion media, and fashion commodities. While these activities are increasingly financialized, the social and emotional character of personal style blogging and its technological and aesthetic practices obscure the conditions and processes of blogging labor. Furthermore, blogging's relations to capital are concealed by the conventional understanding that real work means wage labor and by the stereotype that fashion-minded people are hyperconsumers rather than creators or producers. But, as we know from feminist Marxist scholars of labor, feminized modes of social reproduction enable masculinized economic production.[50] To paraphrase Kylie Jarrett, women's work produces the social relations and social order that support capitalist production.[51]

Outfit posting's technological and aesthetic conventions contribute to the feminization of blogging work. By portraying personal style blogging as effortless, spontaneous, and self-gratifying acts of self-expression, much of the physical, emotional, and intellectual work of blogging is obscured. The same point can be extended to many other kinds of creative labor. But while the construction of blogging labor as effortless work has helped to elevate the status of nonwaged and unpaid bloggers by giving blogging the prestige of creative sectors it has also had the effect of deskilling it in ways that allow it to be seen as just something that girls—or feminized, frivolous fashion people—do. For Asians, the notion of effortless labor has particular racial consequences.

The racialized accusations of a cheap style, cheap work ethic, and cheap success that continue to be made about some of the most influential Asian bloggers, as discussed in chapter 1, suggests that the promise of creative individualism under informational economies is not evenly distributed. The idea of creative individualism is premised, in part, on the notion that increased freedom and creativity to organize work space and time go hand in hand with workers' increased autonomy and individualization. This is the allure of do-it-yourself projects like personal style blogs: they provide opportunities to redo and remake ourselves as individuals who have a distinctive approach to style and a distinctive perspective about fashion, style, and taste. But for Asian bloggers, racial stereotypes about Asian labor color perceptions of them as an unindividuated racial group.

Labor's invisibilization is particularly problematic for Asian bloggers because it resurrects the specter of Asians' historical role in capitalism and, more specifically, in the fashion industry as unskilled, cheap labor. Blogging's conventions might create the image that bloggers have a natural facility for style. But for Asian bloggers, labor's invisibilization potentially deskills and devalues their knowledge and competencies in ways that reinforce economic racial stereotypes and dominant power structures.

When Asian superbloggers' cheap morality and work ethic are cited to justify the devaluation of personal style blogging, what is revealed is a racial division that has long structured women's work. In other words, gender has not been the only basis for defining women's work as a category of exploited labor. What's more, it is not only performed by one gender. Women's work is more accurately understood as an occupational expression of a social status that has long reflected and reinforced dominant racial attitudes and hierarchies.

In the 1880s, for example, large numbers of Asian men performed women's work. In California and Hawaii during this time, most domestic servants were Chinese, Japanese, and Filipino men.[52] In addition to domestic service, many Asian men were employed in feminine labor markets as laundry workers, cooks, and restaurant servers. Cultural stereotypes about feminine Asian men and economic stereotypes that associated them with cheap labor helped to keep Asian men out of higher-paying masculine labor markets. In addition, U.S. immigration acts targeting Asian women, like the Immigration Act of 1875 that barred Chinese, Japanese, and Mongolian immigrants, severely reduced the number of Asian women who might have taken jobs in the domestic sector.[53]

Historically, the racialization of women's work has also benefited white women. As Evelyn Nakano Glenn explains, the nineteenth-century "cult of domesticity" identified the home as the appropriate place for white women, whose proper roles were as wives, mothers, and "household managers." This increased "the need for additional domestic servants in the house-holds of the white middle class."[54] Thus, the making of middle-class white womanhood depended on the subordinated labors of men and women of color. Glenn writes: "Nineteenth century middle-class white women helped to elaborate and refine, rather than overthrow, the domestic 'code.' Instead of questioning the inequitable gender division of labor, white middle-class women delegated the more onerous household tasks onto women of color."[55] Despite major changes in the economy and shifts in labor organization in the twentieth century, the racial stratifications within women's work in the United States persisted.

When white women did enter the labor market, they found jobs in clean, clerical, administrative, and retail occupations. The dirty work was left to women of color. In the home, women of color did the washing, cooking, and cleaning. In manufacturing jobs, Black and Mexican women were hired as sweepers and machine scrubbers. In tobacco factories of the 1910s and 1920s, white women packaged cigarettes while Black women stripped tobacco leaves, earning about one-third of white women's salaries.[56] Today, racialized women's work is globalized, as can be seen in the high proportion of Asian women in labor sectors involving biological and social reproduction—Filipina domestic workers, nannies, and nurses; Indian surrogate mothers; Southeast Asian sex workers; and Filipina and Thai mail-order wives.[57]

In some ways, Asian superbloggers' ascendency suggests that this new fashion labor market is more racially equitable, but top-tier Asian bloggers are not the whole story of the personal style blogosphere. In fact, as I have noted throughout this book, they are only a small part of it. The personal style blogosphere's upper echelon is still largely white, female, straight, and normatively gender-presenting. While Asian superbloggers have apparently made it, their numbers are extremely small, and they bear the brunt of the moral and ethical criticism against bloggers—much of which is racialized (such as the accusation of being cheap labor). White bloggers' racial and class privilege buffers them from such charges. Rather than being an example of a more equitable labor market with free expression and free workers, the personal style blogosphere—as my examination of it has sought to demonstrate—has the same occupational segregation as industrial economies that are built into new digital economies.

# Coda.
## All in the Eyes

When the television journalist and personality Julie Chen publicly revealed that she had had eyelid surgery in her twenties in an effort to increase her professional potential, her story exemplified what is for many Asian Americans an all-too-familiar experience with mainstream perceptions about Asian eyes. Chen recalled one news director telling her: "You will never be on this anchor desk, because you're Chinese. . . . Because of your Asian eyes . . . when you're on camera and you're interviewing someone, you look disinterested, you look bored because your eyes are so heavy, they are so small."[1] Chen also remembered a "big-time" talent agent refusing to represent her unless she had the operation. These moments represent a common racial reality for many Asians in the workforce: their very bodies become obstacles to their career advancement. The physical characteristics of Asian eyes racially marked Chen as a bored and unengaged journalist, a bad employee, and a bad Asian woman. By prompting Chen to undergo cosmetic surgery, people were asking her to remake her image from an uninterested to an interested Asian woman.

Chen's experiences reflect long-held associations of Asian physical features with negative personal characteristics. The encounters she recalled were more than twenty years old by the time she publicly revealed them, but Asian eyes continue to function as a visible sign and stigma of race in the mainstream Western social and cultural imaginary. This is the very reason that Susanna Lau hides or strikes out her eyes in her outfit photos. Yet from this experience of external and internalized anti-Asian racism, an unlikely but highly influential cultural form and practice was invented: the Susie Bubble pose. In Lau's bodily act of negotiating her racial ambivalence, she takes control of how others see her. The pose directs viewers to "Look at the outfit . . . not the face."[2]

The Susie Bubble pose with its signature elsewhere gaze is an act of image management not unlike the identity work Chen and so many other people of color perform as a means of building or enhancing their chances for social, economic, and professional opportunities. At the same time, the Susie Bubble pose represents a new form and practice of racial identity construction created by Asian superbloggers. Through their blogging activities, Asian superbloggers move race from a group-based category (with shared social identities, experiences, and struggles) to a distinctive personal brand that is both individuating and socially, culturally, and economically productive. Asian superbloggers' self-produced taste performances go a long way toward reconfiguring the significance of Asian eyes in popular media discourse.

Today, Asian superbloggers' Asian eyes are interpreted not as physical markers of racial inferiority but as a set of finely honed skills of aesthetic and sartorial judgment. The headline of a New York Times feature story on Lau emphasizes her "eye for detail."[3] The article continues the ocular metaphor, describing Lau's "magpie eye for minutiae: the crosshatching in a swatch of silk; the latticework on a Nigerian shirt." Lau has described her mode of blogging as a kind of labor that centrally involves her eyes: "My eye, my point of view, a certain taste, a certain way of documenting and presenting fashion; that's supposedly what I'm selling."[4] In countless more print and web pages of fashion news articles, blogs, and reader comments, Asian superbloggers' eyes for fashion, style, design, and trends are praised as "well-trained," "discerning," "keen," and "sharp." In each of these descriptions, the significance of Asian eyes lies not in what they look like but in what they can do. If we understand perceptions about Asian eyes as a measure of racial attitudes and as a site of discursive productions about gendered Asian difference, then these latest interpretations of Asian superbloggers' eyes indicate that superbloggers are effecting a transformation of racial signification along the lines that Wendy Chun describes: in the fashion blogosphere, it is not so much "the *what* of race" but "the *how* of race"[5] that is meaningful.

Asian superbloggers' taste performances in their style stories, their distinctive and brand-name blogger poses, their outfit photos, and their outfit posts are practices of racial identity construction and stereotype management. In these digital acts of self-composure, Asian superbloggers use a wide range of discursive, communicative, technological, aesthetic, sartorial, cultural, and commercial practices to fashion new styles of racial embodiment in which Asianness is recoded as individual style. Asian superbloggers' taste work practices make clear that race not only continues to matter in the new fashion media and market but that, if styled properly as a legitimate difference, Asianness has potentially high cultural and commercial value.

The razor's edge on which Asian superbloggers produce and perform their taste identities as a legitimate difference—a style of racialized embodiment and taste that stands out but does not stick out as radically different—sets both the conditions and limits of these bloggers' digital practices. Asian superbloggers embody the paradoxes of their fraught position as a racialized labor force in a deracialized informational economy; as beneficiaries of widespread cultural and commercial shifts that have given rise to the Asian moment in fashion and in global consumer capitalism more broadly, while also being targets of racial discrimination that are rooted in stereotypes about Asian cheapness (in its many forms and registers); and as an elite class of Asian fashion worker whose creative labors are at once distinct from, overlap with, and depend on the sweated labors of an earlier class of industrial Asian fashion (and electronics assembly) workers. The systems and processes that continue to associate cheap labor with Asianness, regardless of the worker's actual racial identity, manifest older and deeper structures of racialized labor that shape contemporary digital media economies and the new social hierarchies inherent in them.

In this book I have argued that in all of the excitement about the digital democratization of the fashion media and fashion industry—demonstrated to a great extent by the rise of Asian superbloggers—the latest Asian fashion worker formation is not indicative of fashion capitalism's newfound social diversity. On the contrary, it reveals the implicit conditionality and limits of mainstream liberal paradigms of racial inclusion and tolerance.

The personal style blogosphere, like many other digital media environments, is based on the logic of liberal multicultural democracy. Increased access to and participation in media technologies and sites by historically minoritized people are celebrated as marks of social political achievement. Thus Asian superbloggers' high levels of visibility, recognition, and success—at the highest levels of contemporary fashion media—have been interpreted as a digital democratic revolution. But this additive model of democracy not only obscures the fashion media complex's sociopolitical asymmetries, it also enables them to persist. This contradiction is constitutive of liberal multiculturalism. As Patricia Richards writes, "the rationale behind neoliberal multiculturalism is less about changing racial hierarchies than it is about creating self-governing . . . subjects that will not challenge [dominant] political-economic goals."[6] The rise of an elite class of Asian bloggers into the upper echelons of fashion media does not signal the democratization of fashion media but rather the increased incorporation into the fashion establishment of those previously excluded from it, people who now serve as an unpaid and underpaid labor force contributing to its production. Asian superbloggers' conditional inclusion in the fashion establishment—conditioned on their expression and embodiment of legitimate difference—paradoxically confirms and perpetuates a tangled set of hierarchies (of race, class, size, and so on) under the cover of multicultural diversity.

Drawing on their considerable resources, connections, and knowledge, Asian superbloggers have the capacity to negotiate their fraught positions in the fashion blogosphere. As I have discussed throughout this book, many of the core practices and conventions of personal style blogging that have been widely adopted across diverse sites of fashion media were invented or popularized by Asian superbloggers. While personal style blogging practices are located in a much broader technological, cultural, and commercial context framed by the globalization of cute aesthetic commodities, the rapid ascension of Asian luxury markets, and the rise of social commerce, these practices have also enabled the creation of a different context of, and new opportunities for, racialized labor in the elite sites of the fashion media complex.

In parsing out and analyzing each of the major elements of personal style blogging—style stories, fashion blogger poses, outfit photos, and outfit posts—I have sought to uncover the racial, gender, class, and sexual dimensions of this new mode and structure of Asian fashion labor. As I have shown, Asian superbloggers construct their class-based, gendered, and queer Asianness in various ways—as a flexible asset enhancing their identity, as Aimee Song does; as a transcendent style of fabulousness, as Bryan Grey Yambao does; and as personal brands of embodiment as exemplified by the Susie Bubble and BryanBoy poses. Superbloggers' articulations of Asianness are structured around a model of racialized eliteness that is valuable and, indeed, value-producing because it is mobile, imitable, and approachable rather than exclusive and out of reach. Superbloggers' considerable audiences, or taste communities, are the result of successfully capitalizing on and perpetuating the memetic culture of social media. Their social and economic mobility is driven by their informational mobility—the widespread reproduction and circulation of their images and identities through outfit photos, outfit posts, and blogger poses. In all these ways, Asian superbloggers have managed to move their racial difference from the particular to the universal. Superbloggers' cultural, communicative, and computational practices work to rearticulate Asianness as a distinctive but not radically different personal brand, an exotic but not foreign commodity.

As I finished writing this book, an article by Robin Givhan, a fashion journalist and winner of the Pulitzer Prize, called "The Golden Era of 'Fashion Blogging' Is Over" sparked another round of predictions about the death of the fashion blog and fashion blogger. Such predictions have been a nearly constant feature of each stage of the fashion blog's brief but intense history. When read carefully, though, Givhan's article is clearly not forecasting the demise of the fashion blog, but its opposite. Givhan observes that the fashion blog's communicative practices; representational conventions; and cultural, ideological, and commercial value systems now extend far beyond the blogosphere into the very heart of the fashion establishment: "Legacy editors [are] watching the runway from the backside of their iPhone cameras as they [share] their up-close views with the virtual world. Critics, instead of reserving their droll commentary for post-show dinner patter, now [spew] it fast and succinctly on Twitter."[7] The fashion blog is not dying, it is joining the mainstream. The fashion blogosphere is now the fashion world. And if the popular media accounts of elite fashion bloggers' rise to household-name status are accurate—albeit probably only in fashionably inclined households—then the fashion blogosphere also pervades more and more of everyday culture.

The persistent predictions of the fashion blog's death reflect the precariousness of the medium. Like all social media platforms, interfaces, and designs, fashion blogs are constantly being remade and altered by system updates; new features for media production, sharing, and privacy; design tweaks; and emerging platforms. For Asian superbloggers, the fashion blog's inherent instability is also experienced in another way. Their fraught position as racialized labor in a supposedly deracialized media economy in which their elite standing is continually challenged by racial economic stereotypes of Asian cheapness, not to mention the fickle tastes of fashion consumers and social media users, means that they are always at risk of the Internet's equivalent of death—cultural irrelevance.

Givhan describes Asian superbloggers as part of "the first generation of bloggers"—she specifically names Bryan Grey Yambao, Susanna Lau, and Tommy Ton.[8] Incredibly, these bloggers are not only still blogging, but they are now recognized as (minor) members of the fashion establishment. Their longevity is facilitated by their structurally advantageous position in relation to the broader cultural, economic, and technological shifts I have described above. But it is also due to Asian superbloggers' deftness in navigating and negotiating the ever-changing terrain of digital fashion media (in large part because they helped to create it). The Asian superbloggers who are the focus of this book have never just taken and posted photos of themselves wearing clothes. They have always engaged in the production of diverse types of media content (such as fashion commentary, reportage, and marketing copy and images) and a wide range of social and commercial relationships. The oft-repeated advice[9] to new bloggers to look beyond themselves and their wardrobes; to have a unique and authentic point of view about fashion beyond their personal tastes and style; to write original articles; and to take an entrepreneurial approach to their blogs by monetizing them, creating a personal brand, and carefully tracking their productivity, web traffic, return on investment, and related analytic data describe the activities that Asian superbloggers—the first-generation bloggers—have been doing since the early days of the fashion blogosphere. The personal style blog as a cultural form and commercial product will, no doubt, continue to change and evolve, driven in large measure by the efforts of Asian superbloggers.

My intention with this book is not to provide a comprehensive account of the Asian superblogger phenomenon. Given the rapid pace at which social media environments change, such a goal is impossible and also not useful. In focusing on the deeper-seated structures of the Asian superblogger phenomenon—the cultural and social economy of digital fashion media spaces, interactions, hierarchies, opportunities, and rewards—I hope that *Asians Wear Clothes on the Internet* offers a useful critical framework for analyzing the always dynamic relations of race, gender, class, and labor to the digital fashion media.

# Notes

## Introduction

1. Joos, "She's Bubblicious."
2. La Ferla, "An Eye for Detail, and Plenty of Pop."
3. Quoted in Gortan, "Fashion Blogs Making Little Miss a Hit."
4. Strugatz, "To Pay or Not to Pay: A Closer Look at the Business of Blogging."
5. Rosman, "Super 'Selfies.' "
6. Apatoff, "Want Your Valentine's Gift to Top Beyoncé's?"
7. S. Lau, "About."
8. "Wendy Nguyen." As with many children of garment workers, Nguyen helped her parents with their work at home. Her job was to "flip collars and pockets."
9. W. Nguyen, "Spring Romance."
10. Entwistle, The Fashioned Body, 4.
11. In this book, I use *fashion industry* as an umbrella term encompassing a broad range of designers, retailers, marketers, advertisers, journalists, and textile and apparel manufacturers, as well as their go-betweens who work to produce, promote, and sell clothes.
12. Bourdieu, "The Sociologist in Question," 27.
13. Bourdieu, Distinction, 6.
14. Affiliate links are hyperlinks that have an additional function. When a viewer clicks on affiliate links, the links take them to another website as well as place "cookies," or small files of data specific to a particular retailer, on the viewer's computer. If the viewer then buys any item from that retailer's site, the blogger earns a cut—typically a 4–8 percent commission. Superbloggers who attract

tens of thousands of readers to their blog posts can make as much as $50,000 a month on affiliate linking alone, according to one article on Fashionista.com (Phelan, "How Personal Style Bloggers Are Raking in Millions"). The article observes that taking into account superbloggers' brand partnerships, guest appearances, and freelance writing and lecturing, they "have the potential to make millions of dollars a year." Of the five superbloggers cited in the article, four are Asian (Craig, Song, Yambao, and Lau).

15. Amed, "The Business of Blogging: Tommy Ton."
16. Quoted in Kansara, "The Business of Blogging: Style Bubble."
17. Florida, "Cities and the Creative Class in Asia."
18. Peter McLaren ("Multiculturalism and the Postmodern Critique") has argued that within the framework of liberal multiculturalism, race and ethnicity are treated as lifestyle issues and cultural choices rather than structural features of society or social group categories.
19. Considine, "For Asian-American Web Stars, Many Web Fans"; Moy, "The Asian Whizkid's Sibling?"; R. Wong, "A Billion Hits and Counting."
20. Lam, "The 'Bamboo Ceiling.'"
21. Kan, "Diane von Furstenberg on China"; Davies, "Asian Century Will Dominate Global Financial Markets."
22. According to the Wikimedia Foundation, which operates Wikipedia, 80 to 90 percent of its editors are male and most are white. Siko Bouterse, director of community resources at Wikimedia Foundation confirmed on *Forum with Michael Krasny* that "the typical Wikipedia editor is a white man in his 30s." ("Wikipedia's Gender and Race Gaps.") See also Wikipedia, "Wikipedia: Systemic Bias" and Knibbs, "Wikipedia Has a Gender Problem."
23. Nakamura, "Don't Hate the Player, Hate the Game," "Economies of Digital Production in East Asia," and "Indigenous Circuits"; Moallem, "Carpets and Computers" and "Nation-on-the Move"; Digital Cultures Research Lab, "DCRL Questions: Nishant Shah"; Vora, "The Transmission of Care."
24. Tu, *The Beautiful Generation*, 9.
25. Quoted in Smith, "More Asian Models on Fashion's Big Stages."
26. La Ferla, "An Eye for Detail, and Plenty of Pop."
27. Collings, "Aimee Song's Secrets to Blogging Success."
28. Throughout this book, unless otherwise noted, currency amounts using the dollar sign refer to U.S. dollars.
29. "The $8 Trillion Internet Economy."
30. Terranova, "Free Labor," 39.
31. Jacob, "Actually, Bloggers DO Influence People to Buy."
32. "Need a Product Endorsement?"
33. Phelan, "How Personal Style Bloggers Are Raking in Millions."
34. Petersen, "Success Story, Japanese American Style."
35. Egan, "Little Asia on the Hill."

36. Egan, "Little Asia on the Hill."
37. Bourdieu, "The Metamorphosis of Tastes," 111.
38. Petersen, "Success Story, Japanese American Style."
39. "Success Story of One Minority Group in the U.S.," *U.S. News and World Report*.
40. Lessin, *Behind the Labels*.
41. Lessin, *Behind the Labels*.
42. George Lipsitz's *Possessive Investment in Whiteness* provides a lucid and detailed account of the economic decline most Americans experienced in the deindustrialization of the 1980s and 1990s.
43. For more on the impact of neoliberal political economic policies on the international division of labor, see Duggan, *Twilight of Equality*; Harvey, *A Brief History of Neoliberalism*.
44. Lipsitz, *Possessive Investment in Whiteness*, 94.
45. Choy and Tajima-Peña, *Who Killed Vincent Chin?*
46. A. Benjamin, "Top 5 Highest-Grossing Fashion Bloggers."
47. Marcus, "Bryan Boy Earns Handsome Rewards for His Blogging."
48. Yambao's stated earnings are widely believed to be an underestimate by a blogger who has built a reputation as a passion-driven artist.
49. Strugatz, "To Pay or Not to Pay."
50. Jenkins et al., *Confronting the Challenges of Participatory Culture*; Watkins, *The Young and the Digital*.
51. Quoted in Soong, "Democracy via Technology?"
52. Quoted in Soong, "Democracy via Technology?"
53. McPherson is now based in Italy but was raised in New York.
54. Thomas, "Are Black Fashion Bloggers Being Ignored?"
55. Florida, Mellander, and Stolarick, "Creativity and Prosperity," 7.
56. Sherman, "Google Wants to Be More Fashionable."
57. Ross, *Nice Work If You Can Get It*, 10.
58. Andrejevic, "Estranged Free Labor," 158.
59. Quoted in Woo, *Glass Ceilings and Asian Americans*, 49.
60. Hesmondhalgh, "User-Generated Content, Free Labour and the Cultural Industries," 271. Indonesia is in fact one of the top ten textile exporting countries in the world; more than 90 percent of its textile products are garments, fabric, and yarn (see "Roadmap for Indonesia's Textile and Textile Products Industry").
61. Jewish immigrants' important role in New York City's garment district is memorialized by a statue of a Jewish tailor on Seventh Avenue (also known as Fashion Avenue) between 39th and 40th Streets.
62. See Chin, *Sewing Women*.
63. Chinatown Study Group, "Chinatown Report: 1969," 52. See also Chin, *Sewing Women*, 19.
64. Chin, *Sewing Women*, 122 and 159.
65. See Bonacich and Appelbaum, *Behind the Label*; Cline, *Overdressed*.

66. Cline, *Overdressed*, 37.

67. Chin, *Sewing Women*, 19.

68. Bonacich and Appelbaum, *Behind the Label*, 4.

69. Cline, *Overdressed*, 55.

70. Spener, Gereffi, and Bair, "Introduction: The Apparel Industry and North American Economic Integration," 5.

71. Bonacich and Appelbaum, *Behind the Label*, 181.

72. Bonacich and Appelbaum, *Behind the Label*, 166.

73. Being coy about his age is just one of the strategies of self-composure that Yambao employs to construct his identity as a fashion celebrity. As with most of these strategies, there is always a degree of tongue-in-cheek humor involved in his self-identification.

74. Yambao, "You Owe It to Your Fans."

75. Yambao, "For the Love of Work."

76. Yambao, "You Owe It to Your Fans."

77. Lessin, *Behind the Labels*.

78. Crary, 24/7, 62.

79. "AAFA Releases Apparel Stats 2012 Report."

80. "Apparel Export Shows 9.7% Decline in Dollar Terms in First Month of FY 2012–13."

81. Wallace, "70 Immigrants Found in Raid on Sweatshop."

82. Bonacich and Applebaum, *Behind the Label*, 165.

83. See Lessin, *Behind the Labels*.

84. Ong, *Neoliberalism as Exception*.

85. Joslin, et al., "Gap, Inc.," 2.

86. Lessin, *Behind the Labels*.

87. Lipsitz, *Possessive Investment in Whiteness*, 74.

88. Worker Rights Consortium, "Global Wage Trends for Apparel Workers, 2001–2011."

89. Center for American Progress, "Garment Worker Wages Declined in Majority of Top Apparel-Exporting Countries over the Last Decade, New Study Reveals."

90. Barthes, *The Fashion System*.

### Chapter 1. The Taste and Aftertaste for Asian Superbloggers

1. Tate, "Marc Jacobs Wrapped around Finger of This Gay Filipino Blogger."

2. At the time, Jacobs was also creative director of the French heritage label Louis Vuitton.

3. Spiridakis, "The Next Level."

4. Keil, "Letter from the Editor," 2.

5. Elton, "Lanvin Paris Fall 2010."

6. "Moxsie's Nod to Blogger Susie Bubble Is a Sign of the Times."

7. Nguyen and Tu, Introduction, 13.

8. For examples of the operation of this discursive construction, see Cowles, "Jason Wu Discusses the Asian American Fashion 'Movement'"; Davies, "Asian Century Will Dominate Global Financial Markets"; J. Lee, "Meet the New Asian Superrich"; Y. Lee, "In America, a New Asian Creative Class"; Matsumoto, "Stinky, Spicy, and Delicious"; Menkes, "The Asian Wave"; Moy, "The Asian Whizkid's Sibling?"; Ozersky, "Talented, Young and Asian American"; E. Wilson, "Asian Americans Climb Fashion Industry" and "Documenting a Growing Force in Fashion."

9. "Philippine Blogger Stirs a Fashion Revolution."

10. Tate, "Marc Jacobs Wrapped around Finger of This Gay Filipino Blogger."

11. Bourdieu, "The Metamorphosis of Taste," 111.

12. Tchen, *New York before Chinatown*, xx.

13. For more on particular instances of Asian chic trends in Western fashion and their significances, see Kondo, *About Face* and "Interview with Nirmal Puwar"; Maira, "Henna and Hip Hop" and "Indo-Chic"; McLarney, "Burqa in Vogue"; Pham, "Paul Poiret's Magical Techno-Oriental Fashions (1911)"; Puwar, "Multicultural Fashion"; Tu, *The Beautiful Generation*.

14. Yano, *Pink Globalization*, 2–3. For a history of cute culture, see Kinsella, "Cuties in Japan."

15. Yano, *Pink Globalization*, 20.

16. Yano, *Pink Globalization*, 37.

17. See "Cute Power!"

18. Pokémon refers to a fictional world of 719 species created by Satoshi Tajiri for Nintendo. The franchise includes video games, books, trading cards, and other toys.

19. Boyes, "UK Paper Names Top Game Franchises."

20. "The Best People of 1999."

21. Yano, *Pink Globalization*, 6.

22. Allison, "Portable Monsters and Commodity Cuteness: Pokemon as Japan's New Global Power," 384.

23. "Cute Power!"

24. Joseph Nye coined the term soft power in *Bound to Lead* and *Soft Power*.

25. I recognize that cute culture encompasses a wide range of qualities from the erotic cute to the creepy cute, but the link between the power of cute culture and Asia's soft power rests on the more traditional characteristics of cute. It is the sweeter and racially gendered connotations of Asian cute that have its critics bristling over the Orientalist implications of this cultural power for Asia's status in the global economy.

26. Yano, *Pink Globalization*, 8.

27. Hjorth, "Odours of Mobility," 45.

28. Lukács, "The Labor of Cute."

29. Lukács, "The Labor of Cute."

30. Quoted in Lukács, "The Labor of Cute."
31. Lukács, "The Labor of Cute."
32. Lukács, "The Labor of Cute."
33. Lukács, "The Labor of Cute."
34. Yambao, "Celebrity Schmelebrity."
35. S. Lau, "FAQ."
36. Yambao, "Holt Renfrew Unveils Fashion Blogger Windows."
37. Quoted in K. Lau, "Meet Tyra's Protege."
38. Though they have never been substantiated, rumors about Yambao's overspending and speculations about credit card schemes have followed him since he began his blog in 2004.
39. Larson, "The Growing Allure of Designed-in-China Fashion."
40. Tu, *The Beautiful Generation*, 11.
41. Tu, *The Beautiful Generation*, 12.
42. Pham, " 'Susie Bubble Is a Sign of the Times.' "
43. FlorCruz, "Shanghai Surpasses New York for Luxury Goods Buying, Despite Chinese Austerity Drive"; Larmer, "Shoppers' Republic of China"; Leonhardt, "Can the Chinese Discover the Urge to Splurge?"; Monaghan and Kaiman, "Why Global Recovery Could Depend on China's Taste for Luxury."
44. In 2014, the French luxury brand Balenciaga (as noted above, now under the directorship of an Asian American designer) introduced a China-only collection of thirteen looks designed exclusively for the Chinese market (see Hyland, "Balenciaga Unveils China-Exclusive Looks in Beijing"). Before Balenciaga, the Italian luxury label Prada and the British shoe designer Rupert Sanderson also created fashion collections tailored for, if not actually to, Chinese bodies and fashion tastes.
45. Boudreau, "U.S. Retailers Tailor Fashions to Asian Tastes."
46. "Thailand Named Emerging 'Hot Spot.' "
47. "HKEx Monthly Market Highlights—November 2011."
48. Gustini, "Why Luxury Brands Love the Hong Kong Stock Exchange"; Dishman, "Prada's IPO"; Paton, "Coach to List on Hong Kong Stock Exchange."
49. See, for example, Chang, "Asia Major" and Branigan, "Chinese Models Stride the Catwalk as the West Eyes China's Rich Fashion Market."
50. See Smith, "More Asian Models on Fashion's Big Stages" and Yang, "Why the Rise of Asia in Fashion Isn't as Beautiful as It Seems."
51. Pham, " 'Diversity' in Fashion Will Never Be Enough."
52. I have written about yellowface in fashion on Threadbared (see Pham, "Unintentionally Eating the Other" and "The Truth of Lagerfeld's Idea of China").
53. Barnes and Lescault, "Millennials Drive Social Commerce."
54. Indvik, "Fashion Retailer Responds to Facebook Fans' Call for 'Real Women' in Photos."
55. Bourne, "Designers Are Finally Creating Clothes for Real Women."
56. "LOFT Employees Model Looks on Facebook."

57. Bourne, "Designers Are Finally Creating Clothes for Real Women."
58. Menkes, "Working the Crowd."
59. Beusman, "Rick Owens Is the Latest Designer to Replace Models with 'Real Women.'"
60. Gurrieri and Cherrier, "Queering Beauty"; Heiss, "Locating the Bodies of Women and Disability in Definitions of Beauty"; Johnston and Taylor, "Feminist Consumerism and Fat Activists."
61. boyd, "Why Youth <3 Social Network Sites," 131. See also Hodkinson and Lincoln, "Online Journals as Virtual Bedrooms?"; Livingstone, "On the Relation between Audiences and Publics"; Papacharissi, "The Presentation of Self in Virtual Life"; Reed, "'My Blog Is Me'"; Schau and Gilly, "We Are What We Post?".
62. Marwick and boyd, "I Tweet Honestly, I Tweet Passionately," 115.
63. Quoted in Kansara, "The Business of Blogging: Style Bubble."
64. Quoted in Smith, "More Asian Models on Fashion's Big Stages."
65. In the context of fashion, representative texts include Hebdige, Subculture; Mercer, "Black Hair/Style Politics"; Miller, Slaves to Fashion; Ramirez, The Woman in the Zoot Suit.
66. Bourdieu, Distinction, 56.
67. Bourdieu, Distinction, 56.
68. Cardiff, "We All Know Fashion Bloggers Have No Integrity, Right?"
69. Phelan, "Can You Trust the Editorial Integrity of Personal Style Blogs?"
70. Menkes, "The Circus of Fashion," 91.
71. Menkes, "The Circus of Fashion," 91.
72. Menkes, "The Circus of Fashion," 91.
73. Menkes, "The Circus of Fashion," 91.
74. Lau, "Fashion Blogger Susie Bubble Makes a Case in Defense of Street Style."
75. Givhan, "Everyone's a Fashion Critic," 316.
76. Chow, The Protestant Ethnic and the Spirit of Capitalism, 29.
77. Bourdieu, "Haute Couture and Haute Culture."
78. Bourdieu, "Haute Couture and Haute Culture," 136, 135.
79. Fabian, Time and the Other.
80. Lorentzen, "Is Fashion Blogging Dead?"; Odell, "Why the Era of Personal Style Blogs Must Come to an End"; Givhan, "The Golden Era of 'Fashion Blogging' Is Over."
81. Odell, "Finding the Next Bryanboy."
82. See Kim, "The Racial Triangulation of Asian Americans"; Glenn, Unequal Freedom; and Jung, Coolies and Cane.
83. Hamlin, Gridneff, and Davison, "Ethiopia Becomes China's China in Global Search for Cheap Labor."
84. Nakamura, "Don't Hate the Player, Hate the Game."
85. Chow, The Protestant Ethnic and the Spirit of Capitalism, 34.
86. Clancy, "Asia 'To Take Over Half Luxury Goods Market.'"

87. Quoted in Clancy, "Asia 'To Take Over Half Luxury Goods Market.'"
88. "Page Law 1875."
89. Representative examples include Stanley Kubrick's *Full Metal Jacket* (1986), David Lynch's *Inland Empire* (2006), and the numerous revivals of *Miss Saigon* (the latest one opened in London in 2014).
90. Harte, "Plain Language from Truthful James."
91. See Okihiro, *Cane Fires*; Palumbo-Liu, *Asian/American.*
92. See Menkes, "Balenciaga Points East with Wang"; Mau, "New Evidence that Alexander Wang's Chinese Connections May Have Helped Land Him Balenciaga"; Cowles, "Will Carine Roitfeld Join Alexander Wang at Balenciaga?"
93. Mau, "New Evidence that Alexander Wang's Chinese Connections May Have Helped Land Him Balenciaga."
94. Pham, "Couture's Chinese Culture Shock."
95. Quoted in S. Lau, "Round the Table."
96. For more on "racial capitalism," see Leong, "Racial Capitalism"; Melamed, *Represent and Destroy*. Also, while they don't use the term *racial capitalism*, Chow's *The Protestant Ethnic and the Spirit of Capitalism* and Amy Hasinoff's "Fashioning Race for the Free Market on *America's Next Top Model*" are great analyses of neoliberal capitalist articulations of race. Hasinoff's essay illustrates how race has become a marketable commodity in the form of flexible labor power. She argues that the television show encourages Black and mixed raced competitors "to turn on and off" markers of racial difference when it is economically advantageous (337). Chow's book, discussed elsewhere in this chapter, provides a trenchant analysis of how biopolitical transactions that are organized around race, ethnicity, and gender hierarchies of value have become the bedrock of global capitalism, in which human rights as well as human bodies are exchanged for profit.
97. Robinson, *Black Marxism*, 23.
98. Wallerstein, *The Modern World-System I*, 119.
99. Quoted in Morris, *Swindon Fifty Years Ago, More or Less*, 49.
100. Melamed, "The Spirit of Neoliberalism," 20.
101. Menkes, "The Circus of Fashion," 94, emphasis added.
102. Menkes may be also hinting at recent questions about Yambao's financial affairs that have appeared in fashion's gossip mill. The rumors alleging that his opulent wardrobe and glamorous lifestyle are funded by credit card fraud are, as far as I can tell, unsubstantiated.
103. Melamed, "The Spirit of Neoliberalism," 20.

### Chapter 2. Style Stories, Written Tastes, and the Work of Self-Composure

1. Barthes, *The Fashion System*, 8.
2. Barthes, *The Fashion System*, 8.
3. Barthes, *The Fashion System*, 9.

4. Barthes, *The Fashion System*, 13.
5. Barthes, *The Fashion System*, 14.
6. Bourdieu, "Haute Couture and Haute Culture," 134.
7. Bourdieu, "Haute Couture and Haute Culture," 134.
8. Menkes, "The Circus of Fashion," 91.
9. Barthes, *The Fashion System*.
10. Medine's blog defines a *man repeller* in this way: "she who outfits herself in a sartorially offensive mode that may result in repelling members of the opposite sex. Such garments include but are not limited to harem pants, boyfriend jeans, overalls, shoulder pads, full length jumpsuits, jewelry that resembles violent weaponry and clogs" ("What Is a Man Repeller?").
11. Song, "Flared Hem Skirt and Chanel Chain Boots in Seoul."
12. Hayles, "Electronic Literature."
13. Song, "Palm Print Playsuit in New York."
14. Heyer, "The Creative Challenge of CD-ROM," 347.
15. Vandendorpe, "Reading on Screen: The New Media Sphere."
16. Aarseth, *Cybertext*, 51.
17. It is pretty well known among bloggers that Google's algorithms for ranking pages penalize or discount sites with a lot of affiliate links. Google justifies this by citing fairness. According to its "Webmaster Guidelines" on affiliate links, its search engine rankings are intended to reward sites with high amounts of unique and high-quality content (affiliate links are examples of duplicate and thin content). However, it is difficult not to see Google's algorithm as a computational end run around the market competition for its own ad program, Google AdSense.
18. Lau, "Chinoiserie Query."
19. See Copping, "Style Bloggers Take Centre Stage"; King, "Bloggers Take Over the Front Row"; Pfeiffer, "Young Bloggers Have Ear of Fashion Heavyweights"; Wells, "Have Laptop, Will Travel"; E. Wilson, "Bloggers Crash Fashion's Front Row"; Wiseman, "Today I'm Wearing . . ."; and Zucker, "Fashion Bloggers, Where They Belong."
20. Lau and Medine directly responded to Menkes on their blogs and about a year later, Lau published an opinion piece in *Vogue* that was framed as a "defense" of bloggers. See Lau, "Sad Clown" and "Fashion Blogger Susie Bubble Makes a Case in Defense of Street Style" and Medine, "Blog Is a Dirty Word."
21. Carbado and Gulati, *Acting White?*, 29.
22. Examples include Song, "White Button Down and Denim Shorts Kinda Day" and "The Boyfriend Sweatshirt."
23. Examples include Song, "The Boyfriend Sweatshirt" and "Summer Boyfriend Jeans."
24. Song, "Summer Essentials" and "The Black and White Striped Button Down."
25. Song, "The Black and White Striped Button Down."

26. Song, "Calamigos Ranch, Malibu" and "Song of Style on Instagram."
27. Song, "Kimono and Over the Knee Boots."
28. Song, "White Lace and Red Shorts."
29. Song, "Black Uniform" and "Leopard on Leopard during Paris Fashion Week."
30. Song, "Polished Casual" and "Pinstripes and Quilted Leather."
31. Song, "Overalls and Heels" and "Flared Hem Skirt and Chanel Chain Boots in Seoul."
32. Lukács, "The Labor of Cute."
33. For a longer discussion of multiculturalism as a valued marketing strategy, see Banet-Weiser, Kids Rule! and The Most Beautiful Girl in the World. Also see Dávila, Latinos, Inc.; Hasinoff, "Fashioning Race for the Free Market on America's Next Top Model."
34. See Goldberg, The Threat of Race; Gray, "Subject(ed) to Recognition"; Perry, More Beautiful and More Terrible.
35. Gray, "Subject(ed) to Recognition," 790.
36. Gray, "Subject(ed) to Recognition," 771.
37. For examples of Song's discussions of twirling, see "Red Valentino" and "Swinging in Green."
38. Chow, The Protestant Ethnic and the Spirit of Capitalism, 25.
39. Chow, The Protestant Ethnic and the Spirit of Capitalism, 111–12.
40. Lau, "Chinoiserie Query."
41. Song, "Yacht Ride in Los Cabos, Mexico" and "Back in Rabat, Morocco."
42. Song, "Kimono Dreams in Huntington Botanical Gardens."
43. Song, "Magical Pink" and "Song of Style on Instagram."
44. Yambao, "X Marks the Spot."
45. Yambao, "Aristocrazy Headquarters Madrid."
46. Yambao, "Anya Hindmarch Ching Chong Edition."
47. Gubar, "Racial Camp in The Producers and Bamboozled," 26.
48. Isherwood, The World in the Evening, 214.
49. Yambao, "Mall Rat Extraordinaire."
50. Yambao, "Filipino Hospitality" and "BryanBoy Loves . . . and Random Cheesemax."
51. Yambao, "Goodbye Third World!"
52. Yambao, "Holt Renfrew Unveils Fashion Blogger Windows."
53. Yambao, " 'Everybody Wants to Be Us.' "
54. Yambao, "An Open Letter to Riccardo Tisci and Givenchy."
55. Yambao, "Raf-ing It Up."
56. Yambao, "Coloured Male Models?"
57. For an example of his racism, misogyny, and sizism, see "Blasphemous: Ashanti in a Balenciaga Dress" in which he insists that the African American singer Ashanti is too big to wear Balenciaga: "I'm an equal opportunity lover and I love everyone regardless of their size. However, some dresses, like skinny jeans,

are simply NOT meant to be worn by women of certain body types. Look how Ashanti stretched the whole thing out! I can't believe it! It's Balenciaga for god's sake!"

58. Yambao routinely uses this title and he is frequently described by others with this title. As examples, see Yambao, "Team Sissyfication!" and Warne, "Interview: Fashion Blogger Bryanboy."

59. Nakata, "Will the Real Bryanboy Please Stand Up?"

60. Yambao, " 'Everybody Wants to Be Us.' "

61. Yambao, "Healthy Options."

62. Sontag, "Notes on "Camp,' " 518.

63. The original title of his blog was *Bryanboy: Le Superstar Fabuleux* [sic]. Although he has dropped the subtitle, the permalinks to individual blog posts includes a version of the original title in the directory name of the URL path.

## Chapter 3. "So Many and All the Same" (but Not Quite)

1. Sozzani, "Bloggers."

2. Finauro, "Bryan Boy a Vogue Italia."

3. Quoted in Knebl, "Bryanboy on Starting His Blog from the Ground Up."

4. De Palol, "About Me."

5. Baenen, "We Will Not Be Deleted."

6. Her first outfit photos remain visible in her blog's archive but their quality is far too low for them to be printed in this book. (As examples see her first two outfit photos, "There Are Two Kinds of People" and "Let the Music Guide You.")

7. See, for example, Lau, "Oooh la la . . . viva la revolution!" and "Let the Music Guide You."

8. Lau's influence could be seen not only in the widespread adoption of mirror shots and outfit photography by other bloggers but also in the invitations she received to industry events hosted by the likes of Chanel, Gucci, and Lanvin, where she was often one of only a few bloggers on the guest list. She was attending these events in 2007 and 2008, well over a year before sightings of bloggers in the front rows of fashion shows became a cause célèbre.

9. Rosman, "Super 'Selfies.' "

10. Yi, "The Camera-Wielding Boyfriends behind Fashion's Most Famous Bloggers."

11. Quoted in Knebl, "Bryanboy on Starting His Blog from the Ground Up."

12. Aboutaleb, "Tommy Ton Accuses Jimmy Choo of Stealing His Style."

13. Marlene, "What Do Bloggers Really Wear."

14. Lou, "Fashion Blogger."

15. Humm, *Snapshots of Bloomsbury: The Private Lives of Virginia Woolf and Vanessa Bell*, viii.

16. Yi, "The Camera-Wielding Boyfriends behind Fashion's Most Famous Bloggers."

17. West, *Kodak and the Lens of Nostalgia*, 35.

18. Quoted in West, *Kodak and the Lens of Nostalgia*, 35.
19. A standard advertising trope for handheld cameras is seen in a 1908 ad in *Harper's* titled "The Baby's Picture." It features a white mother holding a Kodak Brownie camera and kneeling in front of her baby. Part of the advertisement copy reads: "The record of his infant days is incomplete unless there are home pictures" ("The Baby's Picture).
20. Gover, *The Positive Image*.
21. For more on the feminization of amateur photography, see West, *Kodak and the Lens of Nostalgia*; Holland, " 'sweet It Is To Scan . . .' "
22. W. Benjamin, *Illuminations*, 224.
23. De Mul, "The Work of Art in the Age of Digital Recombination."
24. W. Benjamin, *Illuminations*, 220.
25. W. Benjamin, *Illuminations*, 243.
26. In one of those fortuitous moments that can sometimes happen when we are focused on a particular subject or when we are on Facebook, an article came to my attention (via Facebook) that neatly describes the contemporary cultural history of relatability. In the article, called "The Scourge of 'Relatability,' " Rebecca Mead confirms my understanding of the roots of relatability in reality culture when she traces the idea and value to daytime television. Continuing to trace this history, Mead's understanding of "the notion of relatability" leads her to draw a link between reality culture and new fashion and beauty media practices. Our desire for and valuing of relatability, Mead suggests, turns everything into "a selfie: a flattering confirmation of an individual's solipsism."
27. De Mul, "The Work of Art in the Age of Digital Recombination," 102.
28. There are far too many examples to list here, but they include almost any Western fashion media representation in which people of color or racial and ethnic difference are included in some way. Often, the people of color in ads are represented as outside and behind the temporal frame and trajectory of normative Euro-American whiteness. People of color wear traditional ethnic garb that typically blends into or accentuates the exotic backdrop, while white models are in the latest, most fashion forward outfits. The supposed difference between ethnic clothing and fashion is itself based on a racialized temporal construction. Ethnic clothing is defined as an unchanged style, whereas Western fashion is defined by or as change (in terms of trends, seasons, and evolving tastes). Likewise, when Western fashion designers incorporate ethnic designs and embellishments into their collections, they and the fashion media often describe it in temporal terms, as updating or modernizing an ethnic look. For more post-colonial feminist analyses of race and fashion media representation, see Mimi Nguyen's important series of blog posts on Threadbared, called "Background Color," "Background Color, Redux," and "Background Color, Redux II." Also see Pham, "On the Seduction of Proenza Schouler's *Act Da Fool*" and "Why Fashion Should Stop Trying to Be Diverse."

29. Bhabha, "Of Mimicry and Man," 126.
30. Bhabha, "Of Mimicry and Man," 127.
31. Bhabha, "Of Mimicry and Man," 128.
32. L. Liu, "The Female Body and Nationalist Discourse"; McClintock, *Imperial Leather*.
33. McClintock, *Imperial Leather*, 64.
34. Quoted in Fisher, "Gangnam Style, Dissected."
35. Gruger, "PSY's 'Gangnam Style' Video Hits 1 Billion Views."
36. "Psy's 'Gangnam Style' MV becomes Most Liked Video in YouTube History."
37. *Chopped*, Season 19, Episode 1, aired February 4, 2014 and Season 21, Episode 8, aired September 2, 2014.
38. Fisher, "Gangnam Style, Dissected."
39. Quoted in Fisher, "Gangnam Style, Dissected."
40. Kwan, *Crazy Rich Asians*, 26.
41. Kwan, *Crazy Rich Asians*, 78.
42. Kwan, *Crazy Rich Asians*, 59.
43. Kwan, *Crazy Rich Asians*, 195.
44. Kwan, *Crazy Rich Asians*, 46.
45. Kwan, *Crazy Rich Asians*, 17.
46. Kwan, *Crazy Rich Asians*, 133.
47. Kwan, *Crazy Rich Asians*, 234.
48. J. Lee, "Meet the New Asian Superrich."
49. Christensen, "*Crazy Rich Asians* Author Kevin Kwan on the Lavish Culture of Asia's Upper Crust."
50. Quoted in Lau, "Round the Table."
51. Kwan, *Crazy Rich Asians*, 234.
52. For a slightly longer discussion of Lagerfeld's film, see Pham, "The Truth of Lagerfeld's Idea of China."
53. Davey-Attlee, "Why China Is Sitting on Fashion's Front Row"; Amed, "China's Constant Flux."
54. Adam, "The Gendered Time Politics of Globalization," 16–17.
55. Adam, "The Gendered Time Politics of Globalization," 21.
56. See Nakamura and Chow-White, *Race after the Internet*; Chun, *Programmed Visions* and "Race and/as Technology"; Daniels, *Cyber Racism*; Magnet, *When Biometrics Fail*; McPherson, "Digital Possibilities and the Reimagining of Politics, Place, and the Self"; Nakamura, *Cybertypes* and *Digitizing Race*.
57. See Chun, *Programmed Visions*.
58. Chun, "Race and/as Technology," 8.
59. Nakamura and Chow-White, introduction to *Race after the Internet*, 8–9.
60. Yambao, "Healthy Options."
61. Shimakawa, *National Abjection*, 17.

1. Bradley, "How to Pose Like a Fashion Blogger."
2. Smith and Sidel, "Should You Dress Like the CEO?"
3. Carbado and Gulati, "Working Identity."
4. Carbado and Gulati, "Working Identity."
5. Martin, "Diversity and the Virtual Workplace," 630.
6. Martin, "Diversity and the Virtual Workplace," 633.
7. Cherry, "A Taxonomy of Virtual Work," 977.
8. Augé, *Non-Places*, 78.
9. Quoted in Knebl, "Bryanboy on Starting His Blog from the Ground Up."
10. JLJ Group, "China."
11. Quoted in Botz-Bornstein, "Wong Kar-wai's Films and the Culture of the *Kawaii*," 96.
12. Long, "Jason Wu." See also Cowles, "Jason Wu Discusses the Asian American Fashion 'Movement.'"
13. Phelps, "Jason Wu Fall 2012 Ready-to-Wear Review."
14. Lim, "Jason Wu's New Collection."
15. "Video."
16. Alexa Chung is three-eighths Asian, on her father's side.
17. D. Harris, "Some Reflections on the Facial Expressions of Fashion Models," 133.
18. Lakoff and Scherr, *Face Value*, 290.
19. "Float On," 236–41.
20. "Float On," 237.
21. Recent data show that U.S. Black, Latina, Asian, and Native women, especially those who are single mothers, have higher rates of poverty than white women (National Women's Law Center, "Poverty among Women and Families, 2000–2010," 3–4).
22. The irony of posed spontaneity is not lost on fashion bloggers or their audiences. Indeed, the fashion blogosphere's culture of realism motivates many of the parodies of these cryptocasual postures. Such parodies, often created by members of fashion blog audiences and bloggers themselves, appear on many social media platforms. Of course, self-parodies are more like inside jokes that establish a common knowledge shared by members of the in-group. I think they also reflect bloggers' contradictory desires to attain fashion fame while maintaining their indie status. Many parodies of fashion blogger poses are performed with a dose of hipster irony.
23. Castiglione, *The Book of the Courtier*, 67.
24. Adichie, "We Should All Be Feminists."
25. See, for example, Winter, "We Woke Up Like This Too Beyonce!"
26. Goman, *The Silent Language of Leaders*, 63.

27. Goman, *The Silent Language of Leaders*, 170.
28. See Bynner, Chisholm, and Furlong, *Youth, Citizenship and Social Change in a European Context*; Dwyer and Wyn, *Youth, Education and Risk*; A. Harris, *Future Girl*; Rattansi and Phoenix, "Rethinking Youth Identities."
29. Quoted in Kansara, "Fashion 2.0."
30. Walkerdine, Lucey, and Melody, *Growing Up Girl*, 9.
31. Walkerdine, Lucey, and Melody, *Growing Up Girl*, 3.
32. See, for example, Bordo, *Unbearable Weight*; Hellmich, "Do Thin Models Warp Girls' Body Image?"; Mears, "Size Zero High-End Ethnic"; Paquette and Raine, "Sociocultural Context of Women's Body Image"; Pearson, "Fashion and Eating Disorders"; Turner et al., "The Influence of Fashion Magazines on the Body Image Satisfaction of College Women."
33. Bordo, *Unbearable Weight*, 192.
34. Bordo, *Unbearable Weight*, 195.
35. Quoted in Amed, "Top 10 Articles of 2010."
36. Rosman, "Super 'Selfies.' "
37. Wonderful examples of this criticism include Burnham, "Lean In and One Percent Feminism"; T. Harris, "Leaning In While Black"; hooks, "Dig Deep"; Sanders, "The White Privilege behind Sheryl Sandberg's 'Ban Bossy' Campaign."
38. Peters, "The Brand Called You."
39. Henry, "Women and the Creative Industries."
40. Zeveloff, "The 15 Wealthiest People in Fashion."
41. Lau, "Look at Me, Don't Look at Me."
42. Lau, "Monday Larks."
43. Lau, "Look at Me, Don't Look at Me."
44. Lau, "Parisian Reflections (Most Probably Caused by This Sodding Rain)."
45. D. Harris, "Some Reflections on the Facial Expressions of Fashion Models," 130.
46. See Rohlinger, "Eroticizing Men."
47. Entwistle and Mears, "Gender on Display," 324.
48. For more on this point, see Hobson, "The 'Batty' Politic"; Okoye, "Looking Back."
49. Yambao, "Holy Fucking Shiyet Fendi."
50. Yambao, "Fendi: Stop the Fucking Press!"
51. See Yambao, "Fendi: Stop the Fucking Press!"
52. Some of this history is covered on Threadbared. See, for example, Nguyen, "Couture Coincidence"; Pham, "On the Seduction of Proenza Schouler's *Act Da Fool*" and "Unintentionally Eating the Other." See also Pham, "What's in a Name?"
53. Yambao, "Fendi: Stop the Fucking Press!"
54. Yambao, "Holy Fucking Shiyet Fendi."
55. Raustiala and Sprigman, *The Knockoff Economy*.
56. Hiner, *Accessories to Modernity*.

57. Hiner, *Accessories to Modernity*, 183.
58. Dolby, "The Shifting Ground of Race"; Donath, "Signals in Social Supernets"; H. Liu, "Social Network Profiles as Taste Performances"; Nuttall, "Stylizing the Self"; Schenk, "Quantifying Taste."
59. Bourdieu, *Distinction*.
60. Cogent analyses of the racial performances in *America's Next Top Model* include Hasinoff, "Fashioning Race for the Free Market on *America's Next Top Model*"; Joseph, " 'Tyra Banks Is Fat' "; M. Thompson, " 'Learn Something from This!' "
61. Yambao, "Gay Bloggies 2007."
62. Lau, "Chinoiserie Query."
63. See, for example, some of the comments in Lau, "Why Susie Shouldn't Go to LV."
64. Lau is in fact much more ambivalent about her identity than this comment reveals. Throughout her blog she admits to "a love hate relationship with ethnic heritage" that underpins her fashion choices: "I don't really wish to wear my ethnicity on my sleeve . . . for fear of looking like a waitress in a dodgy restaurant or a roleplay actor in a theme park" ("Chinoiserie Query").
65. See Enstad, *Ladies of Labor, Girls of Adventure*; Hebdige, *Subculture*; Miller, *Slaves to Fashion*; Ramirez, *The Woman in the Zoot Suit*; Y. Wong, *Choreographing Asian America*.
66. Hebdige, *Subculture*, 3.

## Chapter 5. Invisible Labor and Racial Visibilities in Outfit Posts

1. Lancelle, "This Week's Most Materialistic Blogger Award Goes to Sterling Style."
2. DiNardo, "Does Fashion Blogging Make You a Shopping Addict?"
3. Everett, "Ramblings on Blogging."
4. Quoted in Schiermer, "Fashion Victims," 86.
5. Veblen, *The Theory of the Leisure Class*.
6. Simmel, "Fashion."
7. Quoted in Schiermer, "Fashion Victims," 90.
8. Schiermer, "Fashion Victims," 86.
9. Kate Winslet has been especially outspoken about photo retouching. When *GQ* digitally altered her image, she admonished the magazine for its "excessive" manipulation and stated, "I do not look like that and more importantly I don't desire to look like that" ("Retouching Is 'Excessive' Says SlimLine CoverGirl Kate Winslet"). Jamie Lee Curtis has also insisted that magazines include unretouched photos alongside digitally altered photos (Sharp, "French Elle").
10. Odell, "Stars Go Makeupless on the Cover of French *Elle*."
11. Hilton, "What's Wrong with Skinny?"
12. Furness, "Nobody Wants a 'Real Person' on the Cover of *Vogue*, Editor Says."
13. Quoted in Waldman, "Lena Dunham Responds to the *Vogue* Haters."

14. Veblen, *The Theory of the Leisure Class*, 63.
15. Veblen, *The Theory of the Leisure Class*, 171.
16. Veblen, *The Theory of the Leisure Class*, 179.
17. Veblen, *The Theory of the Leisure Class*, 50.
18. Veblen, *The Theory of the Leisure Class*, 47.
19. Ong, *Flexible Citizenship*.
20. See Appadurai, *Modernity at Large*; Clifford, *Routes*; Harvey, *The Condition of Postmodernity*; Jameson, *Postmodernism*; Ong, *Flexible Citizenship*.
21. Tishgart, "Tour Style Blogger Aimee Song's Apartment."
22. "Closet Confessions Presents Susie Bubble."
23. E. Thompson, "Time, Work-Discipline, and Industrial Capitalism," 59.
24. For readings on the racial construction of free labor, see Allen, *The Invention of the White Race*, vols. 1 and 2; Roediger, *The Wages of Whiteness*.
25. Harvey, *The Condition of Postmodernity*, 240.
26. Kopytoff, "The Cultural Biography of Things."
27. Kopytoff, "The Cultural Biography of Things"; Appadurai, "Introduction."
28. See Kretz and de Valck, " 'Pixelize Me!' "; Liao, "Virtual Fashion Play as Embodied Identity Re/Assembling"; Palmgren, "Posing My Identity"; Rocamora, "Personal Fashion Blogs."
29. Neely, "oasis."
30. Neely, "casual friday."
31. Neely, "at the flower shoppe."
32. Neely, "pink in beverly hills."
33. It is also possible that not discussing prices is a holdover from before the FTC mandate compelling bloggers to disclose which products or services featured on their blogs they did not pay for. Discussing the prices paid for some items and not for others would have signaled what were the freebies and made the blogger vulnerable to allegations that blog posts had been bought.
34. Houghton, "Google Chrome."
35. Lau, "Sophie Bubble."
36. Quoted in Scherpe, "On Fashion Blogs."
37. Zwick, Bonsu, and Darmody, "Putting Consumers to Work," 185.
38. Americans are among the most overworked. They "work 137 more hours per year than Japanese workers, 260 more hours per year than British workers, and 499 more hours per year than French workers" (Matile, "Survey Finds We're Working More Hours Than We Did Back in '73"). These figures have less to do with work ethics than with employment structures in the United States, where there is no national requirement for time off each week, paid maternity leave, or paid annual vacation time.
39. Lee, McCann, and Messenger, *Working Time around the World*, 53.
40. Toffler, *Powershift* and *The Third Wave*; Ritzer and Jurgenson, "Production, Consumption, Prosumption."

41. "'Jeans Machine' Scanner Sizes You Up."
42. Hochschild, *The Managed Heart*.
43. Neely, "up high."
44. Ross, "The New Geography of Work," 41.
45. Lau, "Words, Words, Words . . ."
46. Deuze, *Media Work*, 11.
47. Chia, "Welcome to Me-Mart," 429.
48. Cited in Tongson, *Relocations*, 23.
49. Yambao, "You Owe It to Your Fans."
50. Glenn, "Cleaning Up/Kept Down," "From Servitude to Service Work," and "Racial Ethnic Women's Labor"; Jarrett, "The Relevance of 'Women's Work'"; MacKinnon, *Towards a Feminist Theory of the State*; Ong, "The Gender and Labor Politics of Postmodernity"; Pascale, "All in a Day's Work a Feminist Analysis of Class Formation and Social Identity."
51. Jarrett, "The Relevance of 'Women's Work.'"
52. Glenn, "Cleaning Up/Kept Down"; Lind, "The Changing Position of Domestic Service in Hawaii."
53. Chan, "The Exclusion of Chinese Women, 1870–1943."
54. Glenn, "Cleaning Up/Kept Down," 1340.
55. Glenn, "Cleaning Up/Kept Down," 1341.
56. Glenn, "Cleaning Up/Kept Down," 1338–39.
57. Bishop and Robinson, *Night Market*; Constable, *Maid to Order in Hong Kong* and *Romance on a Global Stage*; Kelsky, *Women on the Verge*; Manderson and Jolly, *Sites of Desire/Economies of Pleasure*; Parreñas, *Servants of Globalization*; A. Wilson, *The Intimate Economies of Bangkok*.

## Coda

1. Quoted in Rothman, "Julie Chen Admits to Past Plastic Surgery to Change 'Asian Eyes.'"
2. Lau, "Look at Me, Don't Look at Me."
3. La Ferla, "An Eye for Detail, and Plenty of Pop."
4. Quoted in Kansara, "The Business of Blogging: Style Bubble."
5. Chun, "Race and/as Technology," 8.
6. Richards, "Of Indians and Terrorists," 90.
7. Givhan, "The Golden Era of 'Fashion Blogging' Is Over."
8. Givhan, "The Golden Era of 'Fashion Blogging' Is Over."
9. For example, see Ellison, "Love at First Site?"; Lorentzen, "Is Fashion Blogging Dead?"; Odell, "Why the Era of Personal Style Blogs Must Come to an End"; Rahman, "Is the Era of Selfie-Centred Fashion Blogging Coming to an End?"; Reiter, "Is This The End of Fashion Blogging?"

# Bibliography

"The $8 Trillion Internet Economy: By the Numbers." *Week*. November 7, 2011. Accessed January 17, 2015. http://theweek.com/article/index/221181/the-8-trillion -internet-economy-by-the-numbers.

"AAFA Releases Apparel Stats 2012 Report." American Apparel and Footwear Association. October 19, 2012. Accessed January 18, 2015. https://www.wewear.org/aafa -releases-apparelstats-2012-report/.

Aarseth, Espen J. *Cybertext: Perspectives on Ergodic Literature*. Baltimore, MD: Johns Hopkins University Press, 1997.

Aboutaleb, Britt. "Tommy Ton Accuses Jimmy Choo of Stealing His Style." Fashionista .com. January 27, 2010. Accessed January 22, 2015. http://fashionista.com/2010 /01/tommy-ton-accuses-jimmy-choo-of-stealing-his-style.

Adam, Barbara. "The Gendered Time Politics of Globalization: Of Shadowlands and Elusive Justice." *Feminist Review* 70 (2002): 3–29.

Adichie, Chimamanda Ngozi. "We Should All Be Feminists." TED Talk. April 12, 2013. https://www.youtube.com/watch?v=hg3umXU_qWc.

Allen, Theodore W. *The Invention of the White Race*. Vol 1: *Racial Oppression and Social Control*. London: Verso, 1994.

———. *The Invention of the White Race*. Vol. 2: *The Origin of Racial Oppression in Anglo-America*. London: Verso, 1997.

Allison, Anne. "Portable Monsters and Commodity Cuteness: Pokemon as Japan's New Global Power." *Postcolonial Studies* 6, no. 3 (2003): 381–95.

Amed, Imran. "The Business of Blogging: Tommy Ton." Business of Fashion (blog). March 28, 2011. Accessed January 17, 2015. http://www.businessoffashion.com /2011/03/the-business-of-blogging-tommy-ton.html.

————. "China's Constant Flux." Business of Fashion (blog). November 14, 2013. Accessed January 24, 2015. http://www.businessoffashion.com/2013/11/chinas -constant-flux.html.

————. "Top 10 Articles of 2010." Business of Fashion (blog). December 22, 2010. Accessed January 24, 2015. http://www.businessoffashion.com/2010/12/the-best -of-bof-top-10-articles-of-2010.html.

Andrejevic, Mark. "Estranged Free Labor." In Digital Labor: The Internet as Playground and Factory, edited by Trebor Scholz, 149–64. New York: Routledge, 2012.

Apatoff, Alex. "Want Your Valentine's Gift to Top Beyoncé's? Then Your Guy Will Have to Do Better Than Jay Z." People. February 11, 2014. Accessed January 17, 2015. http://stylenews.peoplestylewatch.com/2014/02/11/beyonce-jay-z-marriage -valentines-day-gift/.

Appadurai, Arjun. "Introduction: Commodities and the Politics of Value." In The Social Life of Things: Commodities in Cultural Perspective, edited by Arjun Appadurai, 3–63. Cambridge: Cambridge University Press, 1986.

————. Modernity at Large: Cultural Dimensions of Globalization. Minneapolis: University of Minnesota Press, 1996.

"Apparel Export Shows 9.7% Decline in Dollar Terms in First Month of FY 2012–13." Fibre2 Fashion.com. August 31, 2012. Accessed January 18, 2015. http://www .fibre2fashion.com/industry-article/44/4338/apparel-export-shows2.asp.

Augé, Marc. Non-Places: Introduction to an Anthropology of Supermodernity. Translated by John Howe. London: Verso, 1995.

Aytes, Ayhan. "Return of the Crowds: Mechanical Turk and Neoliberal States of Exception." In Digital Labor: The Internet as Playground and Factory, edited by Trebor Scholz, 79–97. New York: Routledge, 2012.

"The Baby's Picture." Harper's. February 1908. Kodak Advertising Collection. Accessed March 15, 2015. http://www.eastmanhouse.org/features/kodak-advertis ing/.

Baenen, Alison. "We Will Not Be Deleted: Great Moments in Fashion Blogging History." Style.com. May 2010. http://www.style.com/trendsshopping/stylenotes /052010_Fashion_Blog_Landmarks/slideshow/?loop=0&iphoto=8&play=true &cnt=23.

Banet-Weiser, Sarah. Kids Rule! Nickelodeon and Consumer Citizenship. Durham, NC: Duke University Press, 2007.

————. The Most Beautiful Girl in the World: Beauty Pageants and National Identity. Berkeley: University of California Press, 1999.

Barnes, Nora Ganim, and Ava M. Lescault. "Millennials Drive Social Commerce: Turning Their Likes, Follows or Pins into a Sale." Dartmouth: University of Massachusetts. Accessed January 18, 2015. http://www.umassd.edu/cmr/socialmediaresearch/so cialcommerce/.

Barthes, Roland. The Fashion System. Translated by Matthew Ward and Richard Howard. New York: Hill and Wang, 1983.

Benjamin, Allie. "Top 5 Highest-Grossing Fashion Bloggers." Top 5. Accessed March 4, 2015. http://interwebs.top5.com/top-5-highest-grossing-fashion-blog gers/?viewOnSinglePage=true.

Benjamin, Walter. *Illuminations: Essays and Reflections*. Translated by Harry Zohn, edited and with an introduction by Hannah Arendt. New York: Schocken, 2007.

"The Best People of 1999." *Time*. December 20, 1999. Accessed January 18, 2015. http://www.cnn.com/ASIANOW/time/magazine/99/1220/1999bw.people.html.

Beusman, Callie. "Rick Owens Is the Latest Designer to Replace Models with 'Real Women.'" *Jezebel*. February 28, 2014. Accessed January 18, 2015. http://jezebel .com/rick-owens-is-the-latest-designer-to-replace-models-wit-1533372063.

Bhabha, Homi. "Of Mimicry and Man: The Ambivalence of Colonial Discourse." *October* 28 (Spring 1984): 125–33.

Bishop, Ryan, and Lillian Robinson. *Night Market: Sexual Cultures and the Thai Economic Miracle*. New York: Routledge, 1998.

Bonacich, Edna, and Richard Appelbaum. *Behind the Label: Inequality in the Los Angeles Apparel Industry*. Berkeley: University of California Press, 2000.

Bordo, Susan. *Unbearable Weight: Feminism, Western Culture, and the Body*. Berkeley: University of California Press, 1995.

Botz-Bornstein, Thorsten. "Wong Kar-wai's Films and the Culture of the *Kawaii*." *SubStance* 37, no. 2 (2008): 94–109.

Boudreau, John. "U.S. Retailers Tailor Fashions to Asian Tastes." *Los Angeles Times*, December 5, 2011.

Bourdieu, Pierre. *Distinction: A Social Critique of the Judgment of Taste*. Translated by Richard Nice. Cambridge, MA: Harvard University Press, 1984.

———. "Haute Couture and Haute Culture." *Sociology in Question*. Translated by Richard Nice, 132–38. Thousand Oaks, CA: Sage, 1993.

———. "The Metamorphosis of Tastes." *Sociology in Question*. Translated by Richard Nice, 108–16. Thousand Oaks, CA: Sage, 1993.

———. "The Sociologist in Question." *Sociology in Question*. Translated by Richard Nice, 20–35. Thousand Oaks, CA: Sage, 1993.

Bourne, Leah. "Designers Are Finally Creating Clothes for Real Women." *Forbes*. February 23, 2010. Accessed January 18, 2015. http://www.forbes.com/2010/02/23/fash ion-week-designer-clothes-what-to-wear-forbes-woman-style-shopping.html.

boyd, danah. "Why Youth <3 Social Network Sites: The Role of Networked Publics in Teenage Social Life." In *Youth Identity and Digital Media*, edited by David Buckingham, 119–42. Cambridge, MA: MIT Press, 2007.

Boyes, Emma. "UK Paper Names Top Game Franchises." GameSpot. January 10, 2007. Accessed March 18, 2015. http://www.gamespot.com/articles/uk-paper-names-top -game-franchises/1100-6164012/.

Bradley, Stuart. "How to Pose Like a Fashion Blogger." FunStuffCafe.com. Accessed March 17, 2015. http://funstuffcafe.com/how-to-pose-like-a-fashion-blogger-by -stuart-bradley.

Branigan, Tania. "Chinese Models Stride the Catwalk as the West Eyes China's Rich Fashion Market." *Guardian*. May 14, 2011. http://www.theguardian.com/lifeandstyle /2011/may/15/chinese-models-fashion-vogue.

Burnham, Linda. "Lean In and One Percent Feminism." Portside.org. March 26, 2013. Accessed March 16, 2015. http://portside.org/2013-03-26/lean-and-one-percent -feminism.

Bynner, John, Lynne Chisholm, and Andy Furlong, eds. *Youth, Citizenship and Social Change in a European Context*. Aldershot, UK: Ashgate, 1997.

Carbado, Devon W., and Mitu Gulati. *Acting White? Rethinking Race in Post-Racial America*. Oxford: Oxford University Press, 2013.

———. "Working Identity." *Cornell Law Review* 85 (2000): 1259–308.

Cardiff, Ashley. "We All Know Fashion Bloggers Have No Integrity, Right?" Gloss .com. March 12, 2012. Accessed January 19, 2015. http://www.thegloss.com /2012/03/12/fashion/fashion-bloggers-integrity-212.

Castiglione, Baldassare. *The Book of the Courtier*. Translated by George Bull. London: Penguin, 1976.

Center for American Progress. "Garment Worker Wages Declined in Majority of Top Apparel-Exporting Countries over the Last Decade, New Study Reveals." Center for American Progress. July 11, 2013. Accessed January 18, 2015. http://www .americanprogress.org/press/release/2013/07/11/69250/release-garment -worker-wages-declined-in-majority-of-top-apparel-exporting-countries-over -the-last-decade-new-study-reveals/.

Chan, Sucheng. "The Exclusion of Chinese Women, 1870–1943." In *Entry Denied: Exclusion and the Chinese Community in America, 1882–1943*, edited by Sucheng Chan, 94–146. Philadelphia: Temple University Press, 1994.

Chang, Samantha. "Asia Major." *Vogue* (December 2010): 298.

Cherry, Miriam A. "A Taxonomy of Virtual Work." *Georgia Law Review* 45, no. 951 (2011): 951–91.

Chia, Aleena. "Welcome to Me-Mart: The Politics of User-Generated Content in Personal Blogs." *American Behavioral Scientist* 56, no. 4 (2012): 421–38.

Chin, Margaret M. *Sewing Women: Immigrants and the New York City Garment Industry*. New York: Columbia University Press, 2005.

Chinatown Study Group, "Chinatown Report: 1969." Columbia University East Asian Studies Center, New York, 1970.

Chow, Rey. *The Protestant Ethnic and the Spirit of Capitalism*. New York: Columbia University Press, 2002.

Choy, Christine, and Renee Tajima-Peña, dirs. *Who Killed Vincent Chin?* Arlington, VA: Public Broadcasting System, 1987.

Christensen, Lauren. "*Crazy Rich Asians* Author Kevin Kwan on the Lavish Culture of Asia's Upper Crust: 'The Reality Is Simply Unbelievable.'" *Vanity Fair*. June 11, 2013. Accessed January 24, 2015. http://www.vanityfair.com/online/daily/2013 /06/crazy-rich-asians-kevin-kwan-asia-upper-crust.

Chun, Wendy Hui Kyong. *Programmed Visions: Software and Memory*. Cambridge, MA: MIT Press, 2011.

———. "Race and/as Technology." *Camera Obscura* 24, no. 1 70 (2009): 7–35.

Clancy, Rebecca. "Asia 'To Take Over Half Luxury Goods Market.'" *Telegraph*, August 12, 2013. Accessed January 19, 2015. http://www.telegraph.co.uk/finance /newsbysector/retailandconsumer/10236298/Asia-to-take-over-half-luxury-goods -market.html.

Clifford, James. *Routes: Travel and Translation in the Late Twentieth Century*. Cambridge, MA: Harvard University Press, 1997.

Cline, Elizabeth L. *Overdressed: The Shockingly High Cost of Cheap Fashion*. New York: Penguin, 2012.

"Closet Confessions Presents Susie Bubble." Bluefly.com. Accessed March 18, 2015. http://www.bluefly.com/closets/susie_bubble.

Collings, Kat. "Aimee Song's Secrets to Blogging Success." WhoWhatWear.com, February 28, 2014. http://www.whowhatwear.com/aimee-song-of-style-blogging -secrets-tips-fashion-2014.

Considine, Austin. "For Asian-American Web Stars, Many Web Fans." *New York Times*, July 29, 2011.

Constable, Nicole. *Maid to Order in Hong Kong: An Ethnography of Filipina Workers*. Ithaca, NY: Cornell University Press, 1997.

———. *Romance on a Global Stage: Pen Pals, Virtual Ethnography, and "Mail Order" Marriages*. Berkeley: University of California Press, 2003.

Copping, Nicola. " 'I'm in the front row with Anna!' - The famously formidable editor of US Vogue sharing the front row with a laptop-wielding blogger called Bryanboy? What in the fashion world is happening?" *Financial Times*. November 14, 2009, 1.

Cowles, Charlotte. "Jason Wu Discusses the Asian American Fashion 'Movement.' " Cut (blog). *New York Magazine*. March 20, 2012. Accessed January 18, 2015. http:// nymag.com/daily/fashion/2012/03/jason-wu-on-the-asian-american-movement .html.

———. "Will Carine Roitfeld Join Alexander Wang at Balenciaga?" The Cut (blog). *New York Magazine*, January 8, 2013. Accessed January 19, 2015. http://nymag.com /thecut/2013/01/reports-roitfeld-to-join-wang-at-balenciaga.html.

Crary, Jonathan. *24/7: Late Capitalism and the Ends of Sleep*. London: Verso, 2013.

"Cute Power! Asia Is in Love with Japan's Pop Culture." *Newsweek International*, November 8, 1999. Accessed March 11, 2015. http://www.newsweek.com/cute-power -164150.

Daniels, Jesse. *Cyber Racism: White Supremacy Online and the New Attack on Civil Rights*. Lanham, MD: Rowman and Littlefield, 2009.

Davey-Attlee, Florence. "Why China Is Sitting on Fashion's Front Row." CNN. February 26, 2013. Accessed January 24, 2015. http://www.cnn.com/2013/02/26/world /asia/china-london-fashion-week/.

Davies, Paul J. "Asian Century Will Dominate Global Financial Markets." *Financial Times*, April 7, 2014, 20.

Dávila, Arlene. *Latinos, Inc.: The Marketing and Making of a People*. Berkeley: University of California Press, 2012.

De Mul, Jos. "The Work of Art in the Age of Digital Recombination." In *Digital Material: Tracing New Media in Everyday Life and Technology*, edited by Marianne Van Den Boomen et al., 95–106. Amsterdam: Amsterdam University Press, 2009.

De Palol, Erika Marie. "About Me." Fashion Chalet (blog). Accessed January 22, 2015. http://fashionchalet.net/p/about-me.html.

Deuze, Mark. *Media Work*. Cambridge: Polity, 2007.

Digital Cultures Research Lab. "DCRL Questions: Nishant Shah." Vimeo.com. Accessed January 17, 2015. http://vimeo.com/81102111.

DiNardo, Julia. "Does Fashion Blogging Make You a Shopping Addict?" Independent Fashion Bloggers. October 8, 2013. Accessed January 26, 2015. http://heartifb.com/2013/10/08/does-fashion-blogging-make-you-a-shopping-addict.

Dishman, Lydia. "Prada's IPO: First in a Line of Luxury Companies Seeking Hong Kong Investors." *Forbes*. May 23, 2011. Accessed January 18, 2015. http://www.forbes.com/sites/lydiadishman/2011/05/23/pradas-ipo-first-in-a-line-of-luxury-companies-seeking-hong-kong-investors/.

———. "Prada's Potential IPO: When It Pays to Be Fashionably Late." *CBS News*, January 28, 2011. Accesssed March 18, 2015. http://www.cbsnews.com/news/pradas-potential-ipo-when-it-pays-to-be-fashionably-late/.

Doi, Takeo. *The Anatomy of Dependence*. New York: Kodansha, 1973.

Dolby, Nadine. "The Shifting Ground of Race: The Role of Taste in Youth's Production of Identities." *Race, Ethnicity, and Education* 3, no. 1 (2000): 7–17.

Donath, Judith. "Signals in Social Supernets." *Journal of Computer-Mediated Communication* 13, no. 1 (2007): 231–51.

Duggan, Lisa. *Twilight of Equality: Neoliberalism, Cultural Politics, and the Attack on Democracy*. Boston: Beacon, 2003.

Dwyer, Peter, and Johanna Wyn. *Youth, Education and Risk: Facing the Future*. London: Routledge, 2001.

Egan, Timothy. "Little Asia on the Hill." *New York Times*, January 7, 2007.

Ellison, Jo. "Love at First Site?" *Financial Times*, August 23, 2014.

Elton, Tiffany. "Lanvin Paris Fall 2010." TiffanyElton (blog). October 2010. Accessed January 18, 2015. http://tiffanyelton.blogspot.com/2010/10/susie-bubble-you-know-you-are-doing.html#links.

Enstad, Nan. *Ladies of Labor, Girls of Adventure: Working Women, Popular Culture, and Labor Politics at the Turn of the Twentieth Century*. New York: Columbia University Press, 1990.

Entwistle, Joanne. *The Fashioned Body: Fashion, Dress, and Modern Social Theory*. Cambridge: Polity, 2000.

Entwistle, Joanne, and Ashley Mears. "Gender on Display: Peformativity in Fashion Modelling." *Cultural Sociology* 7, no. 3 (2013): 320–35.

Everett, Catherine. "Ramblings on Blogging." *Teen Vogue*. April 4, 2012. Accessed January 26, 2015. http://fashion.teenvogue.com/post/ramblings-on-blogging.

Fabian, Johannes. *Time and the Other: How Anthropology Makes Its Object*. New York: Columbia University Press, 2002.

Finauro, Beatrice. "Bryan Boy a Vogue Italia." *Vogue Italia*. September 24, 2010. Accessed January 22, 2015. http://www.vogue.it/magazine/notizie-del-giorno/2010/09/bryan-boy-a-vogue-italia#ad-image35421.

Fisher, Max. "Gangnam Style, Dissected: The Subversive Message within South Korea's Music Video Sensation." *Atlantic*. August 23, 2012. Accessed January 24, 2015. http://www.theatlantic.com/international/archive/2012/08/gangnam-style-dissected-the-subversive-message-within-south-koreas-music-video-sensation/261462/.

"Float On." *Vogue* (April 2010): 236–41.

FlorCruz, Michelle. "Shanghai Surpasses New York for Luxury Goods Buying, Despite Chinese Austerity Drive." *International Business Times*. February 6, 2014. Accessed January 18, 2015. http://www.ibtimes.com/shanghai-surpasses-new-york-luxury-goods-buying-despite-chinese-austerity-drive-1553742.

Florida, Richard. "Cities and the Creative Class in Asia." *Citylab*. November 17, 2011. January 17, 2015. http://www.theatlanticcities.com/jobs-and-economy/2011/11/cities-creative-class-in-asia/500/.

Florida, Richard, Charlotta Mellander, and Kevin Stolarick. "Creativity and Prosperity: The Global Creativity Index." Toronto: University of Toronto, Martin Prosperity Institute, September 2011. Accessed January 18, 2015. http://martinprosperity.org/media/GCI-Report-reduced-Oct%202011.pdf.

Furness, Hannah. "Nobody Wants a 'Real Person' On the Cover of *Vogue*, Editor Says." *Telegraph*. March 17, 2014. Accessed March 15, 2015. http://fashion.telegraph.co.uk/news-features/TMG10701240/Nobody-wants-a-real-person-on-the-cover-of-Vogue-editor-says.html.

Givhan, Robin. "Everyone's a Fashion Critic." *Harper's Bazaar*, September 2007, 316.

———. "The Golden Era of 'Fashion Blogging' Is Over." The Cut (blog). *New York Magazine*, April 21, 2014. Accessed January 19, 2015. http://nymag.com/thecut/2014/04/golden-era-of-fashion-blogging-is-over.html.

Glenn, Evelyn Nakano. "Cleaning Up/Kept Down: A Historical Perspective on Racial Inequality in 'Women's Work.'" *Stanford Law Review* 43, no. 6 (1991): 1333–56.

———. "From Servitude to Service Work: Historical Continuities in the Racial Division of Paid Reproductive Labor." *Signs* 18, no. 1 (1992): 1–42.

———. "Racial Ethnic Women's Labor: The Intersection of Race, Gender and Class Oppression." *Review of Radical Political Economies* 17, no. 3 (1985): 86–108.

———. *Unequal Freedom: How Race and Gender Shaped American Citizenship and Labor*. Cambridge, MA: Harvard University Press, 2004.

Goldberg, David Theo. *The Threat of Race: Reflections on Racial Neoliberalism*. Malden, MA: Blackwell, 2008.

Goman, Carol Kinsey. *The Silent Language of Leaders: How Body Language Can Help—or Hurt—How You Lead*. San Francisco, CA: Jossey-Bass, 2011.

Gortan, Renata. "Fashion Blogs Making Little Miss a Hit." *Sydney Daily Telegraph*, March 23, 2012.

Gover, C. Jane. *The Positive Image: Women Photographers in Turn of the Century America*. Albany: State University of New York Press, 1988.

Gray, Herman. "Subject(ed) to Recognition." *American Quarterly* 65, no. 4 (2013): 771–98.

Gruger, William. "PSY's 'Gangnam Style' Video Hits 1 Billion Views, Unprecedented Milestone." Billboard.com, December 21, 2012. Accessed January 24, 2015. http://www.billboard.com/biz/articles/news/1483733/psys-gangnam-style-video-hits-1-billion-views-unprecedented-milestone.

Gubar, Susan. "Racial Camp in *The Producers* and *Bamboozled*." *Film Quarterly* 60, no. 2 (2006): 26–37.

Gurrieri, Lauren, and Hélène Cherrier. "Queering Beauty: Fatshionistas in the Fatosphere." *Qualitative Market Research* 16, no. 3 (2013): 276–95.

Gustini, Ray. "Why Luxury Brands Love the Hong Kong Stock Exchange." Wire (blog). *Atlantic*. May 20, 2011. Accessed January 18, 2015. http://www.thewire.com/entertainment/2011/05/why-luxury-brands-love-hong-kong-stock-exchange/37980/.

Hamamoto, Darrell. *Monitored Peril: Asian Americans and the Politics of TV Representation*. Minneapolis: University of Minnesota Press, 1994.

Hamlin, Kevin, Ilya Gridneff, and William Davison. "Ethiopia Becomes China's China in Global Search for Cheap Labor." *Bloomberg*. July 22, 2014. Accessed March 11, 2015. http://www.bloomberg.com/news/articles/2014-07-22/ethiopia-becomes-china-s-china-in-search-for-cheap-labor.

Harris, Anita. *Future Girl: Young Women in the Twenty-First Century*. New York: Routledge, 2004.

Harris, Daniel. "Some Reflections on the Facial Expressions of Fashion Models: 100 Years of *Vogue*." *Salmagundi* 98–99 (Spring–Summer 1993): 128–40.

Harris, Tamara Winfrey. "Leaning In While Black." In These Times. April 19, 2013, http://inthesetimes.com/article/14888/leaning_in_while_black.

Harvey, David. *A Brief History of Neoliberalism*. Oxford: Oxford University Press, 2005.

———. *The Condition of Postmodernity: An Enquiry into the Origins of Cultural Change*. Malden, MA: Blackwell, 1990.

Harte, Bret. "Plain Language from Truthful James." *Overland Monthly* 5, no. 3 (September 1870): 287.

Hasinoff, Amy Adele. "Fashioning Race for the Free Market on *America's Next Top Model*." *Critical Studies in Media Communication* 25, no. 3 (2008): 324–43.

Hayles, N. Katherine. "Electronic Literature: What Is It?" Electronic Literature Organization. January 2, 2007. Accessed January 20, 2015. http://eliterature.org/pad/elp.html.

Hebdige, Dick. *Subculture: The Meaning of Style*. New York: Methuen, 1979.

Heiss, Sarah N. "Locating the Bodies of Women and Disability in Definitions of Beauty: An Analysis of Dove's Campaign for Real Beauty." *Disability Studies Quarterly* (2011). Accessed January 18, 2015. http://dsq-sds.org/article/view/1367/1497.

Hellmich, Nanci. "Do Thin Models Warp Girls' Body Image?" *USA Today*. September 26, 2006. Accessed March 12, 2015. http://usatoday30.usatoday.com/news /health/2006-09-25-thin-models_x.htm.

Henry, Colette. "Women and the Creative Industries: Exploring the Popular Appeal." *Creative Industries Journal* 2, no. 2 (2009): 143–60.

Hesmondhalgh, David. "User-Generated Content, Free Labour and the Cultural Industries." *ephemera* 10, nos. 3–4 (2010): 267–84.

Heyer, Mark. "The Creative Challenge of CD-ROM." In *CD-ROM: The New Papyrus*, edited by Steve Lambert and Suzanne Ropiequet, 347–57. Redmond, OR: Microsoft Press, 1986.

Hilton, Lisa. "What's Wrong with Skinny?" *Daily Beast*. February 8, 2010. Accessed January 26, 2015. http://www.thedailybeast.com/articles/2010/02/08/are-models -too-thin.html.

Hiner, Susan. *Accessories to Modernity: Fashion and the Feminine in Nineteenth Century France*. Philadelphia: University of Pennsylvania Press, 2010.

Hjorth, Larissa. "Odours of Mobility: Mobile Phones and Japanese Cute Culture in the Asia-Pacific." *Journal of Intercultural Studies* 26, nos. 1–2 (2005): 39–55.

"HKEx Monthly Market Highlights—November 2011." Hong Kong Exchange. November 30, 2011. Accessed March 12, 2015. http://www.hkex.com.hk/eng/stat/statrpt /mkthl/mkthl201111.htm.

Hobson, Janell. "The 'Batty' Politic: Toward an Aesthetic of the Black Female Body." *Hypatia* 18, no. 4 (2003): 87–105.

Hochschild, Arlie Russell. *The Managed Heart: Commercialization of Human Feeling*. Berkeley: University of California Press, 1983.

Hodkinson, Paul, and Sian Lincoln. "Online Journals as Virtual Bedrooms? Young People, Identity and Personal Space." *Young* 16, no. 4 (2008): 625–50.

Holland, Patricia. " 'sweet It Is To Scan . . .': Personal Photographs and Popular Photography." In *Photography: A Critical Introduction*, edited by Liz Wells, 113–58. New York: Routledge, 2000.

hooks, bell. "Dig Deep: Beyond Lean In." Feminist Wire. October 28, 2013. Accessed January 24, 2015. http://thefeministwire.com/2013/10/17973/.

Houghton, Matt, dir. "Google Chrome: 'Julie Deane.'" Vimeo.com. Accessed January 26, 2015. http://vimeo.com/70049226.

Humm, Maggie. *Snapshots of Bloomsbury: The Private Lives of Virginia Woolf and Vanessa Bell*. New Brunswick, NJ: Rutgers University Press, 2006.

Hyland, Véronique. "Balenciaga Unveils China-Exclusive Looks in Beijing." The Cut (blog). *New York Magazine*, May 16, 2014. Accessed January 18, 2015. http://nymag .com/thecut/2014/05/balenciaga-unveils-china-exclusive-looks.html.

Indvik, Lauren. "Fashion Retailer Responds to Facebook Fans' Call for 'Real Women' in Photos." Mashable. June 18, 2010. Accessed January 18, 2015. http://mashable .com/2010/06/18/ann-taylor-facebook/.

Isherwood, Christopher. *The World in the Evening*. New York: Random House, 1954.

Jacob, Jennine. "Actually, Bloggers DO Influence People to Buy." Independent Fashion Bloggers. March 24, 2013. Accessed January 18, 2015. http://heartifb.com/2013 /03/25/actually-bloggers-do-influence-people-to-buy/.

Jameson, Fredric. *Postmodernism, or, The Cultural Logic of Late Capitalism*. Durham, NC: Duke University Press, 1991.

Jarrett, Kylie. "The Relevance of 'Women's Work': Social Reproduction and Immaterial Labour in Digital Media." *Television and New Media* 15, no. 1 (2014): 14–29.

" 'Jeans Machine' Scanner Sizes You Up." *Good Morning, America*. April 27, 2011. Accessed March 15, 2015. http://abcnews.go.com/GMA/video/clothing-scanner -determines-shoppers-size-gadget-jean-pants-dress-13467626.

Jenkins, Henry, et al. *Confronting the Challenges of Participatory Culture: Media Education for the 21st Century*. Cambridge, MA: MIT Press, 2009.

JLJ Group. "China: Challenges and Opportunities for US Designer Companies." Council of Fashion Designers of America. June 26, 2009. Accessed January 24, 2015. http://cfda.com/blog/china-challenges-and-opportunities-for-us-designer -companies.

Johnston, Josée, and Judith Taylor. "Feminist Consumerism and Fat Activists: A Comparative Study of Grassroots Activism and the Dove Real Beauty Campaign." *Signs* 33, no. 4 (2008): 941–66.

Joos, Natalie. "She's Bubblicious." Tales of Endearment (blog). March 22, 2011. Accessed January 17, 2015. http://talesofendearment.com/shes-bubblicious.

Joseph, Ralina L. " 'Tyra Banks Is Fat': Reading (Post-) Racism and (Post-) Feminism in the New Millennium." *Critical Studies in Media Communication* 26, no. 3 (2009): 237–54.

Joslin, Richard, et al. "Gap, Inc.: Has the Retailer Lost Its Style?" In *Understanding Business Strategy: Concepts and Cases*, edited by R. Duane Ireland et al., 1–18. Mason, OH: South-Western Cengage Learning, 2008.

Jung, Moon-Ho. *Coolies and Cane: Race, Labor, and Sugar in the Age of Emancipation*. Baltimore, MD: Johns Hopkins University Press, 2006.

Kan, Deborah. "Diane von Furstenberg on China." Scene Asia (blog). Wall Street Journal. June 20, 2012. Accessed January 17, 2015. http://blogs.wsj.com/scene /2012/06/20/diane-von-furstenberg-on-the-china-century/.

Kang, Laura Hyun Yi. *Compositional Subjects: Enfiguring Asian/American Women*. Durham, NC: Duke University Press, 2002.

Kansara, Vikram Alexei. "The Business of Blogging: Style Bubble." Business of Fashion (blog). January 24, 2011. Accessed January 17, 2015. http://www.businessoffashion .com/2011/01/the-business-of-blogging-susie-bubble.html.

———. "Fashion 2.0: L2 Innovation Forum Examines Disruptive Thinking, Listening and Iterative Development." Business of Fashion (blog). November 8, 2010. Accessed March 15, 2015. http://www.businessoffashion.com/2010/11/fashion -2-0-l2-innovation-forum-examines-disruptive-thinking-listening-and-iterative -development.html.

Keil, Raoul. "Letter from the Editor." Schön, July 2011, 2.

Kelsky, Karen. Women on the Verge: Japanese Women, Western Dreams. Durham, NC: Duke University Press, 2001.

Kim, Claire Jean. "The Racial Triangulation of Asian Americans." Politics and Society 27, no. 1 (1999): 105–38.

King, Joyann. "Bloggers Take Over the Front Row." InStyle, September 10, 2009. Accessed March 12, 2015. http://news.instyle.com/2009/09/10/bloggers-take-over -the-front-row/.

Kinsella, Sharon. "Cuties in Japan." In Women, Media, and Consumption in Japan, edited by Lise Skov, 220–54. New York: Routledge, 2013.

Knebl, Claire. "Bryanboy on Starting His Blog from the Ground Up." Teen Vogue. August 2013. Accessed March 14, 2015. http://www.teenvogue.com/fashion/2013-08 /bryanboy-blogging-tips.

Knibbs, Kate. "Wikipedia Has a Gender Problem—Can It Be Fixed?" Digital Trends. May 1, 2013. Accessed January 17, 2015. http://www.digitaltrends.com/web/wikipedia -has-a-gender-problem/.

Kondo, Dorinne. About Face: Performing Race in Fashion and Theater. New York: Routledge 1997.

———. "Interview with Nirmal Puwar." Fashion Theory 7, nos. 3–4 (2003): 253–56.

Kopytoff, Igor. "The Cultural Biography of Things." In The Social Life of Things: Commodities in Cultural Perspective, edited by Arjun Appadurai, 64–91. Cambridge: Cambridge University Press, 1986.

Kretz, Gachoucha, and Kristine de Valck. " 'Pixelize Me!': Digital Storytelling and the Creation of Archetypal Myths through Explicit and Implicit Self-Brand Association in Fashion and Luxury Blogs." In Research in Consumer Behavior, edited by Russell W. Belk, 12:313–29. Emerald Group, 2010.

Kwan, Kevin. Crazy Rich Asians. New York: Penguin, 2013.

La Ferla, Ruth. "An Eye for Detail, and Plenty of Pop." New York Times, December 8, 2010.

Lagerfeld, Karl, dir. Paris-Shanghai: A Fantasy. Film. Performed by Edita Vilkeviciute, Freja Beha, and Baptiste Giabiconi, Chanel. 2009.

Lakoff, Robin Tolmach, and Raquel L. Scherr. Face Value: The Politics of Beauty. Boston: Routledge and Kegan Paul, 1984.

Lam, Andrew. "The 'Bamboo Ceiling': Hollywood Shuns Asians, While New Media Embraces Them." Huffington Post. January 26, 2014. Accessed January 17, 2015. http://www.huffingtonpost.com/andrew-lam/the-bamboo-ceiling_b_4665943 .html.

Lancelle. "This Week's Most Materialistic Blogger Award Goes to Sterling Style." Get Off My Internets. November 9, 2011. Accessed January 24, 2015. http://getoffmyinternets .net/2011/this-weeks-most-materialistic-blogger-award-goes-to-sterling-style.

Larmer, Brook. "Shoppers' Republic of China." *New York Times Magazine*, November 30, 2010, 64–70.

Larson, Christina. "The Growing Allure of Designed-in-China Fashion." *Bloomberg Businessweek*, May 15, 2014. http://www.bloomberg.com/bw/articles/2014-05-15/the -growing-allure-of-designed-in-china-fashions.

Lau, Kristie. "Meet Tyra's Protege: Fashion Blogger Bryanboy Revealed to Be New America's Next Top Model Judge." *Daily Mail*, May 25, 2012.

Lau, Susanna. "About." Style Bubble (blog). July 18, 2013. Accessed January 17, 2015. http://www.stylebubble.co.uk/about.

———. "Chinoiserie Query." Style Bubble (blog). January 31, 2011. Accessed January 21, 2015. http://www.stylebubble.co.uk/style_bubble/2011/01/chinoiserie-query .html.

———. "FAQ." Style Bubble (blog). Accessed January 18, 2015. http://www.stylebub ble.co.uk/faq.

———. "Fashion Blogger Susie Bubble Makes a Case in Defense of Street Style." *Vogue*, February 5, 2014. Accessed January 19, 2015. http://www.vogue.com/vogue-daily /article/fashion-blogger-susie-bubble-makes-a-case-in-defense-of-street-style/#1.

———. "Let the Music Guide You." Style Bubble (blog). March 11, 2006. Accessed January 22, 2015. http://www.stylebubble.co.uk/style_bubble/2006/03/let_the_music _g.html.

———. "Look at Me, Don't Look at Me." Style Bubble (blog). August 14, 2007. Accessed January 24, 2015. http://www.stylebubble.co.uk/style_bubble/2007/08/look -at-me-dont.html.

———. "Monday Larks." Style Bubble (blog). April 19, 2010. Accessed January 24, 2015. http://www.stylebubble.co.uk/style_bubble/2010/04/monday-larks.html.

———. "Oooh la la . . . viva la revolution!" Style Bubble (blog). March 19, 2006. Accessed January 22, 2015. http://www.stylebubble.co.uk/style_bubble/2006/03/oooh _la_laviva_.html.

———. "Parisian Reflections (Most Probably Caused by This Sodding Rain)." Style Bubble (blog). October 9, 2007. Accessed January 24, 2015. http://www.stylebub ble.co.uk/style_bubble/2007/10/parisian-reflec.html.

———. "Party Shirt Time." Style Bubble (blog). December 30, 2011. Accessed January 24, 2015. http://www.stylebubble.co.uk/style_bubble/2011/12/party-shirt-time .html.

———. "Round the Table." Style Bubble (blog). December 2, 2011. Accessed January 19, 2015. http://www.stylebubble.co.uk/style_bubble/2011/12/round-the -table.html.

———. "Sophie Bubble." Style Bubble (blog). March 27, 2013. Accessed January 26, 2015. http://www.stylebubble.co.uk/style_bubble/2013/03/sophie-bubble.html.

———. "There Are Two Kinds of People: The Skirts Over Trousers People and Everyone Else." Style Bubble (blog). March 9, 2006. Accessed March 15, 2015. http://stylebubble.co.uk/style_bubble/2006/03/there_are_two_k.html.

———. "Why Susie Shouldn't Go to LV." Style Bubble (blog). October 8, 2006. http://stylebubble.typepad.com/style_bubble/2006/10/why_susie_shoul.html.

———. "Words, Words, Words . . . ." Style Bubble (blog). August 4, 2009. Accessed January 27, 2015. http://www.stylebubble.co.uk/style_bubble/2009/08/words-words-words.html.

Lee, Janice Y. K. "Meet the New Asian Superrich." Elle. May 22, 2013. Accessed January 18, 2015. http://www.elle.com/life-love/personal-style/books-on-how-to-become-rich-in-asia.

Lee, Sangheon, Deirdre McCann, and Jon C. Messenger. Working Time around the World: Trends in Working Hours, Laws and Policies in a Global Comparative Perspective. Geneva: International Labor Organization, 2007.

Lee, Youyoung. "In America, a New Asian Creative Class." Huffington Post. August 27, 2013. Accessed January 18, 2015. http://www.huffingtonpost.com/youyoung-lee/in-america-a-new-asian-creative-class_b_3822813.html.

Leong, Nancy. "Racial Capitalism." Harvard Law Review 126, no. 8 (2013): 2151–226.

Leonhardt, David. "Can the Chinese Discover the Urge to Splurge?" New York Times Magazine, November 24, 2010, 56–63, 88, 90.

Lessin, Tia, dir. Behind the Labels: Garment Workers on US Saipan. Brooklyn, NY: Witness Video, 2001.

Liao, Christine. "Virtual Fashion Play as Embodied Identity Re/Assembling: Second Life Fashion Bloggers and Their Avatar Bodies." In Reinventing Ourselves: Contemporary Concepts of Identity in Virtual Worlds, edited by Anna Peachey and Mark Childs, 101–27. New York: Springer, 2011.

Lim, Christy. "Jason Wu's New Collection: 'Elegant and Powerful.'" Dumpling, March 21, 2012. Accessed January 24, 2015. http://www.dumplingmag.com/2012/03/jason-wus-new-collection-elegant-and-powerful/.

Lind, Andrew. "The Changing Position of Domestic Service in Hawaii." Social Process in Hawaii 15 (1951): 71–87.

Lipsitz, George. Possessive Investment in Whiteness: How White People Profit from Identity Politics. Philadelphia: Temple University Press, 2006.

Liu, Hugo. "Social Network Profiles as Taste Performances." Journal of Computer-Mediated Communication 13, no. 1 (2007): 252–75.

Liu, Lydia. "The Female Body and Nationalist Discourse: The Field of Life and Death Revisited." In Scattered Hegemonies: Postmodernity and Transnational Feminist Practices, edited by Inderpal Grewal and Caren Kaplan, 37–62. Minneapolis: University of Minnesota Press, 1994.

Livingstone, Sonia. "On the Relation between Audiences and Publics." In Audiences and Publics: When Cultural Engagement Matters for the Public Sphere, edited by Sonia Livingstone, 17–41. Portland, OR: Intellect, 2005.

"LOFT Employees Model Looks on Facebook." Huffington Post. June 21, 2010. Accessed January 18, 2015. http://www.huffingtonpost.com/2010/06/21/ann-taylor-employees-mode_n_619531.html.

Long, Craig David. "Jason Wu: A Silk Road." *Montecristo*. March 19, 2012. Accessed January 24, 2015. http://montecristomagazine.com/magazine/spring-2012/jason-wu.

Lorentzen, Renee. "Is Fashion Blogging Dead?" Refinery29. December 27, 2013. Accessed January 19, 2015. http://www.refinery29.com/2013/12/59713/future-of-fashion-blogging.

Lou, Lana. "Fashion Blogger: OOTD #1." The Truth about Blondes (blog). May 9, 2014. Accessed January 22, 2015. http://thetruthaboutblondes.com/2014/05/09/fashion-blogger-ootd-1/.

Lukács, Gabriella. "The Labor of Cute: Net Idols, Cute Culture and the Social Factory in Contemporary Japan." Talk at Weatherhead East Asian Institute, Columbia University, October 3, 2011. Accessed January 18, 2015. https://itunes.apple.com/fi/itunes-u/labor-cute-net-idols-cute/id535917809?mt=10.

MacKinnon, Catherine A. *Towards a Feminist Theory of the State*. Cambridge, MA: Harvard University Press, 1991.

Magnet, Shoshana. *When Biometrics Fail: Gender, Race, and the Technology of Identity*. Durham, NC: Duke University Press, 2011.

Maira, Sunaina. "Henna and Hip Hop: The Politics of Cultural Production and the Work of Cultural Studies." *Journal of Asian American Studies* 3, no. 3 (2000): 329–69.

———. "Indo-Chic: Late Capitalist Orientalism and Imperial Culture." In *Alien Encounters: Popular Culture in Asian America*, edited by Mimi Thi Nguyen and Thuy Linh Nguyen Tu, 221–43. Durham, NC: Duke University Press, 2007.

Manderson, Leonore, and Margaret Jolly. *Sites of Desire/Economies of Pleasure: Sexualities in Asia and the Pacific*. Chicago: University of Chicago Press, 1997.

Marcus, Bennett. "Bryan Boy Earns Handsome Rewards for His Blogging." The Cut (blog). *New York Magazine*, December 7, 2010. Accessed January 18, 2015. http://nymag.com/thecut/2010/12/bryan_boy_earns_handsome_rewar.html.

Marlene. "What Do Bloggers Really Wear?" Chocolate, Cookies, and Candies (blog). April 4, 2013. Accessed January 22, 2015. http://www.chocolatecookiesandcandies.com/2013/04/what-do-bloggers-really-wear.html.

Martin, Natasha T. "Diversity and the Virtual Workplace: Performance Identity and Shifting Boundaries of Workplace Engagement." *Lewis and Clark Law Review* 16, no. 2 (2012): 605–46.

Marwick, Alice, and danah boyd, "I Tweet Honestly, I Tweet Passionately: Twitter Users, Context Collapse, and the Imagined Audience." *New Media and Society* 13, no. 1 (2011): 114–33.

Matile, Roger. "Survey Finds We're Working More Hours than We Did Back in '73." *Oswego Ledger-Sentinel*. May 10, 2012. Accessed January 27, 2015. http://www.ledgersentinel.com/article.asp?a=10394.

Matsumoto, Nancy. "Stinky, Spicy, and Delicious: The Radical Reinvention of Asian American Food." *Atlantic*. July 16, 2012. Accessed January 18, 2015. http://www .theatlantic.com/national/archive/2012/07/stinky-spicy-and-delicious-the-radical -reinvention-of-asian-american-food/259864/.

Mau, Dhani. "New Evidence that Alexander Wang's Chinese Connections May Have Helped Land Him Balenciaga." Fashionista.com. December 10, 2012. Accessed January 19, 2015. http://fashionista.com/2012/12/did-alexander-wangs-chinese -connections-help-get-him-the-balenciaga-job#awesm=~oHEfYY7K2BuKQz.

McClintock, Anne. *Imperial Leather: Race, Gender, and Sexuality in the Colonial Contest*. New York: Routledge, 1995.

McLaren, Peter. "Multiculturalism and the Postmodern Critique." In *Between Borders: Pedagogy and the Politics of Cultural Studies*, edited by Henry Giroux and Peter McLaren, 192–224. New York: Routledge, 1994.

McLarney, Ellen. "Burqa in Vogue: Fashioning Afghanistan." *Journal of Middle East Women's Studies* 5, no. 1 (2009): 1–20.

Mcpherson, Tara. "Digital Possibilities and the Reimagining of Politics, Place, and the Self." In *Transmedia Frictions: The Digital, the Arts, and the Humanities*, edited by Marsha Kinder and Tara McPherson, 161–79. Berkeley: University of California Press, 2014.

Mead, Rebecca. "The Scourge of 'Relatability.'" *New Yorker*. August 1, 2014. Accessed January 23, 2015. http://www.newyorker.com/culture/cultural-comment/scourge -relatability.

Mears, Ashley. "Size Zero High-End Ethnic: Cultural Production and the Reproduction of Culture in Fashion Modeling." *Poetics* 38, no. 1 (2010): 21–46.

Medine, Leandra. "Blog Is a Dirty Word." ManRepeller (blog). February 18, 2013. Accessed March 15, 2015. http://www.manrepeller.com/2013/02/blog-is-a-dirty-word .html.

———. "What Is a Man Repeller?" ManRepeller (blog). April 25, 2010. Accessed January 20, 2015. http://www.manrepeller.com/2010/04/what-is-man-repeller.html.

Melamed, Jodi. *Represent and Destroy: Rationalizing Violence in the New Racial Capitalism*. Minneapolis: University of Minnesota Press, 2011.

———. "The Spirit of Neoliberalism: From Racial Liberalism to Neoliberal Multiculturalism." *Social Text* 24, no. 4 89 (2006): 1–24.

Menkes, Suzy. "Balenciaga Points East with Wang." *International Herald Tribune*, December 4, 2012.

———. "The Circus of Fashion." *New York Times Magazine*, February 17, 2013, 91–94.

———. "Working the Crowd: An Era of Spontaneous Mass Reaction Is Teaching Designers a Harsh Lesson." *International New York Times*, October 15, 2013.

Mercer, Kobena. "Black Hair/Style Politics." *New Formations* 3 (Winter 1987): 33–54.

Miller, Monica L. *Slaves to Fashion: Black Dandyism and the Styling of Black Diasporic Identity*. Durham, NC: Duke University Press, 2009.

Moallem, Minoo. "Carpets and Computers." (Talk) Tech Museum of Innovation February 19, 2012, San Jose, California.

———. "Nation-on-the Move" (design by Eric Loyer). *Vectors* 3, no. 1 (special issue on difference, Fall 2007).

Monaghan, Angela, and Jonathan Kaiman. "Why Global Recovery Could Depend on China's Taste for Luxury." *Guardian.* May 10, 2014. Accessed January 18, 2015. http://www.theguardian.com/business/2014/may/11/why-global-recovery-china -luxury-western-export-middle-class-consumer.

Morris, William. *Swindon Fifty Years Ago, More or Less: Reminiscences, Notes, and Relics of Ye Old Wiltshire Towne.* Ilford, UK: Woburn, 1971.

"Moxsie's Nod to Blogger Susie Bubble Is a Sign of the Times." *Racked.* August 11, 2010. Accessed January 18, 2015. http://ny.racked.com/archives/2010/08/11/moxie _3_susie_bubble.php.

Moy, Victoria. "The Asian Whizkid's Sibling? The Heartthrob." *Huffington Post.* March 3, 2011. Accessed January 17, 2015. http://www.huffingtonpost.com/victoria-moy /is-america-ready-for-cool_b_830525.html.

Nakamura, Lisa. *Cybertypes: Race, Ethnicity, and Identity on the Internet.* New York: Routledge, 2002.

———. *Digitizing Race: Visual Cultures of the Internet.* Minneapolis: University of Minnesota Press, 2007.

———. "Don't Hate the Player, Hate the Game: The Racialization of Labor in World of Warcraft." *Critical Studies in Media Communication* 26, no. 2 (2009): 128–44.

———. "Economies of Digital Production in East Asia: iPhone Girls and the Transnational Circuits of Cool." *Media Fields Journal* 2 (2011): 1–10.

———. "Indigenous Circuits." *Computer History Museum.* Accessed January 17, 2015. http://www.computerhistory.org/atchm/indigenous-circuits/.

Nakamura, Lisa, and Peter A. Chow-White. "Introduction—Race and Digital Technology: Code, the Color Line, and the Information Society." In *Race after the Internet,* edited by Lisa Nakamura and Peter A. Chow-White, 1–18. New York: Routledge 2012.

Nakata, J. R. "Will the Real Bryanboy Please Stand Up?" *Rogue.* January 21, 2013. Accessed March 14, 2015. http://rogue.ph/features/2013/1/18/will-the-real-bryanboy -please-stand-up.

"Need a Product Endorsement? Look to Bloggers, Not Celebrities." *Business News Daily.* April 19, 2011. Accessed January 18, 2015. http://www.businessnewsdaily.com /882-bloggers-celebrities-influence.html.

Neely, Rumi. "at the flower shoppe." Fashion Toast (blog). June 28, 2012. Accessed March 15, 2015. http://fashiontoast.com/2012/06/at-the-flower-shoppe/.

———. "casual friday." Fashion Toast (blog). June 29, 2012. Accessed March 15, 2015. http://fashiontoast.com/2012/06/casual-friday/.

———. "oasis." Fashion Toast (blog). July 2, 2012. Accessed March 15, 2015. http:// fashiontoast.com/2012/07/oasis-2/.

———. "pink in beverly hills." Fashion Toast (blog). June 27, 2012. Accessed March 15, 2015. http://fashiontoast.com/2012/06/pink-in-beverly-hills/.

———. "up high." Fashion Toast (blog). July 7, 2010. Accessed March 15, 2015. http://fashiontoast.com/2010/07/up-high/.

Nguyen, Mimi Thi. "Background Color." Threadbared (blog). July 19, 2008. Accessed January 23, 2015. https://iheartthreadbared.wordpress.com/2008/07/19/.

———. "Background Color, Redux." Threadbared (blog). July 28, 2008. Accessed January 23, 2015. https://iheartthreadbared.wordpress.com/2008/07/28/background-color-redux/.

———. "Background Color, Redux II." Threadbared (blog), July 31, 2008. Accessed January 23, 2015. http://iheartthreadbared.wordpress.com/2008/07/31/background-color-redux-ii/.

———. "Couture Coincidence." Threadbared (blog). July 23, 2009. Accessed January 24, 2015. http://iheartthreadbared.wordpress.com/2009/07/23/couture-coincidence/.

Nguyen, Mimi Thi, and Thuy Linh N. Tu. Introduction. In Alien Encounters: Popular Culture in Asian America, edited by Mimi Thi Nguyen and Thuy Linh N. Tu, 1–34. Durham, NC: Duke University Press, 2007.

Nguyen, Wendy. "Spring Romance: Coral Midi Dress & Tacori Ambassador." Wendy's Lookbook (blog). May 13, 2013. Accessed January 17, 2015. http://www.wendyslookbook.com/2013/05/spring-romance-coral-midi-dress-tacori-ambassador/.

Nuttall, Sarah. "Stylizing the Self: The Y Generation in Rosebank, Johannesburg." Public Culture 16, no. 3 (2004): 430–52.

Nye, Joseph S., Jr. Bound to Lead: The Changing Nature of American Power. New York: Basic, 1990.

———. Soft Power: The Means to Success in World Politics. New York: Public Affairs, 2004.

Odell, Amy. "Finding the Next Bryanboy." BuzzFeed. February 6, 2013. Accessed January 19, 2015. http://www.buzzfeed.com/amyodell/finding-the-next-bryan-boy.

———. "Stars Go Makeupless on the Cover of French Elle." The Cut (blog). New York Magazine. April 15, 2009. Accessed March 15, 2015. http://nymag.com/thecut/2009/04/stars_go_makeup-less_on_the_co.html.

———. "Why the Era of Personal Style Blogs Must Come to an End." BuzzFeed. June 13, 2013. Accessed January 19, 2015. http://www.buzzfeed.com/amyodell/why-the-era-of-personal-style-blogs-must-come-to-an-end.

Okihiro, Gary. Cane Fires: The Anti-Japanese Movement in Hawaii, 1865–1945. Philadelphia: Temple University Press, 1991.

Okoye, Chukwuma. "Looking Back: Nigerian Video Film Anthropologises the West," Leeds African Studies Bulletin 72 (2010–11): 76–90.

Ong, Aihwa. Flexible Citizenship: The Cultural Logics of Transnationality. Durham, NC: Duke University Press, 1999.

———. "The Gender and Labor Politics of Postmodernity." Annual Review of Anthropology 20 (1991): 279–309.

———. *Neoliberalism as Exception: Mutations in Citizenship and Sovereignty.* Durham, NC: Duke University Press, 2006.

Ozersky, Josh. "Talented, Young and Asian American." *Time,* June 20, 2012. Accessed January 18, 2015. http://ideas.time.com/2012/06/20/talented-young-asian -american/.

"Page Law 1875." Center for Educational Telecommunications. Accessed January 19, 2015. http://www.cetel.org/1875_page.html.

Palmgren, Ann-Charlotte. "Posing My Identity. Today's Outfit, Identity and Gender in Swedish Blogs." *Observatorio* 4, no. 2 (2010): 19–34.

Palumbo-Liu, David. *Asian/American: Historical Crossings of a Racial Frontier.* Stanford, CA: Stanford University Press, 1999.

Papacharissi, Zizi. "The Presentation of Self in Virtual Life: Characteristics of Personal Home Pages." *Journalism and Mass Communication Quarterly* 79, no. 3 (2002): 643–60.

Paquette, Marie-Claude, and Kim Raine. "Sociocultural Context of Women's Body Image." *Social Science and Medicine* 59, no. 5 (2004): 1047–58.

Parreñas, Rhacel Salazar. *Servants of Globalization: Women, Migration, and Domestic Work.* Stanford, CA: Stanford University Press, 2001.

Pascale, Celine-Marie. "All in a Day's Work a Feminist Analysis of Class Formation and Social Identity." *Race, Gender and Class* 8, no. 2 (2001): 34–59.

Paton, Elizabeth. "Coach to List on Hong Kong Stock Exchange." *Financial Times.* November 30, 2011. Accessed March 12, 2015. http://www.ft.com/intl/cms/s/0 /2f27b24e-1b4b-11e1-85f8-00144feabdco.html.

Pearson, Catherine. "Fashion and Eating Disorders: How Much Responsibility Does Industry Have?" *Huffington Post.* September 13, 2011. Accessed January 24, 2015. http://www.huffingtonpost.com/2011/09/13/fashion-eating-disorders-industry -responsibility_n_955497.html.

Perry, Imani. *More Beautiful and More Terrible: The Embrace and Transcendence of Racial Inequality in the United States.* New York: New York University Press, 2011.

Peters, Tom. "The Brand Called You." *Fast Company.* August 31, 1997. Accessed January 24, 2015. http://www.fastcompany.com/magazine/10/brandyou.html.

Petersen, William. "Success Story, Japanese American Style." *New York Times,* January 9, 1966.

Pfeiffer, Alice. "Young Bloggers Have Ear of Fashion Heavyweights." *International Herald Tribune,* September 14, 2009.

Pham, Minh-Ha T. "Couture's Chinese Culture Shock." *American Prospect.* January 27, 2012. Accessed January 19, 2015. http://prospect.org/article/coutures-chinese -culture-shock.

———. " 'Diversity' in Fashion Will Never Be Enough." *Salon,* October 2, 2013. Accessed January 18, 2015. http://www.salon.com/2013/10/02/diversity_in_fashion _will_never_be_enough_partner/.

————. "On the Seduction of Proenza Schouler's *Act Da Fool*." Threadbared (blog). September 7, 2010. Accessed January 17, 2015. http://iheartthreadbared.wordpress.com/2010/09/07/on-the-seduction-of-proenza-schouler's-act-da%C2%Aofool/.

————. "Paul Poiret's Magical Techno-Oriental Fashions (1911): Race, Clothing, and Virtuality in the Machine Age." *Configurations* 21, no. 1 (2013): 1–26.

————. " 'Susie Bubble Is a Sign of the Times': The Embodiment of Success in the Web 2.0 Economy." *Feminist Media Studies* 13, no. 2 (2013): 245–67.

————. "The Truth of Lagerfeld's Idea of China." Threadbared (blog). December 7, 2009. Accessed January 18, 2015. http://iheartthreadbared.wordpress.com/2009/12/07/the-truth-of-lagerfelds-idea-of-china/.

————. "Unintentionally Eating the Other." Threadbared (blog). September 12, 2011. Accessed January 17, 2015. http://iheartthreadbared.wordpress.com/2011/09/12/unintentional-eating/.

————. "What's in a Name?" *American Prospect.* November 3, 2011. Accessed January 24, 2015. http://prospect.org/article/whats-name-3.

————. "Why Fashion Should Stop Trying to Be Diverse." Threadbared (blog). September 30, 2013. Accessed January 18, 2015. http://iheartthreadbared.wordpress.com/2013/09/30/just-stop/.

Phelan, Hayley. "Can You Trust the Editorial Integrity of Personal Style Blogs? A Closer Look at How Bloggers Make Money." Fashionista.com. November 14, 2011. Accessed January 19, 2015. http://fashionista.com/2011/11/can-you-trust-the-editorial-integrity-of-style-bloggers-a-closer-look-at-how-bloggers-make-money/2/.

————. "How Personal Style Bloggers Are Raking in Millions." Fashionista.com. August 20, 2013. Accessed January 17, 2015. http://fashionista.com/2013/08/how-personal-style-bloggers-are-raking-in-millions/.

Phelps, Nicole. "Jason Wu Fall 2012 Ready-to-Wear Review." Style.com. February 10, 2012. Accessed March 12, 2015. http://www.style.com/fashion-shows/fall-2012-ready-to-wear/jason-wu.

"Philippine Blogger Stirs a Fashion Revolution." *Independent,* March 6, 2011. Accessed March 16, 2015. http://www.independent.co.uk/life-style/fashion/philippine-blogger-stirs-a-fashion-revolution-2233756.html.

"Poverty among Women and Families, 2000–2010." National Women's Law Center. September 2011. Accessed March 18, 2015. http://www.nwlc.org/sites/default/files/pdfs/povertyamongwomenandfamilies2010final.pdf.

"Psy's 'Gangnam Style' MV becomes Most Liked Video in YouTube History." AllKPop. September 13, 2012. Accessed January 24, 2015. http://www.allkpop.com/article/2012/09/psys-gangnam-style-mv-becomes-most-liked-video-in-youtube-history.

Puwar, Nirmal. "Multicultural Fashion: Stirrings of another Sense of Aesthetics and Memory." *Feminist Review* 71 (2002): 63–87.

Rahman, Abid. "Is the Era of Selfie-Centred Fashion Blogging Coming to an End?" *South China Morning Post,* May 6, 2014. Accessed January 27, 2015. http://www

.scmp.com/lifestyle/fashion-watches/article/1505079/era-selfie-centred-fashion
-blogging-coming-end.

Ramirez, Catherine S. *The Woman in the Zoot Suit: Gender, Nationalism, and the Cultural Politics of Memory*. Durham, NC: Duke University Press, 2009.

Rattansi, Ali, and Ann Phoenix. "Rethinking Youth Identities: Modernist and Post-modernist Frameworks." *Identity* 5, no. 2 (2005): 97–123.

Raustiala, Kal, and Christopher Sprigman. *The Knockoff Economy: How Imitation Sparks Innovation*. New York: Oxford University Press, 2012.

Reed, Adam. " 'My Blog Is Me': Texts and Persons in UK Online Journal Culture." *Ethnos* 70, no. 2 (2005): 220–42.

Reiter, Grechen. "Is This the End of Fashion Blogging?" Independent Fashion Bloggers. October 24, 2014. Accessed January 27, 2015. http://heartifb.com/2014/10/24/is-this-the-end-of-fashion-blogging/.

"Retouching Is 'Excessive' Says SlimLine CoverGirl Kate Winslet." *Hello*, January 10, 2003. Accessed January 26, 2015. http://www.hellomagazine.com/film/2003/01/10/katewinslet/.

Richards, Patricia. "Of Indians and Terrorists: How the State and Local Elites Construct the Mapuche in Neoliberal Multicultural Chile." *Journal of Latin American Studies* 42, no. 1 (2010): 59–90.

Ritzer, George, and Nathan Jurgenson. "Production, Consumption, Prosumption: The Nature of Capitalism in the Age of the Digital 'Prosumer.' " *Journal of Consumer Culture* 10, no. 1 (2010): 13–36.

"Roadmap for Indonesia's Textile and Textile Products Industry." *Indonesia-Investments*. April 22, 2013. Accessed January 18, 2015. http://www.indonesia-investments.com/news/todays-headlines/roadmap-for-indonesias-textile-and-textile-products-industry/item673.

Robinson, Cedric J. *Black Marxism: The Making of the Black Radical Tradition*. Chapel Hill: University of North Carolina Press, 2000.

Rocamora, Agnès. "Personal Fashion Blogs: Screens and Mirrors in Digital Self-Portraits." *Fashion Theory* 15, no. 4 (2011): 407–24.

Roediger, David R. *The Wages of Whiteness: Race and the Making of the American Working Class*. New York: Verso, 1991.

Rohlinger, Deana A. "Eroticizing Men: Cultural Influences on Advertising and Male Objectification." *Sex Roles* 46, nos. 3–4 (2002): 61–74.

Rosman, Katherine. "Super 'Selfies': The Art of the Phone Portrait." *Wall Street Journal*, June 28, 2012.

Ross, Andrew. "The New Geography of Work: Power to the Precarious?" *Theory, Culture and Society* 25, nos. 7–8 (2008): 31–49.

———. *Nice Work If You Can Get It: Life and Labor in Precarious Times*. New York: New York University Press, 2009.

Rothman, Michael. "Julie Chen Admits to Past Plastic Surgery to Change 'Asian Eyes.' " ABC News.com. September 12, 2013. Accessed January 27, 2015. http://abcnews

.go.com/blogs/entertainment/2013/09/julie-chen-admits-to-past-plastic-surgery
-to-change-asian-eyes/.

Sanders, Joshunda. "The White Privilege behind Sheryl Sandberg's 'Ban Bossy' Campaign." *The Week*, March 13, 2014. Accessed January 24, 2015. http://theweek.com
/article/index/257855/the-white-privilege-behind-sheryl-sandbergs-ban-bossy
-campaign.

Schau, Hope J., and Mary C. Gilly. "We Are What We Post? Self-Presentation in Personal Web Space." *Journal of Consumer Research* 30, no. 3 (2003): 385–404.

Schenk, Jan. "Quantifying Taste: Findings from a Survey on Media and Taste among Teenagers from Six High Schools in Cape Town." Centre for Social Science Research Working Paper No. 250. May 2009. Accessed January 25, 2015. http://www
.cssr.uct.ac.za/sites/cssr.uct.ac.za/files/pubs/WP250.pdf.

Scherpe, Mary. "On Fashion Blogs." Vimeo.com. Accessed January 27, 2015. http://
vimeo.com/8882910.

Schiermer, Bjorn. "Fashion Victims: On the Individualizing and De-Individualizing Powers of Fashion." *Fashion Theory* 14, no. 1 (2010): 83–104.

Sharp, Gwen. "French Elle: Stars without Makeup." Sociological Images. April 30, 2009. Accessed January 26, 2015. http://thesocietypages.org/socimages/2009/04
/30/french-elle-stars-without-makeup/.

Sherman, Lauren. "Google Wants to Be More Fashionable." Fashionista.com. July 24, 2010. Accessed January 18, 2015. http://fashionista.com/2010/07/google-wants
-to-be-more-fashionable/.

Shimakawa, Karen. *National Abjection: The Asian American Body on Stage*. Durham, NC: Duke University Press, 2002.

Simmel, Georg. "Fashion." *American Journal of Sociology* 62, no. 6 (1957): 541–58.

Smith, Ray A. "More Asian Models on Fashion's Big Stages—Change Comes to Runways as Brands Look to China for Growth." *Wall Street Journal*, September 13, 2012.

Smith, Ray A., and Robin Sidel. "Should You Dress Like the CEO?" *Wall Street Journal*. July 25, 2013.

Song, Aimee. "Back in Rabat, Morocco." Song of Style (blog). June 1, 2014. Accessed January 21, 2015. http://www.songofstyle.com/2014/06/back-rabat-morocco.html.

———. "The Black and White Striped Button Down." Song of Style (blog). April 28, 2014, Accessed March 15, 2015. http://www.songofstyle.com/2014/04/black
-white-striped-button.html.

———. "Black Uniform." Song of Style (blog). December 12, 2014. Accessed March 15, 2015. http://www.songofstyle.com/2014/12/black-uniform.html.

———. "The Boyfriend Sweatshirt." Song of Style (blog). June 12, 2013. Accessed March 15, 2015. http://www.songofstyle.com/2013/06/the-boyfriend-sweatshirt
.html.

———. "Calamigos Ranch, Malibu." Song of Style (blog). April 21, 2014. Accessed March 15, 2015. http://www.songofstyle.com/2014/04/calamigos-ranch.html.

———. "Flared Hem Skirt and Chanel Chain Boots in Seoul." Song of Style (blog). November 26, 2013. Accessed March 15, 2015. http://www.songofstyle.com/2013/11/flared-hem-skirt-and-chanel-chain-boots-seoul.html.

———. "Leopard on Leopard during Paris Fashion Week." Song of Style (blog). October 6, 2014. Accessed March 14, 2015. http://www.songofstyle.com/2014/10/leopard-on-leopard-during-paris-fashion-week.html.

———. "Kimono and Over the Knee Boots." Song of Style (blog). November 28, 2014. Accessed March 14, 2015. http://www.songofstyle.com/2014/11/kimono-and-over-the-knee-boots.html.

———. "Kimono Dreams in Huntington Botanical Gardens." Song of Style (blog). October 15, 2013. Accessed January 21, 2015. http://www.songofstyle.com/2013/10/kimono-dreams-huntington-botanical-gardens.html.

———. "Magical Pink." Song of Style (blog). April 24, 2013. Accessed January 21, 2015. http://www.songofstyle.com/2013/04/magical-pink.html.

———. "Overalls and Heels." Song of Style (blog). May 2, 2014. Accessed March 14, 2015. http://www.songofstyle.com/2014/05/overalls-heels.html.

———. "Palm Print Playsuit in New York." Song of Style (blog). June 19, 2014. Accessed January 20, 2015. http://www.songofstyle.com/2014/06/palm-print-playsuit-new-york.html.

———. "Pinstripes and Quilted Leather." Song of Style (blog). November 9, 2013. Accessed March 14, 2015. http://www.songofstyle.com/2013/11/pinstripes-quilted-leather.html.

———. "Polished Casual." Song of Style (blog). September 2, 2013. Accessed March 14, 2015. http://www.songofstyle.com/2013/09/polished-casual.html.

———. "Red Valentino." Song of Style (blog). October 16, 2013. Accessed March 14, 2015. http://www.songofstyle.com/2013/10/red-valentino.html.

———. "Song of Style on Instagram." Song of Style (blog). August 2, 2013. Accessed January 20, 2015. http://www.songofstyle.com/2013/08/song-of-style-on-instagram.html.

———. "Summer Boyfriend Jeans." Song of Style (blog). August 19, 2013. Accessed March 14, 2015. http://www.songofstyle.com/2013/08/summer-boyfriend-jeans.html.

———. "Summer Essentials." Song of Style (blog). July 8, 2010. Accessed March 14, 2015. http://www.songofstyle.com/2010/07/summer-essentials.html.

———. "Swinging in Green." Song of Style (blog). October 9, 2013. Accessed March 14, 2015. http://www.songofstyle.com/2013/10/swinging-green.html.

———. "White Button Down and Denim Shorts Kinda Day." Song of Style (blog). May 28, 2014. Accessed March 15, 2015. http://www.songofstyle.com/2014/05/white-button-denim-shorts-kinda-day.html.

———. "White Lace and Red Shorts." Song of Style (blog). April 18, 2014. Accessed March 15, 2015. http://www.songofstyle.com/2014/04/whitelace.html.

———. "Yacht Ride in Los Cabos, Mexico." Song of Style (blog). May 7, 2014. Accessed January 21, 2015. http://www.songofstyle.com/2014/05/yacht-ride-los-cabos-mexico.html.

Sontag, Susan. "Notes on 'Camp.'" Partisan Review 31, no. 4 (1964): 515–30.

Soong, C. S. "Democracy via Technology? Interview with Jodi Dean." Against the Grain. KPFA, October 26, 2009.

Sozzani, Franca. "Bloggers: A Culture Phenomenon or an Epidemic Issue?" Vogue Italia Editor's Blog (blog). January 28, 2011. Accessed January 22, 2015. http://www.vogue.it/en/magazine/editor-s-blog/2011/01/january-28th.

Spener, David, Gary Gereffi, and Jennifer Bair. "Introduction: The Apparel Industry and North American Economic Integration." In Free Trade and Uneven Development: The North American Apparel Industry after NAFTA, edited by Gary Gereffi, David Spener, and Jennifer Bair, 3–22. Philadelphia: Temple University Press, 2002.

Spiridakis, Elizabeth. "The Next Level: Boys with Birkins." T (blog). New York Times Magazine. February 5, 2009. Accessed January 18, 2015. http://tmagazine.blogs.nytimes.com/2009/02/05/the-next-level-boys-with-birkins/.

Strugatz, Rachel. "To Pay or Not to Pay: A Closer Look at the Business of Blogging." Women's Wear Daily. June 5, 2012.

"Success Story of One Minority Group in the U.S." U.S. News and World Report, December 26, 1966, reprinted in Roots: An Asian American Reader, edited by Amy Tachiki, Eddie Wong, Franklin Odo, and Buck Wong, 6–9. Los Angeles: University of California, Los Angeles, Asian American Studies Center, 1971.

Tate, Ryan. "Marc Jacobs Wrapped around Finger of This Gay Filipino Blogger." Gawker (blog). February 12, 2008. Accessed January 18, 2015. http://gawker.com/5003058/marc-jacobs-wrapped-around-finger-of-this-gay-filipino-blogger.

Tchen, John Kuo Wei. New York before Chinatown: Orientalism and the Shaping of American Culture, 1776–1882. Baltimore, MD: Johns Hopkins University Press, 1999.

Terranova, Tiziana. "Free Labor." In Digital Labor: The Internet as Playground and Factory, edited by Trebor Scholz, 33–57. New York: Routledge, 2012.

"Thailand Named Emerging 'Hot Spot.'" Women's Wear Daily, October 11, 2012.

Thomas, Geneva S. "Are Black Fashion Bloggers Being Ignored?" Clutch. February 24, 2010. Accessed January 18, 2015. http://clutchmagonline.com/newsgossipinfo/are-black-fashion-bloggers-being-ignored.

Thompson, E. P. "Time, Work-Discipline, and Industrial Capitalism." Past and Present 38 (December 1967): 56–97.

Thompson, Mary. "'Learn Something From This!': The Problem of Optional Ethnicity on America's Next Top Model." Feminist Media Studies 10, no. 3 (2010): 335–52.

Tishgart, Sierra. "Tour Style Blogger Aimee Song's Apartment." Teen Vogue. November 2012. Accessed March 15, 2015. http://www.teenvogue.com/my-life/my-room/2012-11/aimee-song-bedroom/?slide=1.

Toffler, Alvin. *Powershift: Knowledge, Wealth, and Violence at the Edge of the 21st Century*. New York: Bantam, 1990.

————. *The Third Wave*. New York: William Morrow, 1980.

Tongson, Karen. *Relocations: Queer Suburban Imaginaries*. New York: New York University Press, 2011.

Tu, Thuy Linh N. *The Beautiful Generation: Asian Americans and the Cultural Economy of Fashion*. Durham, NC: Duke University Press, 2010.

Turner, Sherry, et al. "The Influence of Fashion Magazines on the Body Image Satisfaction of College Women: An Exploratory Analysis." *Adolescence* 32, no. 127 (1997): 603–14.

Vandendorpe, Christian. "Reading on Screen: The New Media Sphere." In *A Companion to Digital Literary Studies*, edited by Ray Siemens and Susan Schreibman, chapter 10. Oxford: Blackwell, 2008. http://www.digitalhumanities.org/companionDLS/.

Veblen, Thorstein. *The Theory of the Leisure Class*. New York: Macmillan, 1912.

"Video: Latest Collection by Jason Wu Show Chinese Roots." *Globe and Mail*. February 11, 2012. Accessed January 24, 2015. http://www.theglobeandmail.com/life/life-video /video-latest-collection-by-jason-wu-show-chinese-roots/article545576/.

Vora, Kalindi. "The Transmission of Care: Affective Economies and Indian Call Centers." In *Intimate Labors: Cultures, Technologies, and the Politics of Care*, edited by Eileen Boris and Rhacel Salazar Parreñas, 33–48. Stanford, CA: Stanford Social Sciences, 2010.

Waldman, Katy. "Lena Dunham Responds to the *Vogue* Haters." *Slate*. January 17, 2014. Accessed January 26, 2015. http://www.slate.com/blogs/xx_factor/2014 /01/17/lena_dunham_response_to_vogue_photoshop_criticism_fashion _magazines_are.html.

Walkerdine, Valerie, Helen Lucey, and June Melody. *Growing Up Girl: Psychosocial Explorations of Gender and Class*. London: Palgrave, 2001.

Wallace, Bill. "70 Immigrants Found in Raid on Sweatshop: Thai Workers Tell Horror Stories of Captivity." *San Francisco Chronicle*, August 4, 1995.

Wallerstein, Immanuel. *The Modern World-System I: Capitalist Agriculture and the Origins of the European World-Economy in the Sixteenth Century*. Berkeley: University of California Press, 2011.

Warne, Jade. "Interview: Fashion Blogger Bryanboy." Yahoo! Lifestyle. September 11, 2009. Accessed March 15, 2015. https://au.lifestyle.yahoo.com/marie-claire/fashion /news/a/6183321/interview-fashion-blogger-bryanboy/.

Watkins, S. Craig. *The Young and the Digital: What the Migration to Social Network Sites, Games, and Anytime, Anywhere Media Means for Our Future*. Boston: Beacon, 2009.

"Webmaster Guidelines." Google. Accessed March 15, 2015. https://support.google .com/webmasters/answer/35769?hl=en#quality_guidelines.

Wells, Rachel. "Have Laptop, Will Travel: Bloggers Arrive on Fashion's Front Row." *Age*. May 4, 2008. Accessed March 12, 2015. http://www.theage.com.au/news/fashion /bloggers-arrive-on-fashions-front-row/2008/05/03/1209235234242.html.

"Wendy Nguyen." *Lucky*, n.d. Accessed January 17, 2015. http://www.luckymag.com /blogconference/speaker-bios/speaker-bios-spring-12/Wendy-Nguyen.

West, Nancy Martha. *Kodak and the Lens of Nostalgia*. Charlottesville: University of Virginia Press, 2000.

Wikipedia. "Wikipedia: Systemic Bias." Accessed January 17, 2015. https://en.wikipedia .org/wiki/Wikipedia:Systemic_bias.

"Wikipedia's Gender and Race Gaps." *Forum with Michael Krasny*. KQED Public Media for Northern California, March 13, 2015.

Wilson, Ara. *The Intimate Economies of Bangkok: Tomboys, Tycoons, and Avon Ladies in the Global City*. Berkeley: University of California Press, 2004.

Wilson, Eric. "Asian Americans Climb Fashion Industry." *New York Times*, September 4, 2010.

———. "Bloggers Crash Fashion's Front Row." *New York Times*. December 24, 2009. Accessed March 12, 2015. http://www.nytimes.com/2009/12/27/fashion/27BLOGGERS .html?_r=0.

———. "Documenting a Growing Force in Fashion." *New York Times*, April 24, 2013.

Winter, Katy. "We Woke Up Like This Too Beyonce!." *Daily Mail*, March 21, 2014. Accessed January 24, 2015. http://www.dailymail.co.uk/femail/article-2585203 /We-woke-like-Beyonce-Stars-including-Kim-Kardashian-Rihanna-rush-post -flawless-early-morning-selfies-like-Queen-Bey.html.

Wiseman, Eva. "Today I'm Wearing. . . ." *Guardian*, February 7, 2009. Accessed January 19, 2015. http://www.theguardian.com/lifeandstyle/2009/feb/08/susie-lau -fashion-blogs.

Wong, Ryan. "A Billion Hits and Counting: Asian Americans and YouTube." Hyperallergic. July 18, 2012. Accessed January 17, 2015. http://hyperallergic.com/54441 /a-billion-hits-and-counting-asian-americans-and-youtube/.

Wong, Yutian. *Choreographing Asian America*. Middletown, CT: Wesleyan University Press, 2010.

Woo, Deborah. *Glass Ceilings and Asian Americans: The New Face of Workplace Barriers*. Lanham, MD: AltaMira, 2000.

Worker Rights Consortium. "Global Wage Trends for Apparel Workers, 2001–2011." Center for American Progress. July 11, 2013. Accessed January 18, 2015. http:// americanprogress.org/issues/labor/report/2013/07/11/69255/global-wage-trends -for-apparel-workers-2001-2011/.

Yambao, Bryan Grey. "Anya Hindmarch Ching Chong Edition." BryanBoy (blog). June 22, 2007. Accessed January 21, 2015. http://www.bryanboy.com/bryanboy_le_su perstar_fab/2007/06/anya-hindmarch.html.

———. "Aristocrazy Headquarters Madrid." BryanBoy (blog). May 1, 2014. Accessed January 21, 2015. http://www.bryanboy.com/bryanboy_le_superstar_fab/2014/05 /aristocrazy-headquarters-madrid.html.

———. "Blasphemous: Ashanti in a Balenciaga Dress." BryanBoy (blog). July 19, 2008. Accessed March 17, 2015. http://www.bryanboy.com/bryanboy_le_superstar_fab /2008/07/blasphemous-ashanti-in-a-balenciaga-dress.html.

———. "BryanBoy Loves . . . and Random Cheesemax." BryanBoy (blog). December 24, 2005. http://www.bryanboy.com/bryanboy_le_superstar_fab/2005/12/bryan boy_loves__1-10.html.

———. "BryanBoy Loves Marc Jacobs." BryanBoy (blog). February 6, 2008. Accessed March 12, 2015. http://www.bryanboy.com/bryanboy_le_superstar_fab/2008/02 /bryanboy-love-1-2.html.

———. "Celebrity Schmelebrity. Fuck the Haters. Eat Your Fucking Hearts Out." BryanBoy (blog). June 3, 2006. Accessed January 18, 2015. http://www.bryanboy.com /bryanboy_le_superstar_fab/2006/06/celebrity_schme.html.

———. "Coloured Male Models? Menswear Milan FW08–09." BryanBoy (blog). January 13, 2008. Accessed January 21, 2015. http://www.bryanboy.com/bryanboy_le _superstar_fab/2008/01/where-are-the-c.html.

———. " 'Everybody Wants to Be Us.' " BryanBoy (blog). April 25, 2006. Accessed January 21, 2015. http://www.bryanboy.com/bryanboy_le_superstar_fab/2006/04 /everybody_wants.html.

———. "Everything About Me Is Fake and I'm Perfect." BryanBoy (blog). May 14, 2011. Accessed March 14, 2015. http://www.bryanboy.com/bryanboy_le_superstar_fab /2011/05/everything-about-me-is-fake-and-im-perfect.html.

———. "Fendi: Stop the Fucking Press!" BryanBoy (blog). August 15, 2006. Accessed March 14, 2015. http://www.bryanboy.com/bryanboy_le_superstar_fab/2006/08 /stop_the_fuckin.html.

———. "Filipino Hospitality." BryanBoy (blog). December 13, 2005. Accessed March 12, 2015. http://www.bryanboy.com/bryanboy_le_superstar_fab/2005/12 /filipino_hospit.html.

———. "For the Love of Work." BryanBoy (blog). January 25, 2009. Accessed January 18, 2015. http://www.bryanboy.com/bryanboy_le_superstar_fab/2009/01/for -the-love-of-work.html.

———. "Gay Bloggies 2007." BryanBoy (blog). October 26, 2007. Accessed March 18, 2015. http://www.bryanboy.com/bryanboy_le_superstar_fab/2007/10/gay-bloggies -20.html.

———. "Goodbye Third World!" BryanBoy (blog). November 28, 2006. Accessed January 21, 2015. http://www.bryanboy.com/bryanboy_le_superstar_fab/2006 /11/goodbye_third_w.html.

———. "Healthy Options." BryanBoy (blog). March 31, 2014. Accessed January 22, 2015. http://www.bryanboy.com/bryanboy_le_superstar_fab/2014/03/healthy -options.html.

———. "Holt Renfrew Unveils Fashion Blogger Windows." BryanBoy (blog). June 24, 2009. Accessed January 18, 2015. http://www.bryanboy.com/bryanboy_le_super star_fab/2009/06/holt-renfrew-unveils-fashion-blogger-windows.html.

———. "Holy Fucking Shiyet Fendi." BryanBoy (blog). May 4, 2006. Accessed January 24, 2015. http://www.bryanboy.com/bryanboy_le_superstar_fab/2006/05/resurrection.html.

———. "Mall Rat Extraordinaire." BryanBoy (blog). September 6, 2005. Accessed January 21, 2015. http://www.bryanboy.com/bryanboy_le_superstar_fab/2005/09/mall_rat_extrao.html.

———. "An Open Letter to Riccardo Tisci and Givenchy." BryanBoy (blog). April 16, 2007. Accessed January 21, 2015. http://www.bryanboy.com/bryanboy_le_superstar_fab/2007/04/an_open_letter__1.html.

———. "Raf-ing It Up." BryanBoy (blog). June 16, 2014. Accessed January 21, 2015. http://www.bryanboy.com/bryanboy_le_superstar_fab/2014/06/raf-simons-spring-summer-2014.html.

———. "Team Sissyfication." BryanBoy (blog). November 10, 2007. Accessed March 14, 2015. http://www.bryanboy.com/bryanboy_le_superstar_fab/2007/11/team-sissyficat.html.

———. "X Marks the Spot." BryanBoy (blog). April 23, 2014. Accessed January 21, 2015. http://www.bryanboy.com/bryanboy_le_superstar_fab/2014/04/alexander-wang-sweater.html.

———. "You Owe It to Your Fans." BryanBoy (blog). June 5, 2011. Accessed January 18, 2015. http://www.bryanboy.com/bryanboy_le_superstar_fab/2011/06/you-owe-it-to-your-fans.html.

Yang, Jeff. "Why the Rise of Asia in Fashion Isn't As Beautiful as It Seems." Wall Street Journal (blog). September 17, 2012. http://blogs.wsj.com/speakeasy/2012/09/17/why-the-rise-of-asia-in-fashion-isnt-as-beautiful-as-it-seems/.

Yano, Christine R. Pink Globalization: Hello Kitty's Trek across the Pacific. Durham, NC: Duke University Press, 2013.

Yi, David. "The Camera-Wielding Boyfriends behind Fashion's Most Famous Bloggers." Fashionista.com. April 8, 2014. Accessed January 21, 2015. http://fashionista.com/2014/04/fashion-blogger-boyfriends.

Zeveloff, Julie. "The 15 Wealthiest People in Fashion." Business Insider. September 10, 2012. Accessed March 15, 2015. http://www.businessinsider.com/the-15-wealthiest-people-in-fashion-2012-9.

Zucker, Sara. "Fashion Bloggers, Where They Belong: In the Front Row." Mediaite. September 29, 2009. Accessed January 21, 2015. http://www.mediaite.com/online/fashion-bloggers-where-they-belong-in-the-front-row/.

Zwick, Detlev, Samuel K. Bonsu, and Aron Darmody. "Putting Consumers to Work: 'Co-Creation' and New Marketing Govern-Mentality." Journal of Consumer Culture 8, no. 2 (2008): 163–96.

# Index

Note: When discussed as individuals, designers are alphabetized under their last names (Jacobs, Mark). Brands are alphabetized under the brand name (Michael Kors). Italic page numbers refer to figures.

Apple, 159
Arras, 81
artists, 111, 163; fashion bloggers as, 7, 16, 51, 203n48; graffiti artists, 8
Ashanti, 210n57
Asia. *See individual countries*
Asian American studies, 27
Asian creative class, 6–9, 19, 43, 51, 88
Asian decade, 10, 15, 51–52
Asian diaspora, 4, 6, 165
Asian diaspora studies, 27
Asian exclusion laws, 28. *See also* Page Act
Asian Republican Coalition, 96
*Atlantic*, 53
Atlantic-Pacific, 84
attention economy, 11, 16
Aubrey, John, 76
Augé, Marc, 135
Australia, 1, 121. *See also* Sydney
Australian Fashion Foundation, 149
Australian Fashion Week, 64
Azalea, Iggy, 163

Bag Snob, 2, 107
Balenciaga, 52, 75, 86, 178, 206n44, 210n57
Bangladesh, 32, 35, 52, 71–72, 176
Banks, Tyra, 164
Barbados, 139
Bart, Ivan, 15
Barthes, Roland, 37, 81–83, 86, 95
Beha, Freja, 54, 124
*Behind the Labels*, 31, 34
Beijing, 53
Benjamin, Walter, 114–15
Beyoncé, 2, 142–43
Bhabha, Homi, 117–19
Bieber, Justin, 120, 163
*The Biggest Loser*, 146
biopolitics, 168, 208n96

Black communities, 156, 214n21; Black models, 24, 139, 208n96; Black workers, 73, 134, 190. *See also* African Americans
Blogger, 24
BlogHer, 17
Bluefly, 174
Bluehost, 102
*Bon*, 75
Bonacich, Edna, 30, 33
Bordo, Susan, 146
Bourdieu, Pierre, 37, 44, 68–69, 81–83, 86–87, 95; on taste, 5, 19, 59–60, 163
Bouterse, Siko, 202n22
Bowles, Hamish, 67
boyd, danah, 57
Bradley, Stuart, 132, 150
brand ambassadors, 2, 54, 147
brand storytelling, 57
Brazil, 120, 139
Breaking Media Corporation, 61
British Chinese people, 28–29, 165
British Guiana, 71
BryanBoy, 62, 77, 101–2, 105, 107, 136, 211n63; Marc Jacobs's relationship with, 41, 63. *See also* Yambao, Bryan Grey
BryanBoy pose, 5, 38, 139, 150–51, 156–63, 157, 166, 197; Fendi's use of, 5, 117, 158
Bubble, Susie, 1, 42–43, 62, 70, 82, 105. *See also* Lau, Susanna; Susie Bubble pose
The Budget Fashionista, 23, 107
Bulgaria, 24
The Business of Fashion, 4, 6

California, 3, 43, 71, 74–75, 86–87, 95, 98, 108, 121, 157, 189; fashion labor in, 30, 33. *See also* El Monte; Los Angeles; University of California at Berkeley
Cambodia, 35

Odell, Amy, 70
Ong, Aihwa, 33–34, 172
Orientalism, 45, 128, 155, 166
outfit photos, 37–38, 82–84, 95,
    105–28, 108, 109, 124–27, 149–52,
    168, 178, 180, 194–95, 197, 211n8
outfit posts, 37, 83–86, 88–91, 95, 98,
    104, 114, 152, 167–91
Owens, Rick, 57

Page Act, 73, 190
Palin, Sarah, 116
Paris, 52, 77, 121
Paris Fashion Week, 42, 160
Paris-Shanghai: A Fantasy, 54, 124
parodies, 110, 112, 132, 214n22
Pascale Monvoisin, 178
passing, 94–95, 103, 134–35
patriotism: new patriotism, 34
pedestrian.tv, 1
Peng Liyuan, 52
Perry, Imani, 97
personal branding, 58, 97, 99, 150,
    160–61, 164–66, 197–98
personal style story, 37–38, 81–104,
    111, 141, 168, 195, 197
Peru, 35
Phan, Michelle, 8
Philippines, 4, 20, 33–35, 44, 50,
    99–102. See also Manila
Photobucket, 157
photoshopping, 169–70, 216n9
Pierce, Richard, 20
Pikachu, 45–46
pink-collar work, 8
Pinterest, 129
Poiblanc, Ludivine, 77
Poiret, Paul, 45
Pokémon, 45–46, 137, 205n18
Pokémon: The First Movie, 46
Polo, 20
Portugal, 139

posing, 37–38, 49, 62, 92, 112–13, 115,
    129–66, 177–78, 195, 197, 214n22;
    elsewhere gaze, 47, 129, 150–56, 153,
    154, 164, 194; pigeon-toed stance,
    47, 129, 144–45, 150; sugar bowl
    pose, 47, 129, 145; teapot pose, 129,
    145; the Tilt, 132, 150. See also Bryan-
    Boy pose; Susie Bubble pose
postracism, 8–9, 43, 68, 76, 78–79, 96;
    in fashion industry, 11, 16, 23, 36,
    43–44, 126–27, 164
Prada, 45, 53, 103, 206n44
product reviews, 3, 55, 57, 174
Proenza Schouler: PS11 handbag, 178
Project Runway, 174
prosumption, 183
protestant ethnic, 97
Psy (Park Jaesang): "Gangnam Style,"
    120–23
Puerto Ricans, 28, 32

queer bloggers, 5, 41, 104; race and,
    43–44, 78, 100, 156–63, 165–66, 197.
    See also gay men

race, 3, 63, 95, 122–23, 175–76, 193–99;
    as aesthetic strategy, 4–5, 8, 37,
    103, 156, 159; BryanBoy pose and,
    156–63; cheapness and, 71–79, 104,
    189–91; in digital capitalism, 6–7,
    9–11, 39, 71, 127, 151, 202n22,
    203n42; in fashion industry, 10–18,
    20–23, 26–28, 32–36, 44, 59, 64,
    67, 75–78, 83, 101–2, 104, 124,
    126–27, 138–39, 150–51, 161, 164,
    180–81, 212n28; gender and, 39,
    45–50, 73, 78, 97, 98–99, 118, 147,
    183, 190, 205n25; identity work and,
    133–36; in liberalism, 19, 64, 68,
    202n18; mixed-race identity, 1, 43;
    in neoliberalism, 97, 196, 208n96; in
    personal style superblogosphere, 12,

social media (*continued*)
haul vlogging and, 169; thank you economy and, 144. *See also individual platforms*
soft power, 46
Sokol, Colin, 108–9
Som, Peter, 52
Song, Aimee, 3, 90, 164, 172, 197, 201n14; closet confessional, 174; fashion industry's relation to, 2, 25, 54; income, 16, 21–22; outfit posts by, 84, 85, 89, 180; style stories of, 37, 86–87, 93–99, 103. *See also* Song of Style
Song of Style, 89
Sozzani, Franca, 105–6, 113–14
sponsorships, 11, 25, 91, 174, 184
Springman, Christopher, 161
Sri Lanka, 52, 71
Stefani, Gwen, 163
St. Louis World's Fair, 156
Street Etiquette, 23
Street Peeper, 3
street style blogs, 3–4, 6, 23, 110
StumbleUpon, 25
*Style*, 42
Style Bubble, 2, 15, 63, 82, 108, 149
Style Council, 75
Style Salvage, 109, 152
style stories, 37–38, 81–104, 111, 141, 168, 195, 197
Sui, Anna, 52
Susie Bubble pose, 38, 139, 150–57, 153, 154, 160, 163–66, 194, 197
sweated labor, 11, 29, 39, 171, 176, 179, 195
Sydney, 121
Szarkowski, John, 111

Tacori, 2
Taiwan, 24, 46
Taiwanese Americans, 2, 6, 75

Tajiri, Satoshi, 205n18
Tao Okamoto, 54
Target, 33, 110
taste, 15, 18, 36, 122–23, 136, 138, 150, 177, 179–80, 188–89, 206n44, 212n28; Bourdieu on, 5, 19, 59–60, 163; of personal style bloggers, 1, 3–10, 12, 22, 26, 37–39, 41–79, 82–87, 89, 91–93, 96–100, 103–4, 106, 110, 112–19, 124–28, 133, 155, 160, 163–66, 194–95, 197–98. *See also* racial aftertastes
Technorati, 17, 24
*Teen Vogue*, 106, 109, 167, 174
Teller, Jürgen, 41
temporality, 69–70, 118–19, 137–38, 175–76, 212; of personal style blogs, 39, 112–14, 124–25, 176–80. *See also* snapshot aesthetics
Terranova, Tiziana, 17
Terry, Jennifer, 187
Thailand, 32–33, 35, 52–54, 71–72, 139, 190
thank you economy, 144, 146–47
Third World, 30, 43, 72, 99–100, 102–3, 165–66
Threadbared, 4, 206n52
*Time* magazine, 46
*Time Out London*, 179
The Tiny Closet, 142
Tisci, Riccardo, 101
Toffler, Alvin, 183
Tokyo Stock Exchange, 53
tolerance, 18–19, 36, 44, 55, 58, 59–60, 64, 67–69, 97, 134, 196
Ton, Tommy, 6–7, 25, 67, 110. *See also* Jak & Jil
TopShop, 1, 88
transnationalism, 8, 14, 17, 19, 21, 45–46, 59, 126, 165
Trinidad, 71
trolling, 58

Worth, Charles Fredrick, 152
Wu, Jason, 52, 138

Xiaodan, Zheng, 52
Xiaoyu, Lu, 52

Yahoo, 23, 55
Yambao, Bryan Grey, 5, 25, 42, 43, 61,
   64, 65, 67, 105, 109, 127–28, 136,
   201n14; audiences of, 50; cuteness
   and, 47; humor, 204n73; income, 21,
   51; Marc Jacobs relationship with,
   41–43, 42, 86; media coverage of, 54,
60, 62–63, 65, 67, 77; origin story,
30–31; outfit posts, 84, 85, 106–7,
112–13; style stories by, 37, 95, 99–104;
use of BryanBoy pose, 139, 151.
*See also* BryanBoy; BryanBoy pose
Yano, Christine, 45–46
yellowface, 54, 124, 155, 206n52
Yelp, 55
YouTube, 7–8, 24, 87, 120, 180
Yuhao, Zhang, 52

Zeuner, Jennifer, 178
Zhu, Feng, 52